Country Houses

208 Unique Home Plans with Country Style

HOME PLANNERS, LLC
Wholly owned by Hanley-Wood, Inc.
TUCSON, ARIZONA

About the Designers

The Blue Ribbon Designer Series™ is a collection of books featuring home plans of a diverse group of outstanding home designers and architects known as the Blue Ribbon Network of Designers. This group of companies is dedicated to creating and marketing the finest possible plans for home construction on a regional and national basis. Each of the companies exhibits superior work and integrity in all phases of the stock-plan business including modern, trendsetting floor planning, a professionally executed blueprint package and a strong sense of service and commitment to the consumer.

Design Basics, Inc.

For nearly a decade, Design Basics, a nationally recognized home design service located in Omaha, has been developing plans for custom home builders. Since 1987, the firm has consistently appeared in *Builder* magazine, the official magazine of the National Association of Home Builders, as the top-selling designer. The company's plans also regularly appear in numerous other shelter magazines such as *Better Homes and Gardens, House Beautiful* and *Home Planner*.

Design Traditions

Design Traditions was established by Stephen S. Fuller with the tenets of innovation, quality, originality and uncompromising architectural techniques in traditional and European homes. Especially popular throughout the Southeast, Design Traditions' plans are known for their extensive detail and thoughtful design. They are widely published in such shelter magazines as *Southern Living* magazine and *Better Homes and Gardens*.

Alan Mascord Design Associates, Inc.

Founded in 1983 as a local supplier to the building community, Mascord Design Associates of Portland, Oregon began to successfully publish plans nationally in 1985. With plans now drawn exclusively on computer, Mascord Design Associates quickly received a reputation for homes that are easy to build yet meet the rigorous demands of the buyers' market, winning local and national awards. The company's trademark is creating floor plans that work well and exhibit excellent traffic patterns. Their motto is: "Drawn to build, designed to sell."

Larry E. Belk Designs

Through the years, Larry E. Belk has worked with individuals and builders alike to provide a quality product. After listening to over 4,000 dreams and watching them become reality all across America, Larry's design philosophy today combines traditional exteriors with upscale interiors designed for contemporary lifestyles. Flowing, open spaces and interesting angles define his interiors. Great emphasis is placed on providing views that showcase the natural environment. Dynamic exteriors reflect Larry's extensive home construction experience, painstaking research and talent as a fine artist.

Larry W. Garnett & Associates, Inc.

Starting as a designer of homes for Houston-area residents, Garnett & Associates has been marketing designs nationally for the past ten years. A well-respected design firm, the company's plans are regularly featured in *House Beautiful, Country Living, Home* and *Professional Builder*. Numerous accolades, including several from the Texas Institute of Building Design and the American Institute of Building Design, have been awarded to the company for excellence in architecture.

Home Planners

Headquartered in Tucson, Arizona, with additional offices in Detroit, Home Planners is one of the longest-running and most successful home design firms in the United States. With over 2,500 designs in its portfolio, the company provides a wide range of styles, sizes and types of homes for the residential builder. All of Home Planners' designs are created with the care and professional expertise that fifty years of experience in the home-planning business affords. Their homes are designed to be built, lived in and enjoyed for years to come.

Donald A. Gardner, Architects, Inc.

The South Carolina firm of Donald A. Gardner was established in response to a growing demand for residential designs that reflect constantly changing lifestyles. The company's specialty is providing homes with refined, custom-style details and unique features such as passive-solar designs and open floor plans. Computer-aided design and drafting technology resulting in trouble-free construction documents places the firm at the leading edge of the home plan industry.

The Sater Design Collection

The Sater Design Collection has a long established tradition of providing South Florida's most diverse and extraordinary custom designed homes. Their goal is to fulfill each client's particular need for an exciting approach to design by merging creative vision with elements that satisfy a desire for a distinctive lifestyle. This philosophy is proven, as exemplified by over 50 national design awards, numerous magazine features and, most important, satisfied clients. The result is an elegant statement of lasting beauty and value.

EDITORS NOTE: For many, the term "country" evokes stronger images than those of weather vanes and gingham. As you study the plans on the following pages, you will realize these homes define country on a much grander scale. This definition extends to the planning and construction aids developed to insure a successful home-building project—start to finish. To lend a hand with planning the cost of your new country home, our Quote One® estimating service is available for many of our plans. This invaluable service provides detailed information regarding the cost to build a particular home plan in a specific region of the United States. The Quote One® logo has been placed on the plan pages for easy reference. For additional information regarding this unique service, please see page 214.

Table of Contents

Published by Home Planners, LLC
Wholly owned by Hanley-Wood, Inc.
Editorial and Corporate Offices:
3275 West Ina Road, Suite 110
Tucson, Arizona 85741

Distribution Center:
29333 Lorie Lane
Wixom, Michigan 48393

Rickard D. Bailey, CEO and Publisher
Cindy Coatsworth Lewis, Director of Publishing
Paulette Mulvin, Senior Editor
Jan Prideaux, Editor
Paul Fitzgerald, Senior Designer
Karen Leanio, Graphic Designer

Photo Credits
Front Cover: © Andrew D. Lautman
Back Cover: © Andrew D. Lautman

First Printing, September, 1996

10 9 8 7 6 5 4 3

Printed in the United States of America

Library of Congress Catalog Card Number: 96-75929

ISBN softcover: 1-881955-32-X

On the front cover: Design 2973 displays a light, airy porch that extends a warm country
welcome to family and friends alike. For more information about this design, see page
79.
On the back cover: Design 2174. Page 37 provides a closer look.

Design 9812

First Floor: 1,580 square feet
Second Floor: 595 square feet
Total: 2,175 square feet
Bonus Room: 290 square feet

◆ This home features a front porch which warmly welcomes family and visitors, as well as protecting them from the weather—a true Southern original. Inside, the spacious foyer leads directly to a large vaulted great room with a massive fireplace. The dining room also receives the vaulted ceiling treatment. A grand kitchen offers both storage and large work areas opening up to the breakfast room. In the privacy and quiet of the rear of the home is the master suite with its garden bath, His and Hers vanities, and oversized closet. The second floor provides two additional bedrooms with a shared bath along with a balcony overlook to the foyer below. Ample amounts of storage space or an additional bedroom can be created in space over the garage. This home is designed with a basement foundation.

Width 48'-6"
Depth 70'-11"

Design by
Design Traditions

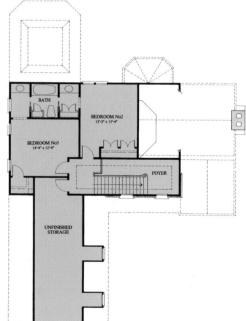

Cost to build? See page 214 to order complete cost estimate to build this house in your area!

REAR ELEVATION

4

Width 64'
Depth 64'-4"

Design by
Design Traditions

QUOTE ONE®

Cost to build? See page 214
to order complete cost estimate
to build this house in your area!

Design 9831

Square Footage: 2,150
Expandable Lower Level: 2,150

◆ This home draws its inspiration from both French and English country homes. From the foyer and across the spacious great room, French doors give a generous view of the covered rear porch. The adjoining dining room is subtly defined by the use of columns and a large triple window. The kitchen, with its generous work island, adjoins the breakfast area, which leads to a keeping room with fireplace, vaulted ceiling and abundant windows. A bedroom to the front of the first floor may act as guest quarters or a study. It shares a bath with another family bedroom. The home is completed by a quiet master suite located at the rear. It contains a bay window, a garden tub and His and Hers vanities. Space on the lower level can be developed later. This home is designed with a basement foundation.

Design 9813

First Floor: 1,724 square feet
Second Floor: 700 square feet
Total: 2,424 square feet

◆ This cozy English cottage might be found hidden away in a European garden. All the charm of gables, stonework and multi-level rooflines combine to create this home. To the left of the foyer you will see the sunlit dining room, highlighted by a dramatic tray ceiling and expansive windows with transoms. This room and the living room flow together to form one large entertainment area. In the gourmet kitchen are a work island, an oversized pantry and a sunny breakfast room with a gazebo ceiling. The great room features a pass-through wet bar, a fireplace and bookcases or an entertainment center. The master suite enjoys privacy at the rear of the home. An open-rail loft above the foyer leads to additional bedrooms with walk-in closets, private vanities and a shared bath. This home is designed with a basement foundation.

Design by
Design Traditions

Cost to build? See page 214 to order complete cost estimate to build this house in your area!

QUOTE ONE®

Width 47'-10"
Depth 63'-10"

Design by
Design Traditions

OPEN TO BELOW

GALLERY

BEDROOM NO. 3
12'-0" X 11'-4"

BATH

LOFT
12'-0" X 9'-10"

BEDROOM NO. 2
12'-0" X 12'-0"

DECK

MASTER BEDROOM
15'-4" X 15'-4"

GREAT ROOM
15'-8" X 16'-7"

BREAKFAST
10'-6" X 10'-0"

GUEST BEDROOM
13'-6" X 12'-0"

MASTER BATH

KITCHEN
10'-6" X 15'-0"

W.I.C.

GUEST BATH

W.I.C.

UP

DN

LAUNDRY
9'-4" X 6'-0"

FOYER
6'-8" X 12'-6"

DINING ROOM
12'-0" X 13'-6"

TWO CAR GARAGE
21'-4" X 21'-4"

STUDY
13'-4" X 11'-2"

STOOP

QUOTE ONE®

Cost to build? See page 214
to order complete cost estimate
to build this house in your area!

Width 58'-4"
Depth 54'-10"

Design 9821

First Floor: 2,070 square feet
Second Floor: 790 square feet
Total: 2,860 square feet

◆ A striking combination of
wood frame, shingles and
glass creates the exterior of
this classic cottage. The foyer
opens to the main-level layout.
To the left of the foyer is a
study with a warming hearth
and a vaulted ceiling. To the
right is the formal dining
room. A great room with an
attached breakfast area is near
the kitchen. A guest room is
nestled in the rear of the plan
for privacy. The master suite
provides an expansive tray
ceiling, a glass sitting area and
easy passage to the outside
deck. Upstairs, two bedrooms
are accompanied by a sunken
loft for a quiet getaway. This
home is designed with a basement foundation.

COPYRIGHT 1993

Design 8050

First Floor: 1,844 square feet
Second Floor: 841 square feet
Total: 2,685 square feet

◆ Two shed dormers and a front porch, perfect for evening relaxation, evoke the charm of the country farmhouse in a home designed for the constraints of a suburban lot. Inside, impact is created at the front door with a dining room defined by columns and connecting arched openings. The conveniently designed kitchen features a work island and eating bar. The family room, with its corner fireplace, has access to a rear covered porch. Three bedrooms and a bath are located on the second floor. A large area, perfect for a game room or craft room, is located over the garage and makes this plan a great pick for the growing family.

Design by
Larry E. Belk
Designs

Width 62'-6"
Depth 52'-10"

QUOTE ONE®

Cost to build? See page 214
to order complete cost estimate
to build this house in your area!

COVERED PORCH

GREAT ROOM
19-4 X 17-6
12 FT CLG

MASTER BATH

SHLV LIN

COVERED PORCH

9 FT CLG

BRKFST RM
12-6 X 9-8
10 FT CLG

SEE THRU FP

MASTER BEDRM
16-8 X 14-8
9 FT CLG

KITCHEN
12-4 X 14-6

FOYER
10 FT CLG

10 FT CLG

DINING ROOM
15-6 X 11-6
10 FT CLG

BATH 2

UTIL
11-6 X 5-6

PANTRY

PORCH

BEDRM 2
11-4 X 11-8
9 FT CLG

GARAGE

STORAGE

Width 64'-4"
Depth 62'

BEDRM 3
13-6 X 12-0

OPEN TO FOYER BELOW

BALCONY

GAME ROOM
16-8 X 15-4

BATH 3

LIN

SLOPE
PLANT LEDGE

BEDRM 4
11-4 X 11-4

Quote One®
Cost to build? See page 214
to order complete cost estimate
to build this house in your area!

Design by
Larry E. Belk
Designs

Design 8037

First Floor: 1,930 square feet
Second Floor: 791 square feet
Total: 2,721 square feet

◆ A delightful elevation with swoop roof captures the eye and provides just the right touch for this inviting home. Inside, an angled foyer with a volume ceiling directs attention to the enormous great room. The dining room is detailed with massive round columns connected by arches and shares a through-fireplace with the great room. The master suite includes an upscale master bath and access to a private covered porch. Bedroom 2 is located nearby and is perfect for a nursery or home office/study. The kitchen features a large cooktop island and walk-in pantry. The second floor is dominated by an oversized game room. Two family bedrooms, each with a walk-in closet, a bath and a linen closet complete the upstairs. Please specify crawlspace or slab foundation when ordering.

Design 9067

First Floor: 1,999 square feet
Second Floor: 933 square feet
Total: 2,932 square feet

◆ The wraparound veranda and simple lines give this home an unassuming elegance that is characteristic of its Folk Victorian heritage. Opening directly to the formal dining room, the two-story foyer offers extra space for large dinner parties. Double French doors lead to the study with raised paneling and a cozy fireplace. Built-in bookcases conceal a hidden security vault. The private master suite features a corner garden tub, glass-enclosed shower and a walk-in closet. Overlooking the family room and built-in breakfast nook is the central kitchen. A rear staircase provides convenient access to the second floor from the family room. The balcony provides a view of the foyer below and the Palladian window. Three additional bedrooms complete this exquisite home.

Design by
Larry W.
Garnett &
Associates, Inc.

Width 79'-8"
Depth 59'

QUOTE ONE®

Cost to build? See page 214 to order complete cost estimate to build this house in your area!

Design 9585

First Floor: 1,337 square feet
Second Floor: 1,025 square feet
Total: 2,362 square feet

◆ An octagonal tower, a wrap-around porch and a wealth of amenities combine to give this house its charming Victorian appeal. The tower furnishes more than a pretty face, containing a sunny den on the first floor and a delightful bedroom on the second floor. To the right of the foyer, the formal living room and dining room unite to provide a wonderful place to celebrate special occasions and holidays. A large kitchen featuring an island cooktop easily serves both the formal dining room and the adjoining nook. Here, family members will appreciate the built-in desk for use in meal planning or paying bills. The spacious family room completes the casual living area and supplies easy access to the rear porch. Upstairs, two bedrooms share a full hall bath while the master bedroom revels in its own luxurious private bath. A two-car garage accommodates the family vehicles.

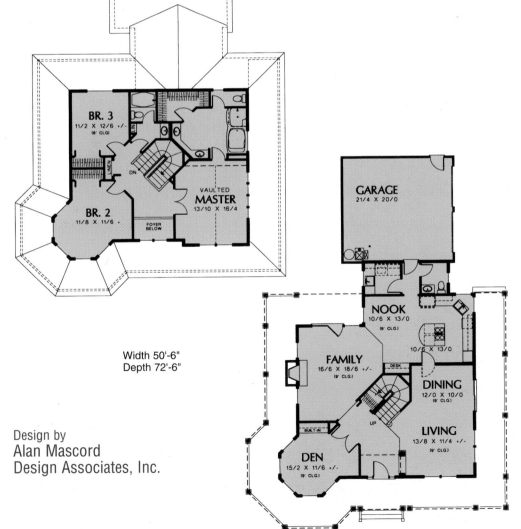

Width 50'-6"
Depth 72'-6"

Design by
Alan Mascord
Design Associates, Inc.

BR. 3
11/2 X 12/6 +/-
(8' CLG)

BR. 2
11/8 X 11/6 +/-

VAULTED
MASTER
13/10 X 16/4

FOYER
BELOW

DN

LINEN

GARAGE
21/4 X 20/0

NOOK
10/6 X 13/0
(9' CLG)

10/6 X 13/0

FAMILY
16/6 X 18/6 +/-
(9' CLG)

DESK

DINING
12/0 X 10/0
(9' CLG)

BUILT-IN

UP

LIVING
13/8 X 11/4 +/-
(9' CLG)

DEN
15/2 X 11/6 +/-
(9' CLG)

*This home, as shown in the photograph, may differ from the actual blueprints.
For more detailed information, please check the floor plans carefully.*

Design 9055

First Floor: 997 square feet
Second Floor: 1,069 square feet
Total: 2,066 square feet

◆ With its exceptional detail and proportions, this home is reminiscent of the Queen Anne Style. Turned posts resting on brick pedestals support a raised-gable entry to the veranda. The foyer opens to a living area with a bay-windowed alcove and a fireplace with flanking bookshelves. A large walk-in pantry and box window at the sink enhance the kitchen. Natural light fills the breakfast area through a full-length bay window and a French door. Upstairs, the master bedroom offers unsurpassed elegance and convenience. The sitting area has an eleven-foot ceiling and arch-top windows. The bath area features a large walk-in closet, His and Hers lavatories and plenty of linen storage. Plans for a two-car detached garage are included.

QUOTE ONE®

Cost to build? See page 214 to order complete cost estimate to build this house in your area!

Design by
Larry W.
Garnett &
Associates, Inc.

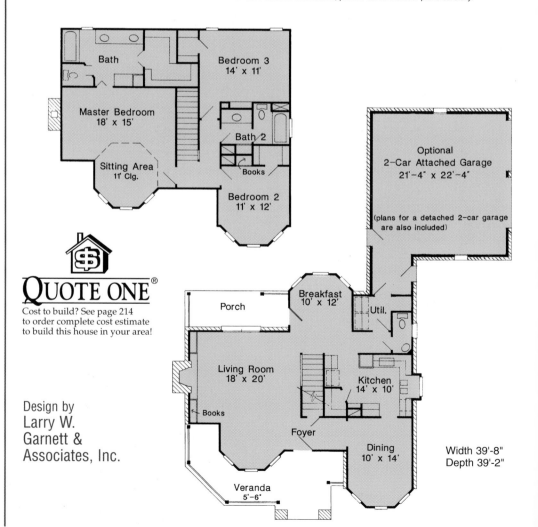

Width 39'-8"
Depth 39'-2"

Width 52'
Depth 46'

QUOTE ONE®

Cost to build? See page 214
to order complete cost estimate
to build this house in your area!

Design by
Home Planners

Design 3683

First Floor: 1,139 square feet
Second Floor: 576 square feet
Total: 1,715 square feet

L **D**

◆ Abe Lincoln most likely would have looked upon this log home as a palace. A rustically royal welcome extends from the wraparound porch, inviting one and all into a comfortable interior. To the right of the foyer, a two-story great room enhanced by a raised-hearth fireplace sets a spirited country mood. A snack bar joins the living area with an efficient, U-shaped kitchen and an attached nook. Two family bedrooms, a full bath and a utility room complete the first floor. The second-floor master suite features amenities that create a private, restful getaway. Curl up in the window seat with a good book or enjoy fresh air from your own private balcony. A walk-in closet, a soothing master bath and a loft/study for quiet contemplation complete this special retreat.

This home, as shown in the photograph, may differ from the actual blueprints.
For more detailed information, please check the floor plans carefully.

Design 2946

First Floor: 1,581 square feet
Second Floor: 1,344 square feet
Total: 2,925 square feet

L **D**

◆ Here's a traditional farm-house design that's made for down-home hospitality, casual conversation, and the good grace of pleasant company. The star attractions are the large covered porch and terrace, perfectly relaxing gathering points for family and friends. Inside, the design is truly a hard worker—separate living and family rooms, each with its own fireplace; a formal dining room; a large kitchen and breakfast area with a bay window; a private study; a workshop and a mud room. The second floor contains a spacious master suite with twin closets and three family bedrooms that share a full bath.

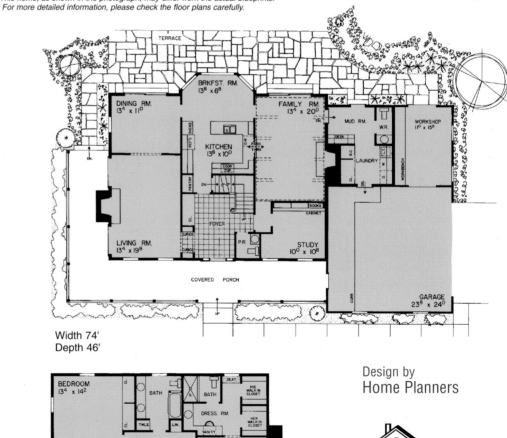

Width 74'
Depth 46'

Design by
Home Planners

QUOTE ONE®

Cost to build? See page 214
to order complete cost estimate
to build this house in your area!

This home, as shown in the photograph, may differ from the actual blueprints.
For more detailed information, please check the floor plans carefully.

Design by
Home Planners

Width 59'-6"
Depth 46'

Quote One®

Cost to build? See page 214
to order complete cost estimate
to build this house in your area!

Design 2774

First Floor: 1,366 square feet
Second Floor: 969 square feet
Total: 2,335 square feet

L **D**

◆ Here's a great farmhouse
adaptation with all the most
up-to-date features. There is
the quiet corner living room
which has an opening to the
sizable dining room. This
room will enjoy plenty of natural light from the delightful
bay window overlooking the
rear yard. The kitchen features
many built-ins and a pass-
through to the beam-ceilinged
breakfast room. Sliding glass
doors to the terrace are found
here and in the family room.
The service entrance to the
garage is flanked by a clothes
closet and a large walk-in
pantry. Four bedrooms and
two baths are located on the
second floor. The master bedroom has a dressing room and
double vanity.

Photo by Andrew D. Lautman

This home, as shown in the photograph, may differ from the actual blueprints. For more detailed information, please check the floor plans carefully.

Design 3699

First Floor: 1,356 square feet
Second Floor: 490 square feet
Total: 1,846 square feet

L **D**

 Split-log siding and a rustic balustrade create country charm with this farmhouse-style retreat. An open living room features a natural stone fireplace and a cathedral ceiling with exposed rough-sawn beams and brackets. A generous kitchen and dining area complete the living area and share the warmth of a fireplace. A laundry room is conveniently close to the master bedroom, which offers generous closets and a complete bath with double vanities and a shower. A second full bath and a nearby family bedroom complete the main floor. Upstairs, a spacious loft can serve as an office or study, an area for hobbies or recreation, or extra sleeping space. A full bath and a large storage area are nearby.

Design by
Home Planners

Width 50'-7"
Depth 38'

QUOTE ONE®

Cost to build? See page 214
to order complete cost estimate
to build this house in your area!

Countryside Cottages & Manors

Master Bedroom 15⁰x16⁰

Breakfast 14⁹x12⁹

Porch

Kitchen 14⁹x10⁰

Great Room 21⁰x15⁰

Dining Room 11⁹x14³

Porch

Two Car Garage 22⁰x26⁹

Width 55'
Depth 77'

Design by
Design Traditions

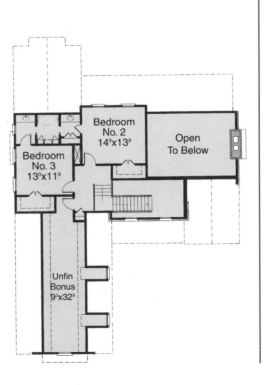

Bedroom No. 2 14⁹x13⁹

Open To Below

Bedroom No. 3 13⁰x11⁹

Unfin Bonus 9³x32⁹

Design 7800

First Floor: 1,831 square feet
Second Floor: 651 square feet
Total: 2,482 square feet
Bonus Room: 394 square feet

◆ This purely country home characterizes all the charm of rural America. From the covered porch entrance, the front door opens to a formal dining room and great room with a fireplace. A rear porch offers outdoor livability to the great room. The U-shaped kitchen and adjoining breakfast room are nearby and offer space for casual eating. Located on the first floor for privacy, the master bedroom features two large walk-in closets and a master bath designed for relaxation. A laundry room and a powder room complete this floor. Upstairs are two family bedrooms—each with a walk-in closet—and a shared bath with separate dressing areas. A large bonus space that might make another bedroom or handy study is also contained on the second floor. This plan is designed with a basement foundation.

Design 9868

First Floor: 1,725 square feet
Second Floor: 650 square feet
Total: 2,375 square feet

◆ This example of Classic American architecture features a columned front porch and wood framing. Bay window detailing and an arched dormer above the porch complete the picture. Straight ahead from the foyer, the great room is largely glass, and opens to the vaulted breakfast area which leads outdoors to the patio. The dining room and living room share a hearth and an open design with bay window treatments for interest and natural light. The master bedroom at the right rear of the home features a large bay window and a master bath with dual vanities, an individual shower and walk-in closets. The upper level is comprised of a gallery and a loft open to the great room and foyer below. Beyond the loft are two bedrooms that share a bath and an unfinished bonus room. This home is designed with a basement foundation.

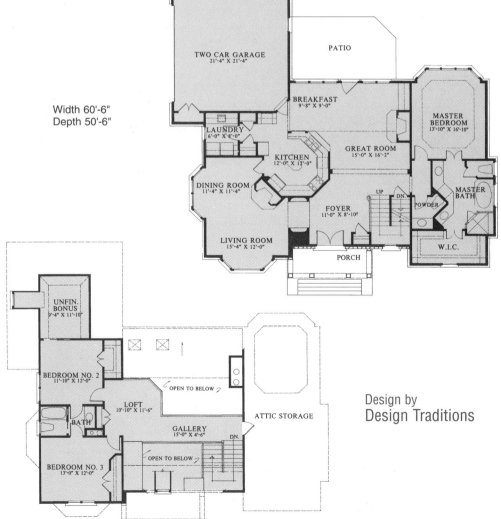

Width 60'-6"
Depth 50'-6"

Design by
Design Traditions

DECK

Width 57'-6"
Depth 46'-6"

BREAKFAST
9'-4" X 10'-6"

TWO STORY
GREAT ROOM
16'-8" X 15'-4"

MEDIA ROOM
12'-0" X 12'-0"

KITCHEN
15'-8" X 14'-0"

STORAGE

UP   DN.

POWDER   WET BAR

LAUNDRY
6'-2" X 7'-6"

TWO-CAR GARAGE
21'-4" X 21'-4"

DINING ROOM
12'-0" X 13'-0"

UP

TWO STORY
FOYER
10'-6" X 13'-0"

LIVING ROOM
12'-0" X 12'-2"

PORCH

SITTING

MASTER
BEDROOM
16'-0" X 13'-0"

OPEN TO BELOW

BALCONY

BEDROOM NO. 2
12'-0" X 11'-4"

BATH

DN.

DN.

MASTER
BATH

BATH

OPEN TO
BELOW

BEDROOM NO. 3
12'-0" X 11'-4"

W.I.C.

BEDROOM NO. 4
11'-2" X 12'-0"

SECRET
ROOM

REAR ELEVATION

Design by
Design Traditions

$
QUOTE ONE®

Cost to build? See page 214
to order complete cost estimate
to build this house in your area!

Design 9869

First Floor: 1,475 square feet
Second Floor: 1,460 square feet
Total: 2,935 square feet

◆ Through this home's columned entry, the two-story foyer opens to the living room with wet bar. The media room features a fireplace and is accessed from both the living room and the main hall. The two-story great room with fireplace is open to the breakfast area, kitchen and rear staircase, making entertaining a pleasure. The kitchen design is ideal, with a breakfast bar and a preparation island; the laundry room is nearby. The upper level begins with the balcony landing overlooking the great room. The master bedroom features a bayed sitting area and a tray ceiling. The master bath has dual vanities, a corner garden tub, a separate shower, a large walk-in closet and an optional secret room. Across the balcony, Bedrooms 2 and 3 share a bath. Bedroom 4 has its own private bath. This home is designed with a basement foundation.

Design 9972

First Floor: 1,809 square feet
Second Floor: 1,690 square feet
Total: 3,499 square feet

◆ Though charming, the front porch of this country cottage provides more than just a pretty facade. Rain or shine, the protective cover will inspire you to enjoy the outdoors. Inside, space for formal entertaining is provided by the living room/study and dining room that flank the foyer. A guest bedroom and an adjacent bath are conveniently located to the rear of the living room/study. An island cooktop enhances the efficient, U-shape kitchen which easily serves the breakfast room, the dining room, and the great room with its centered fireplace. The second floor contains three family bedrooms, two full baths, and a relaxing master suite with twin walk-in closets and a lavish master bath. This home is designed with a basement foundation.

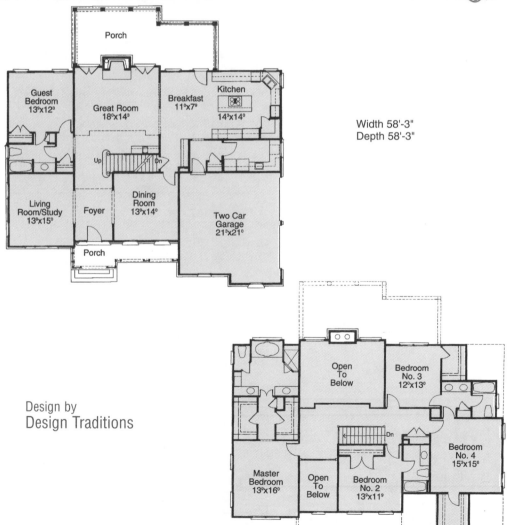

Width 58'-3"
Depth 58'-3"

Design by
Design Traditions

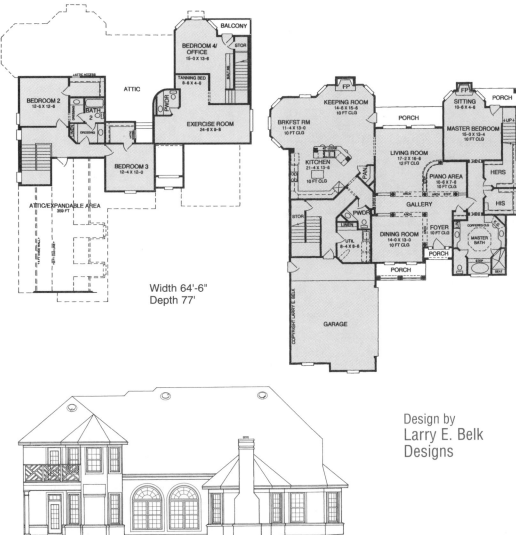

BALCONY

BEDROOM 4/
OFFICE
15-0 X 13-6

STOR

ATTIC ACCESS

TANNING BED
8-6 X 4-0

ATTIC

BEDROOM 2
12-6 X 12-6

BATH
2

LINEN

PWDR

BALT RM

DRESSING

EXERCISE ROOM
24-6 X 9-8

BEDROOM 3
12-4 X 12-0

ATTIC/EXPANDABLE AREA
359 FT

Width 64'-6"
Depth 77'

KEEPING ROOM
14-6 X 15-6
10 FT CLG

FP

SITTING
10-6 X 4-6

FP

PORCH

BRKFST RM
11-4 X 13-0
10 FT CLG

PORCH

MASTER BEDROOM
15-0 X 13-4
10 FT CLG

UP

KITCHEN
21-4 X 13-6

LIVING ROOM
17-2 X 16-6
12 FT CLG

LEDGE

PAN

PIANO AREA
10-6 X 7-8
10 FT CLG

HERS

10 FT CLG

STOR

GALLERY

HIS

PWDR

ARCH

ARCH

STEP

ARCH

ARCH

LINEN

DINING ROOM
14-0 X 13-0
10 FT CLG

FOYER
10 FT CLG

COFFERED CLG

UTIL
8-4 X 8-6

MASTER
BATH

PORCH

SEAT

PORCH

GARAGE

PORCH

Design by
Larry E. Belk
Designs

REAR

Design 8152

First Floor: 2,499 square feet
Second Floor: 1,260 square feet
Total: 3,759 square feet

◆ An eclectic facade graces this home designed with a unique twist. The master suite features private stairs that lead to an office above. An adjacent exercise room offers plenty of room for work out equipment and features an alcove for a tanning bed. A rear stair off the garage leads to Bedrooms 2 and 3 which are completely separate from the office and exercise area. Downstairs, a series of columns and arches defines the formal living and dining rooms. A dramatic curved area provides a special showcase for a baby grand piano and highlights the formal areas of the home. The kitchen, breakfast room and keeping room provide an open space for informal entertaining. Please specify slab or crawlspace foundation when ordering.

Design 9970

First Floor: 1,980 square feet
Second Floor: 1,317 square feet
Total: 3,297 square feet

◆ Centuries ago, the center
column played a vital role in
the support of a double-arched
window such as the one that
graces this home's exterior.
Today's amenities combined
with the well-seasoned architecture of Europe offer the best
of both worlds. The contemporary floor plan begins with a
soaring foyer that opens onto
the formal living and dining
rooms. Casual living is enjoyed at the rear of the plan in
the L-shaped kitchen, the family room and the light-filled
breakfast/sunroom. A guest
bedroom is tucked behind the
family room for privacy.
Upstairs, an exquisite master
suite features a lavish bath
and a huge walk-in closet.
Two family bedrooms, a full
bath and unfinished bonus
space complete the second
floor. This home is designed
with a basement foundation.

Width 58'-9"
Depth 66'-9"

Design by
Design Traditions

Width 47'
Depth 49'-6"

DECK

MEDIA ROOM
12'-0" X 15'-6"

TWO STORY
GREAT ROOM
14'-0" X 18'-0"

BREAKFAST
10'-0" X 10'-0"

KITCHEN
12'-6" X 11'-6"

UP

DN

UP

LAUNDRY

POWDER

TWO STORY
FOYER
10'-6" X 10'-8"

DINING ROOM
12'-0" X 11'-6"

LIVING ROOM
13'-4" X 10'-6"

TWO CAR GARAGE
21'-10" X 22'-0"

STOOP

BEDROOM NO. 2
12'-0" X 12'-0"

OPEN TO BELOW

SITTING

MASTER BEDROOM
19'-8" X 13'-6"

BALCONY

W.I.C.

W.I.C.

DN

MASTER
BATH

BATH

BEDROOM NO. 3
12'-0" X 12'-6"

OPEN TO
BELOW

W.I.C.

UNFIN. BONUS
12'-0" X 11'-4"

Quote One®

Cost to build? See page 214
to order complete cost estimate
to build this house in your area!

Design by
Design Traditions

Design 9864

First Floor: 1,395 square feet
Second Floor: 1,210 square feet
Total: 2,605 square feet

◆ The well-balanced use of stucco and stone combined with box-bay window treatments and a covered entry make this English country home especially inviting. The two-story foyer opens on the right to the attractive living and dining rooms with large windows. The step-saving kitchen and breakfast areas flow easily into the two-story great room and a media room with a see-through fireplace. The second floor offers a pleasing combination of open design and privacy. The master bedroom has a modified tray ceiling and is complete with a sitting area. The master bath with a double vanity, separate shower and water closet leads to a large walk-in closet. Double vanities are also found in the full bath off the hall. Bedrooms 2 and 3 are ample in size and feature walk-in closets. This home is designed with a basement foundation.

23

Design 8088

First Floor: 1,904 square feet
Second Floor: 792 square feet
Total: 2,696 square feet

◆ This charming cottage has all the accoutrements of an English manor. Inside, the angled foyer directs the eye to the arched entrances of the formal dining room and the great room with its fireplace and patio access. The kitchen features an island cooktop, a large walk-in pantry and a utility area with access to the garage. Plenty of counter and cabinet space assure a great layout. The master bedroom and a guest bedroom (or possible study) are located at the opposite end of the house for privacy. The master bedroom includes access to a private porch and a master bath with a corner whirlpool tub, a separate shower and a tremendous walk-in closet. Two additional bedrooms, a full bath, a game room and an upper deck are located on the second floor. Please specify crawlspace or slab foundation when ordering.

Design by
Larry E. Belk
Designs

Width 67'-8"
Depth 64'-10"

Quote One®

Cost to build? See page 214 to order complete cost estimate to build this house in your area!

Design 2854

First Floor: 1,261 square feet
Second Floor: 950 square feet
Total: 2,211 square feet

L **D**

◆ This charming Tudor-style home truly demonstrates a person's home is their castle. Though technically a story and a half, the second floor offers so much livability, it's more like a two-story plan. The first floor is solidly designed for efficiency and contains a living room with a fireplace, a large formal dining room, a beam-ceilinged family room, an efficient U-shaped kitchen, a study with a sunny bay window and a covered porch. In addition to a large master suite, two kids' rooms and a second full bath, the second floor includes a cozy spot that could serve as a home office, a nursery or a play area.

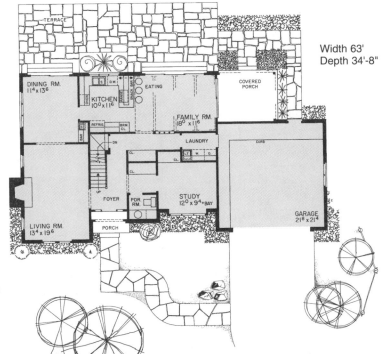

Width 63'
Depth 34'-8"

Design by
Home Planners

Photo by Nick Kelsh

Design 2855

First Floor: 1,372 square feet
Second Floor: 1,245 square feet
Total: 2,617 square feet

L **D**

◆ This elegant Tudor house is perfect for the family who wants to move up in living area, style and luxury. As you enter this home you will find a large living room with a fireplace on your right. Adjacent, the formal dining room has easy access to both the living room and the kitchen. The kitchen/breakfast room has an open plan and access to the rear terrace. Sunken a few steps, the spacious family room is highlighted with a fireplace and access to the rear covered porch. Note the optional planning of the garage storage area. Plan this area according to the needs of your family. Upstairs, your family will enjoy three bedrooms and a full bath, along with a spacious master bedroom suite, complete with a window seat, two closets and a lavish bath.

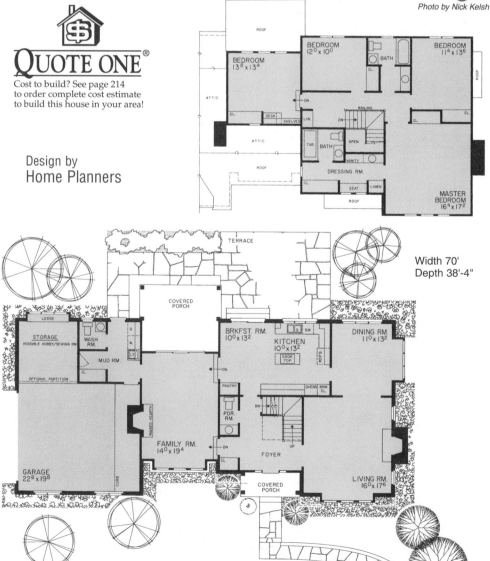

QUOTE ONE®

Cost to build? See page 214
to order complete cost estimate
to build this house in your area!

Design by
Home Planners

Width 70'
Depth 38'-4"

Design by
Design Traditions

Width 50'
Depth 50'-6"

Design 9819

First Floor: 1,678 square feet
Second Floor: 1,677 square feet
Total: 3,355 square feet

◆ This English Manor home features a dramatic brick-and-stucco exterior accented by a gabled roofline and artful half-timbering. Inside, the foyer opens to the formal living room accented with a vaulted ceiling and boxed bay window. The dining room flows directly off the living room and features its own angled bay window. Through the double doors lies the center of family activity. An entire wall of glass, accented by a central fireplace, spans from the family room through to the breakfast area and kitchen. For your guests, a bedroom and bath are located on the main level. The second floor provides two additional bedrooms and a bath for children. The master suite—with its tray ceiling, fireplace and private study—is a pleasant retreat. This home is designed with a basement foundation.

27

Design 9975

First Floor: 2,357 square feet
Second Floor: 1,021 square feet
Total: 3,378 square feet

◆ Baronial in attitude, the Chateau style reflects the Renaissance elegance of its namesake castles in France. Here, the basic formality of the Chateau style has been purposely mellowed for modern-day living: the roof line is simplified, and massive masonry construction is replaced by a stucco finish. The two-story foyer is made for grand entrances, with a marble floor and a sweeping staircase. The foyer opens to the formal dining room and leads to the great room with its fireplace, vaulted ceiling and wet bar. Also located on the first floor is the master suite, which has twin walk-in closets, and a quaint keeping room with a fireplace adjoining the kitchen and breakfast areas. Upstairs you will find three generous bedrooms and two baths, one private, plus a bonus room. This home is designed with a basement foundation.

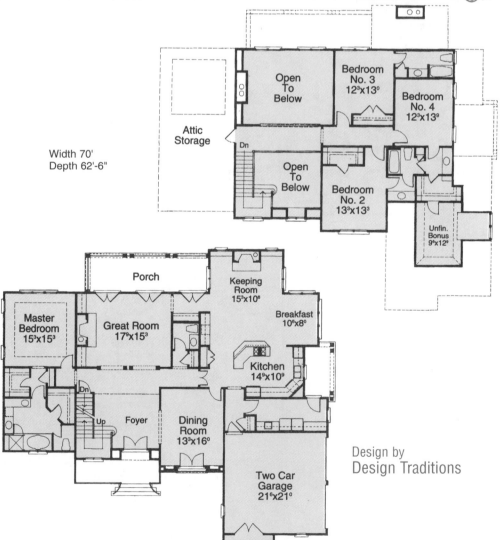

Width 70'
Depth 62'-6"

Attic Storage

Open To Below

Bedroom No. 3
12³x13⁰

Bedroom No. 4
12³x13⁹

Open To Below

Bedroom No. 2
13³x13³

Unfin. Bonus
9⁹x12⁹

Dn

Porch

Keeping Room
15³x10⁰

Breakfast
10⁶x8⁰

Master Bedroom
15³x15³

Great Room
17⁹x15³

Kitchen
14⁹x10⁹

Dn

Up

Foyer

Dining Room
13³x16⁰

Two Car Garage
21⁶x21⁰

Design by
Design Traditions

Quote One®

Cost to build? See page 214 to order complete cost estimate to build this house in your area!

Width 63'
Depth 51'

Design by
Design Traditions

Design 9816

First Floor: 1,900 square feet
Second Floor: 800 square feet
Total: 2,700 square feet

◆ Through the blending of stucco and stacked stone, this Country French home represents a specific architectural motif with the repeated arch pattern evident in the windows and doorway transom. The foyer is flanked by the spacious dining room and study which is accented by a warming fireplace. Adjacent to the great room is the breakfast area; its generous use of windows and its volume ceiling make it feel more like a sunroom extension for the spacious kitchen. The master suite of this home is located on the main level, providing the ultimate in convenience and privacy. A large accommodating bath offers separate vanities and individual closet areas. The upstairs of this livable plan has three bedrooms, large walk-in closets and a shared bath which allows for maximum privacy. This home is designed with a basement foundation.

COPYRIGHT 1993 LARRY E. BELK

Design 8044

First Floor: 1,897 square feet
Second Floor: 1,219 square feet
Total: 3,116 square feet
Bonus Room: 451 square feet

Design 8045

First Floor: 1,844 square feet
Second Floor: 1,103 square feet
Total: 2,947 square feet

◆ A stucco finish and front porch with a metal roof dress up this home designed for the growing family. A large kitchen, breakfast room and family room are open and adjacent to one another. The family room features a corner fireplace and provides access to the covered porch in the rear. A two-story living room and a dining room are available for more formal entertaining. The master bedroom is located downstairs. A luxuriously appointed master bath includes His and Hers walk-in closets, and a corner whirlpool tub. Either a three- (Design 8044) or four-bedroom (Design 8045) upstairs is available. Please specify crawlspace or slab foundation when ordering.

Design by
Larry E. Belk
Designs

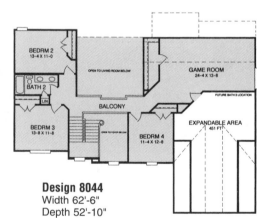

Design 8044
Width 62'-6"
Depth 52'-10"

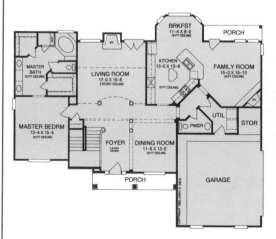

Design 8045
Width 61'-8"
Depth 52'

30

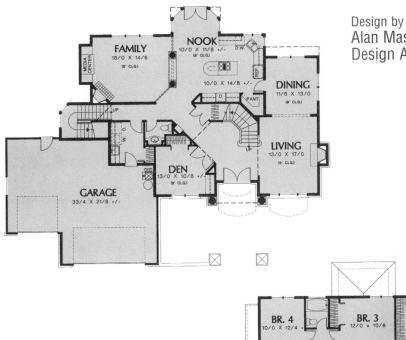

Design by
Alan Mascord
Design Associates, Inc.

Design 9559

First Floor: 1,763 square feet
Second Floor: 1,469 square feet
Total: 3,232 square feet
Bonus Room: 256 square feet

◆ European hospitality comes to mind with this home's high, hipped roof and detailed facade of stone and stucco. This traditional floor plan places the formal living and dining rooms together for elegance in entertaining and the casual areas to the rear of the home. The central kitchen is accessible to the formal dining room while being open to the breakfast nook and family room. The family room has a corner fireplace and a built-in media center. A den and powder room complete this floor. Upstairs, the master suite is situated to one side for privacy. An extra-large master bathroom with dual vanities and a corner spa tub precedes a huge walk-in closet. Three family bedrooms—two that share a private bath—a bonus room, a rear stair, and a hall bath round out this floor.

Width 70'
Depth 57'

Design 9862

Square Footage: 2,170

◆ This classic cottage features a stone-and-wood exterior with an arch-detailed porch and a box-bay window. From the foyer, double doors open to the den with built-in bookcases and a fireplace. A full bath nearby allows it to serve as an optional guest room. The family room is centrally located, just beyond the foyer. Its hearth is framed by windows overlooking the porch at the rear of the home. The master bedroom opens onto the rear porch. The master bath, with a large walk-in closet, double vanities, a corner tub and a separate shower, completes this relaxing retreat. Left of the family room awaits a sun room with access to the covered porch. A breakfast area complements the attractive and efficient kitchen. Two secondary bedrooms with large closets share a full bath featuring double vanities. This home is designed with a basement foundation.

Design by
Design Traditions

Quote One®

Cost to build? See page 214 to order complete cost estimate to build this house in your area!

Width 62'
Depth 61'-6"

Design by
Design Traditions

QUOTE ONE®
Cost to build? See page 214
to order complete cost estimate
to build this house in your area!

PORCH

BREAKFAST
13'-4" X 9'-0"

BEDROOM/
OFFICE
10'-4" X 11'-0"

KITCHEN
13'-4" X 10'-6"

GREAT ROOM
17'-0" X 17'-8"

DN.

BATH

LAUNDRY

TWO CAR GARAGE
20'-6" X 19'-6"

DINING ROOM
11'-4" X 12'-10"

FOYER
5'-4" X
12'-10"

PORCH

Width 61'
Depth 70'-6"

MASTER
BATH

MASTER BEDRDOOM
16'-4" X 13'-6"

BEDROOM NO. 2
10'-4" X 12'-0"

BATH

BEDROOM/
STUDY
11'-2" X 12'-0"

34

Design 9853
Square Footage: 2,090

◆ This traditional home features board-and-batten and
cedar shingles in an attrac-
tively proportioned exterior.
The foyer opens to both the
dining room and great room
beyond with French doors
opening onto the porch.
Through the double doors to
the right of the foyer is the
combination bedroom/study.
A short hallway leads to a full
bath and a secondary bed-
room with ample clo___
The master bed___
cious, wi___
b___

Design 9855

Square Footage: 2,935

◆ This spacious one-story easily accommodates a large family, providing all the luxuries and necessities of life. For formal occasions, there is a grand dining room just off the entry foyer. It features a vaulted ceiling and is just across the hall from the gourmet kitchen. The great room offers a beautiful ceiling treatment and access to the rear deck. For more casual times, the breakfast nook and adjoining keeping room with a fireplace fill the bill. The master suite is spacious and filled with amenities that include sitting room, a walk-in closet and access to the rear deck. The family bedrooms share a bath. Each of these bedrooms has its own lavatory. This home designed with a foundation.

MASTER BATH

SITTING RM.
11'-6" X 10'-0"

DECK

KEEPING ROOM
15'-3" X 15'-3"

VLT. CLG.

MASTER SUITE
18'-0" X 16'-0"

W.I.C.

GREAT ROOM
15'-6" X 17'-3"

KITCHEN
14'-0" X 13'-3"

BREAKFAST
14'-0" X 13'-0"

DN.

BEDROOM NO. 3
12'-0" X 12'-0"

W.I.C.

W.I.C.

POWDER

LAUNDRY

BATH

FOYER

BEDROOM NO. 2
13'-3" X 11'-6"

DINING ROOM
13'-3" X 18'-6"

2-CAR GARAGE
21'-6" X 21'-6"

STOOP

VLT. CLG.

Design by
Design Traditions

Width 71'
Depth 66'

DECK

BREAKFAST
12'-0"x 13'-6"

DN.

GREAT ROOM
20'-6"x 18'-6"

SITTING
12'-0"x 12'-0"

W.I.C.

MASTER BATH

MASTER SUITE
16'-6"x 15'-0"

W.I.C.

KITCHEN
14'-3"x 13'-6"

POWDER

BEDROOM NO.3
12'-0"x 12'-0"

FOYER

LAUNDRY
9'-0" X 8'-6"

DINING ROOM
13'-6" X 14'-6"

BATH

STORAGE

STOOP

BEDROOM NO.2
12'-3"x 14'-0"

TWO CAR GARAGE
21'-6"x 27'-6"

Width 73'-6"
Depth 78'

Design by
Design Traditions

Design 9854
Square Footage: 2,770

◆ This English cottage with cedar shake exterior displays the best qualities of a traditional design. With the bay window and recessed entry, visitors will feel warmly welcomed. The foyer opens to both the dining room and the great room with its fireplace and built-in cabinetry. Surrounded by windows, the breakfast room opens to a gourmet kitchen and a laundry room conveniently located near the garage entrance. To the right of the foyer is a hall powder room. Two bedrooms with large closets are joined by a full bath with individual vanities and a window seat. Through double doors at the end of a short hall, the master suite awaits with a tray ceiling and an adjoining sunlit sitting room. The master bath has His and Hers closets, separate vanities, an individual shower and a garden tub with bay window. This home is designed with a basement foundation.

Design 9966

Square Footage: 2,796

◆ Country details brighten the exterior of this one-story design and grace it with a warmth and charm that says "home." The floor plan includes a formal dining room and an all-purpose great room that opens to the kitchen and the keeping room. A bayed breakfast room is completely enclosed in glass. A master bedroom suite is found to the rear of the plan for privacy. It holds access to the rear covered porch and sports an extra large walk-in closet and detailed bath. The family bedrooms share a full bath but each has its own lavatory. A two-car, side-load garage has extra room for storage. This home is designed with a basement foundation.

Porch

Keeping Room
10⁹x12⁰

Breakfast
10⁰x10⁹

Great Room
18⁹x21⁹

Master Bedroom
17⁶x16⁰

Kitchen
18⁶x10⁰

Bedroom No. 2
12⁰x13⁰

Two Car Garage
21³x21³

Dining Room
13³x13⁹

Foyer

Dn

Porch

Bedroom No. 3
12⁰x13³

Design by
Design Traditions

Width 70'-9"
Depth 66'-6"

Traditional Country Spirit

Photo by Andrew D. Lautman

This home, as shown in the photograph, may differ from the actual blueprints. For more detailed information, please check the floor plans carefully.

Width 72'-10"
Depth 40'-10"

Design by
Home Planners

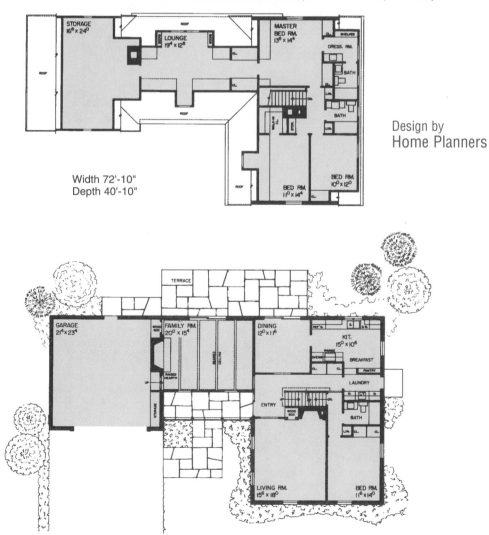

Design 2174

First Floor: 1,506 square feet
Second Floor: 1,156 square feet
Total: 2,662 square feet

L **D**

◆ Come home to country tradition every time you enter this charming two-story home. The appeal of the exterior is wrapped up in a myriad of features. They include the interesting roof lines, the delightful window treatment and a covered front porch. The comfort of the interior is represented by a long list of convenient living features. There is a formal area consisting of a living room with a fireplace and a dining room. The family room has a raised-hearth fireplace, a wood box and a beam ceiling. Also on the first floor is a kitchen with a breakfast area, a laundry and a bedroom with an adjacent bath. Three bedrooms, a lounge and two baths are found upstairs, plus plenty of closets and bulk storage over the garage.

37

Design 8118

First Floor: 1,905 square feet
Second Floor: 855 square feet
Total: 2,760 square feet

◆ An inviting front porch supplies a warm country touch to this appealing two-story home. Classic columns flank the entrance to the spacious living room. The island kitchen, bay-windowed breakfast room and large family room are open to one another, providing an expansive family retreat. The family room features a corner fireplace and access to the rear porch. The downstairs master bedroom includes a bath tailor-made for the working couple with His and Hers vanities and closets, a separate shower and a corner whirlpool tub. Upstairs three roomy bedrooms and a bath, as well as a uniquely shaped balcony, complete the plan. An additional 336 feet is available for future expansion. Please specify crawlspace or slab foundation when ordering.

Design by
Larry E. Belk
Designs

Width 62'-6"
Depth 52'-10"

COPYRIGHT LARRY E. BELK

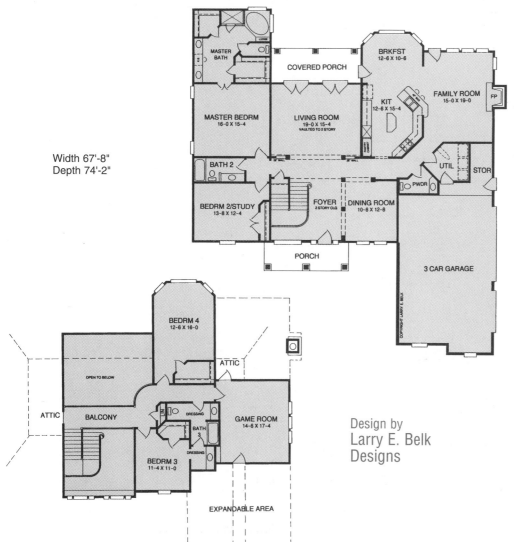

Width 67'-8"
Depth 74'-2"

MASTER BATH

COVERED PORCH

BRKFST
12-6 X 10-6

MASTER BEDRM
16-0 X 15-4

LIVING ROOM
19-0 X 15-4
VAULTED TO 2 STORY

KIT
12-6 X 15-4

FAMILY ROOM
15-0 X 19-0

FP

BATH 2

BEDRM 2/STUDY
13-8 X 12-4

FOYER
2 STORY CLG

DINING ROOM
10-8 X 12-8

PWDR

UTIL

STOR

3 CAR GARAGE

PORCH

COPYRIGHT LARRY E. BELK

BEDRM 4
12-6 X 16-0

ATTIC

OPEN TO BELOW

ATTIC

BALCONY

DRESSING

BATH 3

DRESSING

GAME ROOM
14-6 X 17-4

BEDRM 3
11-4 X 11-0

Design by
Larry E. Belk
Designs

EXPANDABLE AREA

Design 8075

First Floor: 2,469 square feet
Second Floor: 1,013 square feet
Total: 3,482 square feet

◆ Stacked stone, siding and brick supply textured character to this outstanding four-bedroom home. Inside, the two-story foyer opens to the living room and covered porch beyond. The kitchen, with a large work island, the breakfast room and the family room are conveniently grouped to provide a large area for informal entertaining. The master suite includes a master bath replete with all the amenities including a whirlpool tub, a shower, His and Hers vanities and walk-in closets. A second bedroom is located nearby and is perfect for a nursery, a guest bedroom or a study. Upstairs, two additional bedrooms share a bath designed with a private vanity area for each bedroom. The expandable area over the three-car garage provides a great opportunity to add an in-home office, exercise room or hobby room. Please specify crawlspace or slab foundation when ordering.

Design 8161

First Floor: 2,028 square feet
Second Floor: 558 square feet
Total: 2,586 square feet

◆ From the curb, this inviting entrance beckons family and friends to enter. The two-story foyer features a ledge perfect for displaying a special picture or tapestry. Arched openings form the entrance to the formal dining room and great room. An angled, see-through fireplace serves the great room, breakfast room and kitchen areas. The kitchen features an abundance of cabinet and counter space, a walk-in pantry and a built-in desk. A sitting area and a luxurious master bath enhance the private master suite. An adjacent secondary bedroom serves well as a guest room, a nursery or a study. Upstairs, two family bedrooms, a full bath and an expandable area complete the layout. Please specify slab or crawlspace foundation when ordering.

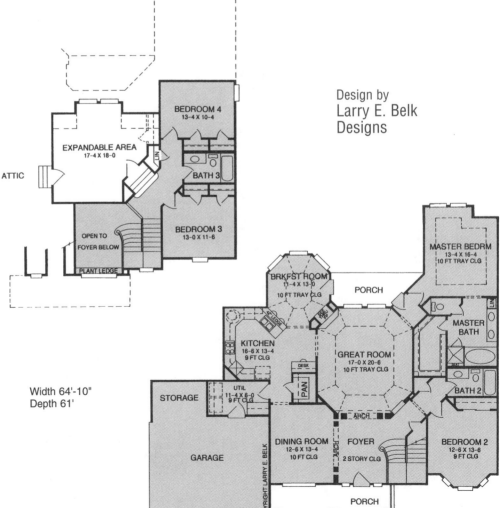

Design by
Larry E. Belk
Designs

Width 64'-10"
Depth 61'

GAME ROOM
16-6 X 16-6
8 FT CLG

ATTIC ACCESS

OPEN TO FOYER
BELOW

BEDROOM 3
11-4 X 13-4
9 FT CLG

BATH 3

ATTIC

BALCONY

STEP

BEDROOM 4
11-4 X 15-5
9 FT CLG

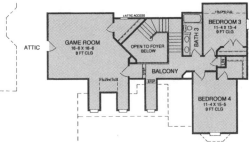

KEEPING ROOM
15-4 X 11-0
10 FT CLG

GREAT ROOM
15-4 X 17-6
10 FT CLG

HIS

MSTR
BATH

HERS

PORCH

BREAKFAST
17-6 X 10-0
10 FT CLG

MASTER BEDROOM
16-6 X 14-6
9 FT CLG

KITCHEN
15-4 X 14-6

FOYER
2 STORY CLG

10 FT CLG

DINING ROOM
15-0 X 13-4
10 FT CLG

VESTIBULE

UTIL

PANTRY

PORCH

BATH
2

BEDROOM 2
11-4 X 14-6
9 FT CLG

GARAGE

STORAGE

Width 67'-2"
Depth 62'-10"

Design by
Larry E. Belk
Designs

GAME ROOM
19-0 X 17-0
8 FT CLG

ATTIC ACCESS

OPEN TO FOYER
BELOW

LEDGE

BEDROOM 3
11-4 X 12-6
9 FT CLG

BATH 3

ATTIC

BALCONY

STEP

LINEN

BEDROOM 4
11-4 X 14-0
9 FT CLG

Optional Second Floor

Design 8115

First Floor: 2,199 square feet
Second Floor: 1,061 square feet
Total: 3,260 square feet

◆ Take one farmhouse—blend architectural features of the past with modern luxuries— and, voila! you have a perfect country home. Inside, an angled foyer opens through columns with arched openings to the dining room and the great room. The kitchen includes a walk-in pantry, an island cooktop and a breakfast bar. A bay window adds to the breakfast/keeping room with its built-in media center and two-way fireplace. The master suite features a secluded porch, a whirlpool tub, a separate shower and two walk-in closets. The other first-floor bedroom can be used as a study or a guest bedroom. An alternative second-floor plan increases the game room size. Please specify crawlspace or slab foundation when ordering.

Design 8003

First Floor: 1,961 square feet
Second Floor: 791 square feet
Total: 2,752 square feet

◆ The combination of stacked stone, brick and siding add warmth to this eye-catching elevation. Inside, the large, angled foyer provides unobstructed views into the great room and dining room. A see-through fireplace between the great room and dining room adds elegance and completes a stunning dining room separated from the foyer by large arches supported by round columns. The kitchen includes a bay window and continues with the ten-foot ceilings found throughout the kitchen area. The home is designed with two bedrooms downstairs. The second bedroom is multi-functional and can be used as a nursery or office/study. All bedrooms downstairs have nine-foot ceilings. Upstairs features two bedrooms and a large game room. Please specify crawlspace or slab foundation when ordering.

Width 64'-4"
Depth 62'

Design by
Larry E. Belk
Designs

This home, as shown in the photograph, may differ from the actual blueprints. For more detailed information, please check the floor plans carefully.

Photo by Andrew D. Lautman

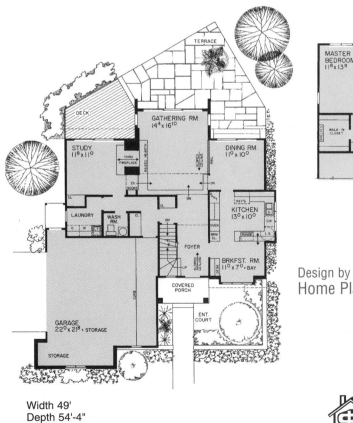

Width 49'
Depth 54'-4"

Design by
Home Planners

ALTERNATE KITCHEN / DINING RM. / BREAKFAST RM. FLOOR PLAN

Design 2826
First Floor: 1,112 square feet
Second Floor: 881 square feet
Total: 1,993 square feet

D

◆ This is an outstanding example of the type of informal, traditional-style architecture that has captured the modern imagination. Notice the spacious sunken gathering room with sliding glass doors to the rear terrace. It shares a through-fireplace with the quiet study, which offers access to a rear deck. Formal and informal dining areas are nicely separated by a roomy U-shaped kitchen. Upstairs, the master bedroom suite is sure to please, while two family bedrooms and a lounge fulfill the family's needs.

QUOTE ONE®
Cost to build? See page 214
to order complete cost estimate
to build this house in your area!

Design 3330

First Floor: 1,394 square feet
Second Floor: 320 square feet
Total: 1,714 square feet

◆ Outdoor enthusiasts will enjoy the covered porches, deck and terrace that highlight this delightful 1½-story home. Amenities include a private hot tub on the wooden deck that is accessible via sliding glass doors in both bedrooms, and a two-story gathering room. The first-floor master suite provides a private retreat. Here, sliding glass doors open onto a deck with a soothing hot tub. A large walk-in closet and dressing room enhance the connecting bath. An optional second-floor plan allows for a 503 square-foot lounge or a second master bedroom with a balcony.

Width 55'
Depth 56'

Design by
Home Planners

Floor Plans

MASTER BEDROOM
13⁰ x 16⁰

UPPER LIVING RM.

SLOPED CEILING

STUDIO
11⁰ x 14⁰

BATH

BALCONY
RAILING

WALK-IN CLOSET
WALK-IN CLOSET

UPPER FOYER
SLOPED CEILING
DN.

CL.

ROOF
SLOPED CEILING

OPEN

Width 55'-4"
Depth 52'-4"

Quote One®

Cost to build? See page 214
to order complete cost estimate
to build this house in your area!

TERRACE

BRKFST. RM.
13⁰ x 11⁰

DINING RM.
10⁴ x 12⁴

LIVING RM.
16⁰ x 16⁸

MEDIA RM./ BEDROOM
11⁰ x 13⁰

SECOND FLOOR LINE

LINEN

CL.

BATH

KITCHEN
11⁰ x 10⁰

COOK TOP
REF'S.

LAUND.
ETAGERE
CL.

FOYER
UP DN.
CL.

RAILING

COVERED PORCH

OPEN

BEDROOM
14⁰ x 13⁶

GARDEN COURT

GARAGE
21⁴ x 21⁴ + STOR.

STORAGE

CURB

LAMPPOST

Design by
Home Planners

Design 2927

First Floor: 1,425 square feet
Second Floor: 704 square feet
Total: 2,129 square feet

D

◆ This charming Early American adaptation offers a warm welcome—inside and out. The first floor features a convenient kitchen with a pass-through to the breakfast room. There's also a formal dining room just steps away in the rear of the house. An adjacent rear living room enjoys its own fireplace. Other features include a rear media room (or optional third bedroom) and a complete second-floor master suite. A downstairs bedroom enjoys an excellent front view. Other features include a garden court, a covered porch and a two-car garage with extra storage.

Design 9586

First Floor: 1,108 square feet
Second Floor: 798 square feet
Total: 1,906 square feet
Bonus Room: 262 square feet

◆ This charming Cape Cod, with three dormers and a covered porch, offers a warm welcome to family and visitors alike. Graceful bay windows fill the formal living room, located to the right of the foyer, and the formal dining room, found to the left, with sunlight. At the rear of the plan, the U-shaped kitchen combines well with the nook and the family room to provide maximum space for casual gatherings. A powder room and a utility room complete the first floor. Upstairs, two family bedrooms share a full hall bath. The master suite is filled with amenities that include a tray ceiling and a private bath with a walk-in closet, a spa tub and a separate shower. A bonus room located over the garage can be developed at a later date as needed.

Design by
Alan Mascord
Design Associates, Inc.

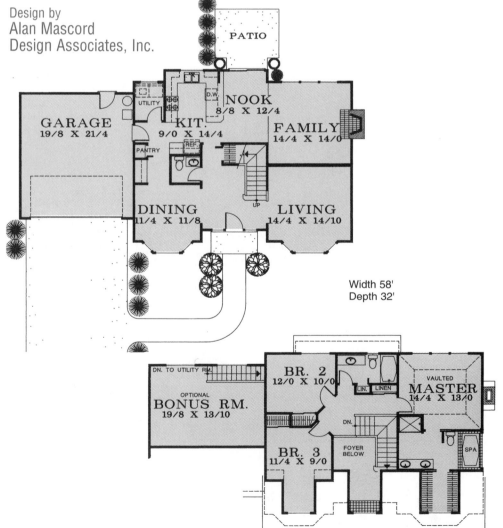

Width 58'
Depth 32'

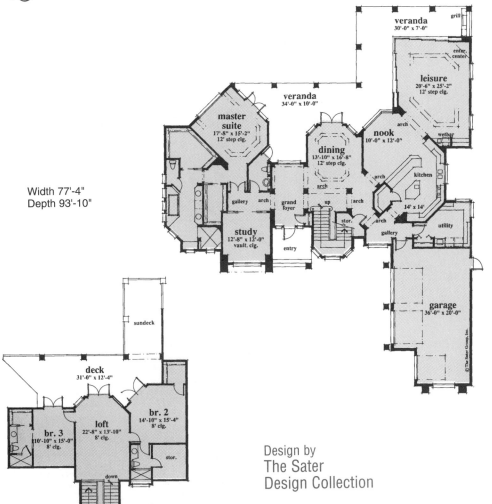

Width 77'-4"
Depth 93'-10"

veranda
30'-0" x 7'-0"

grill

enter.
center

leisure
20'-6" x 25'-2"
12' step clg.

veranda
34'-0" x 10'-0"

master
suite
17'-8" x 15'-2"
12' step clg.

dining
13'-10" x 16'-8"
12' step clg.

nook
10'-0" x 12'-0"

wetbar

arch

arch

gallery

arch

grand
foyer

up

arch

kitchen

14' x 14'

study
12'-8" x 12'-0"
vault. clg.

entry

stor.

arch

gallery

utility

garage
36'-0" x 20'-0"

© The Sater Group, Inc.

sundeck

deck
31'-0" x 12'-4"

br. 3
10'-10" x 15'-0"
8' clg.

loft
22'-8" x 13'-10"
8' clg.

br. 2
14'-10" x 15'-4"
8' clg.

stor.

down

Design by
The Sater
Design Collection

Design 6649

First Floor: 3,035 square feet
Second Floor: 945 square feet
Total: 3,980 square feet

◆ Rich custom details in this lovely transitional home provide luxury for the most discriminating homeowners. To the left of the foyer is the private master suite. The lavish bath contains a large walk-in closet for her, dual vanities and a compartmented toilet. An adjacent study combines well with the master suite. The dining room is perfect for formal occasions and the nearby kitchen with its island prep center and eating nook are ideal for casual meals. Completing this area is a leisure room with a built-in wet bar. The second floor accommodates a loft, two bedrooms with private baths, a large deck and a sun deck.

Design 9542

First Floor: 1,465 square feet
Second Floor: 1,103 square feet
Total: 2,568 square feet
Bonus Room: 303 square feet

◆ Here's traditional style at its best! The bay-windowed den with built-in bookshelves is conveniently located to the front of the plan, making it ideal for use as an office or home-based business. To the left, the formal area contains a living and dining room, both with a tray ceiling. Cooks will find the kitchen a delight, with its sunlit corner sink, cooktop island, large pantry and built-in planning desk. A bumped-out eating nook opens to the rear yard through double doors. Completing the first floor is a spacious family room with a fireplace. The second floor contains the sleeping zone. A master suite with a re-laxing spa tub, a separate shower and a huge walk-in closet is sure to please. Bedrooms 2 and 3 share a full bath. The three-car garage provides ample space for a work-shop.

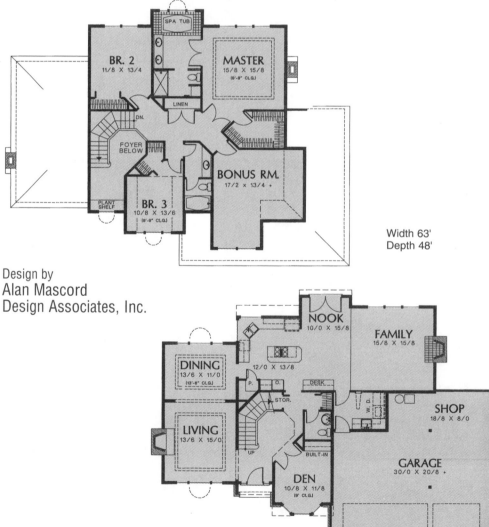

Design by
Alan Mascord
Design Associates, Inc.

Width 63'
Depth 48'

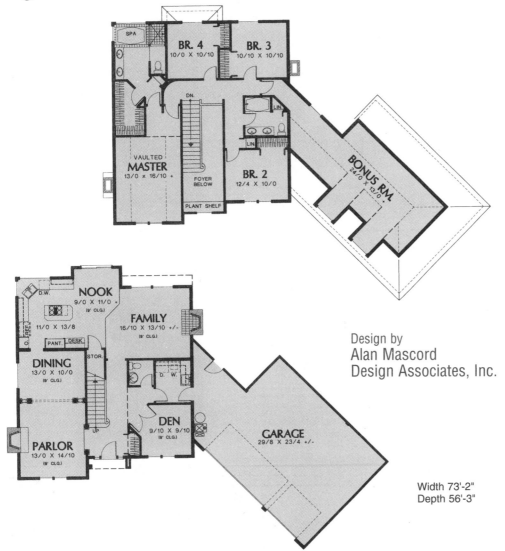

Design by
Alan Mascord
Design Associates, Inc.

Design 9584

First Floor: 1,308 square feet
Second Floor: 1,141 square feet
Total: 2,449 square feet
Bonus Room: 508 square feet

◆ Set at an angle, this home starts off with distinction. Just off the foyer and down a step, the formal parlor presents a welcoming atmosphere with its large window and warming fireplace. The island kitchen has convenient access to both the formal dining room and the sunny nook and looks out onto the large family room graced with yet a second fireplace. A den with double French doors completes this level. Upstairs, three secondary bedrooms share a hall bath with a double-bowl vanity while the vaulted master suite enjoys a huge walk-in closet and a private bath enhanced with a relaxing spa tub, separate shower, double-bowl vanity and compartmented toilet.

Width 73'-2"
Depth 56'-3"

Design 3615

First Floor: 1,355 square feet
Second Floor: 582 square feet
Total: 1,937 square feet

L

◆ A portico makes a strong architectural statement and provides shelter for this home's front entrance. The central foyer with its two-story ceiling and dramatic glass area routes traffic directly to all zones. To the left of the foyer is the formal dining room which is but a step from the angular kitchen. The great room has a high volume ceiling. Its raised-hearth fireplace is flanked by doors opening onto the deck. To the right of the foyer is the master suite. The master bath is compartmented and includes separate vanities, a walk-in closet, a whirlpool, a stall shower with seat, linen storage and access to the rear deck. Upstairs are two family bedrooms, a full hall bath and a balcony overlooking the great room below.

Design by
Home Planners

Width 65'
Depth 55'-8"

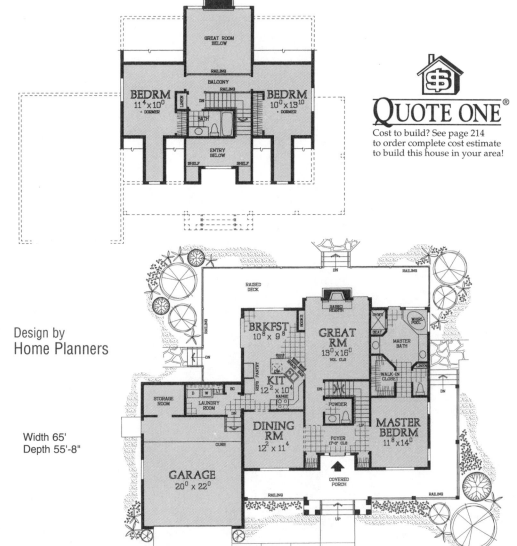

QUOTE ONE®

Cost to build? See page 214 to order complete cost estimate to build this house in your area!

Labels on floor plan:
COVERED PORCH
BRKFST 11⁰ x 9⁶
LAUNDRY ROOM
COVERED PATIO — SLOPED CEILING
SITTING/EXERCISE
MASTER BATH
SHWR
SEAT
LIN
WHIRL POOL
RAISED HEARTH
SNACK BAR
KIT 11⁰ x 13⁸
WALK-IN CLOSET
PANTRY
LINEN
FAMILY RM 16⁰ x 16⁸ — SLOPED CEILING
RAISED HEARTH
MORNING BAR
ENT. CENTER
MASTER SUITE 16⁶ x 15⁰
BEDRM 13² x 12⁰
WH
HVAC
HALLWAY
ARCH
LOW WALL
POWDER
WALK-IN CLOSET
BATH
LIN
ARCH
CHINA
SHELF
SHELF
BOOKSHELF
WALK-IN CLOSET
BEDRM 11⁴ x 13⁴
DINING RM 10⁴ x 12²
FOYER 11'-0" CEILING
LIVING RM 15⁴ x 12² — 11'-0" CEILING
COVERED PORCH
RAILING

Design 3613

Square Footage: 2,407

L

◆ A projecting portico with an archway supported by two sets of twin columns provides shelter, as well as an appealing front entrance. The dramatic central foyer has a high ceiling and an abundance of natural light. At the center of the plan is the family room with its sloped ceiling. It has a raised-hearth fireplace and an entertainment center. It looks over a low wall into the kitchen. The snack bar is nearby. French doors open to the covered patio. This plan offers the increasingly popular feature of split-sleeping facilities. There are two bedrooms and a bath for the children. At the opposite end of the plan is the master suite, where the focal point is the raised-hearth fireplace, which can be enjoyed on three sides—even from the whirlpool!

Design by
Home Planners

QUOTE ONE®

Cost to build? See page 214
to order complete cost estimate
to build this house in your area!

Width 65'-4"
Depth 55'

Design 3491
Square Footage: 2,098

L **D**

◆ This is a fine home for a
young family or for empty-
nesters. The versatile bed-
room/study offers room for
growth or a quiet haven for
reading. The U-shaped kitchen
includes a handy nook with a
snack bar and easy accessibility to the dining room and the
gathering room—perfect for
entertaining. The master bedroom includes its own private
outdoor retreat, a walk-in
closet and an amenity-filled
bathroom. An additional bedroom and a large laundry
room with an adjacent walk-in
pantry complete the plan.

Width 64'
Depth 69'-8"

Design by
Home Planners

QUOTE ONE®

Cost to build? See page 214
to order complete cost estimate
to build this house in your area!

PATIO

MASTER BEDRM
17⁴ x 14⁰

LIVING RM
17⁰ x 15⁴

DINING RM
10⁰ x 12⁶

BEDRM
14⁴ x 12⁰

WALK-IN CLOSET

LINEN

BC

LINEN

BATH

MASTER BATH

SNACK BAR

DW   SINK

RANGE

KIT
19⁰ x 11²

PANTRY

REFG

FOYER

SHOWER

D

W

GARDEN TUB

LAUNDRY

BEDRM
14⁴ x 14⁴

COVERED PORCH

RAILING

GARAGE
21⁴ x 20⁴

QUOTE ONE®

Cost to build? See page 214
to order complete cost estimate
to build this house in your area!

Design by
Home Planners

Width 64'-8"
Depth 54'-7"

Design 3652

Square Footage: 2,076

L **D**

◆ Multi-pane windows, mock-shutters and a covered front porch exhibit the charm of this home's facade. Inside, the foyer is flanked by a spacious, efficient kitchen to the right and a large, convenient laundry room to the left. Directly ahead is the living room which is graced by a warming fireplace. To the right of the living room is the formal dining room and both rooms share a snack bar and direct access to the kitchen. Sleeping quarters are split, with two family bedrooms and a full bath on the right side of the plan and the deluxe master suite on the left. The master bath offers such luxuries as a walk-in closet, twin vanities, a garden tub and a separate shower.

Design 3651

Square Footage: 2,213

L D

◆ This home's two projecting wings with low-pitched, overhanging roofs provide a distinctive note. The compact, efficient floor plan assures convenient living patterns. In the kitchen, a planning desk, an island cooking counter with storage below, double ovens, a pantry, fine counter space and a handy snack bar capture attention. The open planning of the living and dining rooms provides one big, spacious area for functional family living. The master bedroom has French doors to provide outdoor living potential.

Design by
Home Planners

Quote One®

Cost to build? See page 214 to order complete cost estimate to build this house in your area!

Width 60'
Depth 68'

This home, as shown in the photograph, may differ from the actual blueprints. For more detailed information, please check the floor plans carefully.

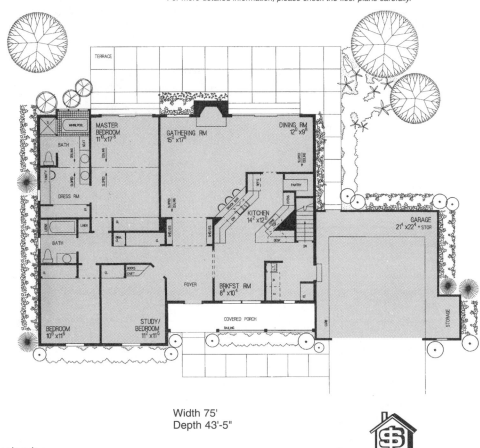

Width 75'
Depth 43'-5"

Design by
Home Planners

Design 2947
Square Footage: 1,830

L **D**

◆ This charming, one-story traditional home greets visitors with a covered porch. A galley-style kitchen shares a snack bar with the spacious gathering room where a fireplace is the focal point. An ample master suite includes a luxury bath with a whirlpool tub and a separate dressing room. Two additional bedrooms, with one that could double as a study, are located at the front of the home.

QUOTE ONE®

Cost to build? See page 214 to order complete cost estimate to build this house in your area!

Design 3487

Square Footage: 1,835

L

◆ Country living is the focus of this charming design. A cozy covered porch invites you into the foyer with the sleeping area on the right and the living area straight ahead. From the front-facing breakfast room, enter the efficient kitchen with its corner laundry room, large pantry, snack bar pass-through to the gathering room and entry to the dining area. The massive gathering room and dining room feature sloped ceilings, an impressive fireplace and access to the rear terrace. Terrace access is also available from the master bedroom with its sloped ceiling and a master bath that includes a whirlpool tub. A study at the front of the house can also be converted into a third bedroom.

Design by
Home Planners

Width 71'
Depth 43'-5"

Colonial Country Heritage

Design by
Design Traditions

Bedroom No. 2
11³x14⁰

Master Bedroom
16⁰x15³

Dn

Bedroom No. 3
12⁹x11⁹

Open To Below

Bedroom No. 4
12⁹x12³

Breakfast/Sunroom
11³x9⁰

Deck

Kitchen
11³x16⁰

Great Room
21³x15⁹

Width 57'
Depth 46'-4"

Two Car Garage
21⁹x21⁰

Dn Up

Dining Room
12⁶x14⁰

Foyer

Living Room
12⁶x12⁰

Design 9980

First Floor: 1,448 square feet
Second Floor: 1,491 square feet
Total: 2,939 square feet

◆ The semi-circular fanlight in the low-pitched gable echoes the one over the door, furthering the symmetry that dignifies the exterior of this impressive traditional home. Formal living areas are entered from the foyer—to the right is the living room and to the left, the dining room. Holiday banquets and dinner parties are simplified with a butler's pantry that links the dining room to the kitchen. Here, an island cooktop aids meal preparation and invites conversation with the family in the adjacent breakfast/sunroom and great room. This is sure to be a favorite place to kick back and relax. The second floor holds a spacious master suite, three secondary bedrooms—Bedroom 4 enjoys its own private bath—and three full baths. This home is designed with a basement foundation.

Design 7267

First Floor: 1,598 square feet
Second Floor: 1,675 square feet
Total: 3,273 square feet

◆ Main and second level covered porches accompanied by intricate detailing and many multi-pane windows create a splendid Southern mansion appearance. The prominent entry opens to formal dining and living rooms. The grand family room is warmed by a fireplace and views a screen porch with a cozy window seat. The roomy breakfast area provides access to a screen porch and a three-car garage. French doors open to the second floor's master bedroom suite. It features decorative ceiling details, His and Hers walk-in closets, a large dressing area, dual lavs, a whirl-pool bath and a separate shower area.

Design by
Design Basics, Inc.

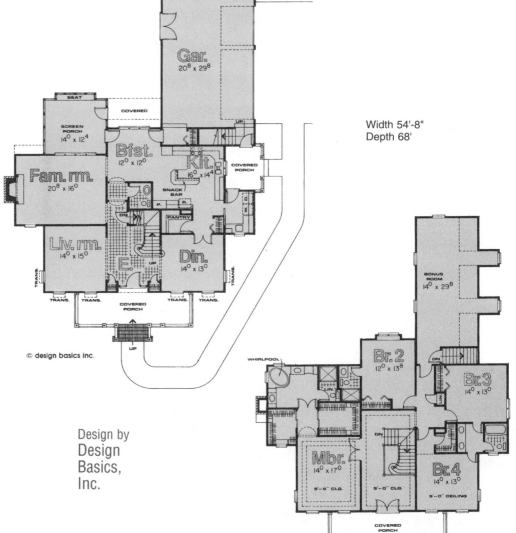

Width 54'-8"
Depth 68'

© design basics inc.

Design 9982

First Floor: 2,174 square feet
Second Floor: 1,113 square feet
Total: 3,287 square feet

◆ Front and back porches and a dash of old Southern charm give this home its warm appeal. The foyer is flanked by a dining room and a living room (or a study). You'll also find a great room with a fireplace for family livability. The kitchen and breakfast room are not far away from here. The first-floor master suite contains porch access, a luxurious private bath and a large walk-in closet. Upstairs, secondary bedrooms accommodate family or guests. This home is designed with a basement foundation.

Design by
Design Traditions

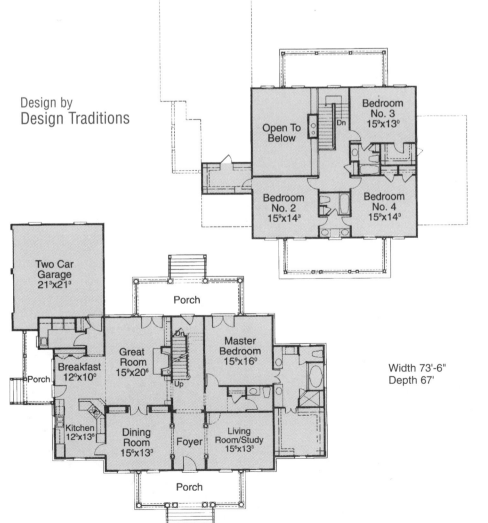

Width 73'-6"
Depth 67'

Design 2659

First Floor: 1,023 square feet
Second Floor: 1,008 square feet
Third Floor: 476 square feet
Total: 2,507 square feet

L **D**

◆ The facade of this three-storied, pitch-roofed house has a symmetrical placement of windows and a restrained but elegant central entrance. The central hall, or foyer, expands midway through the house to a family kitchen. Off the foyer are two rooms, a living room with a fireplace and a study. The windowed third floor attic can be used as a study and a studio. Three bedrooms are housed on the second floor, including a deluxe master suite with a pampering bath.

Design by
Home Planners

QUOTE ONE®

Cost to build? See page 214 to order complete cost estimate to build this house in your area!

Width 49'-8"
Depth 32'

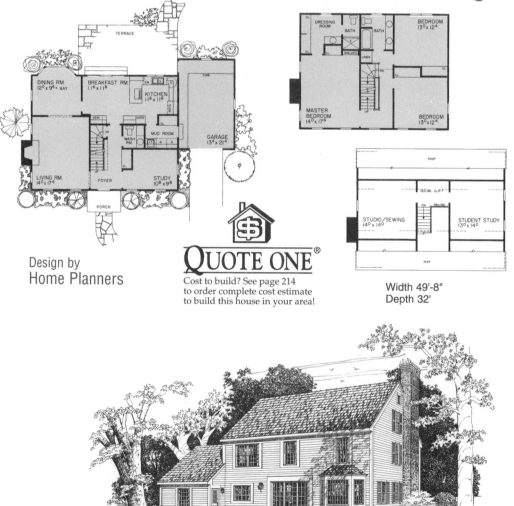

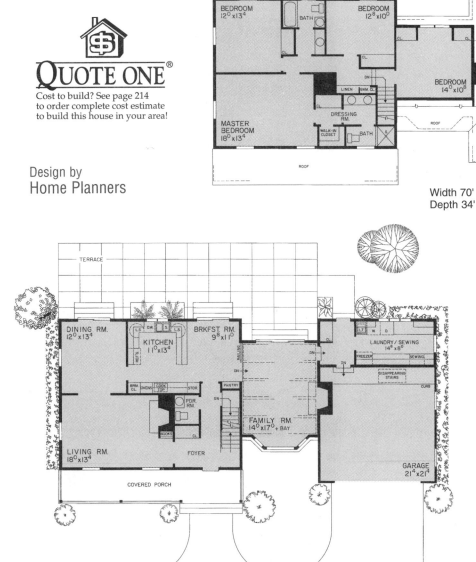

Design by
Home Planners

BEDROOM
12⁰x13⁴

BATH

BEDROOM
12⁸x10⁰

ROOF

CL

CL

ATTIC

CL

DN

LINEN BRM. CL.

BEDROOM
14⁰x10⁸

DRESSING RM.

MASTER BEDROOM
18⁰x13⁴

WALK-IN CLOSET

BATH

ROOF

ROOF

Width 70'
Depth 34'

TERRACE

DINING RM.
12⁰x13⁴

KITCHEN
11⁰x13⁴

BRKFST. RM.
9⁸x11⁰

REF'G.

BRM. CL.

OVENS

COOK TOP

STOR

PANTRY

PDR. RM.

BOOKS

CL

DN

DN

DN

RAILING

LT W D

LAUNDRY / SEWING
14⁶x8⁰

FREEZER

SEWING

DISAPPEARING STAIRS

CURB

CL

FAMILY RM.
14⁰x17⁰ + BAY

LIVING RM.
18⁰x13⁴

FOYER

COVERED PORCH

GARAGE
21⁴x21⁴

Design 2908

First Floor: 1,427 square feet
Second Floor: 1,153 square feet
Total: 2,580 square feet

L **D**

◆ This Early American farmhouse offers a contemporary
floor plan filled with amenities. Exterior enhancements
include the covered front
porch with pillars and rails,
double chimneys and a building attachment. The first-floor
attachment includes a family
room with a bay window that
connects the main house to a
two-car garage. The second
floor contains the master suite
with private bath and three
family bedrooms that share a
full bath. Special features of
this home include fireplaces in
the family room and living
room, a laundry/sewing room
with washer/dryer space, a
large rear terrace and an en-
try-hall powder room.

Design 3510

First Floor: 1,120 square feet
Second Floor: 1,083 square feet
Third Floor: 597 square feet
Total: 2,800 square feet

◆ Sweeping front and rear raised covered porches with solid columns, delicately detailed railings and wide centered stairs to formal and informal areas characterize this farmhouse. Designed to accommodate a relatively narrow building site, the efficient floor plan delivers outstanding livability for the active family. The kitchen/family room area is spacious and has a corner fireplace. Sliding glass doors provide access to the rear porch. In the master suite, a corner fireplace and a dressing area with a large walk-in closet and a separate vanity set the tone. Third-floor living possibilities include a home office, hobby area, studio or clutter room for family storage.

Quote One®

Cost to build? See page 214 to order complete cost estimate to build this house in your area!

Design by
Home Planners

Width 40'
Depth 40'

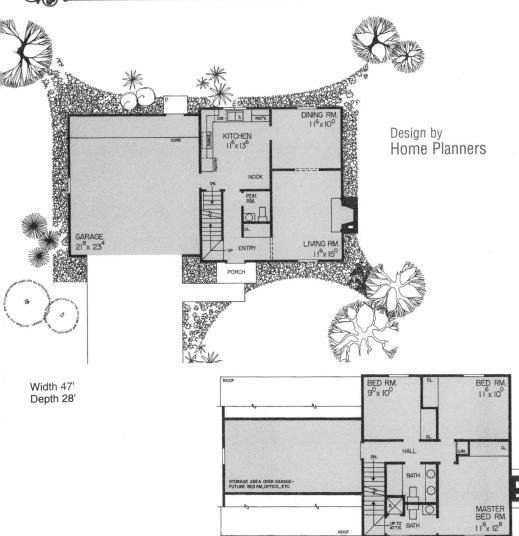

Width 47'
Depth 28'

GARAGE
21⁸ x 23⁴

KITCHEN
11⁶ x 13⁶

DINING RM.
11⁶ x 10⁰

NOOK

PDR. RM.

LIVING RM.
11⁶ x 15⁰

ENTRY

PORCH

STORAGE AREA OVER GARAGE-
FUTURE BED RM., OFFICE, ETC.

BED RM.
9⁰ x 10⁰

BED RM.
11⁶ x 10⁰

HALL

BATH

LIN.

MASTER
BED RM.
11⁶ x 12⁸

BATH

UP TO ATTIC

Design by
Home Planners

Design 2622

First Floor: 624 square feet
Second Floor: 624 square feet
Total: 1,248 square feet
Bonus Room: 247 square feet

◆ This Colonial adaptation provides a functional design that allows for expansion in the future. A cozy fireplace in the living room adds warmth to this space as well as the adjacent dining area. The roomy L-shaped kitchen features a breakfast nook and an over-the-sink window. Upstairs, two secondary bedrooms share a full bath with a double vanity. The master bedroom is on this floor as well. Its private bath contains access to attic storage. An additional storage area over the garage furnishes options for future development that may include a bedroom, an office, a study or an exercise room.

Design 9121

First Floor: 1,266 square feet
Second Floor: 639 square feet
Total: 1,905 square feet

◆ Complete with dormers and a covered front porch, the facade details of this home are repeated at the side-loaded garage, making it a perfectly charming plan from any angle. From the raised foyer, step down into the living room. This area opens to a dining room which has a French door to the rear yard. Close by is a kitchen with a pantry and access to a utility room and the garage. The master suite is on the first floor for convenience and offers two large walk-in closets. Upstairs there are two secondary bedrooms and a full compartmented bath. An entry near the garage leads to a staircase to optional storage room.

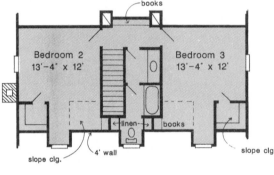

books

Bedroom 2
13'-4" x 12'

Bedroom 3
13'-4" x 12'

linen

books

slope clg.

4' wall

slope clg.

8' ceiling throughout second floor unless otherwise noted

QUOTE ONE®

Cost to build? See page 214 to order complete cost estimate to build this house in your area!

Design by
Larry W.
Garnett &
Associates, Inc.

Width 50'-4"
Depth 64'-4"

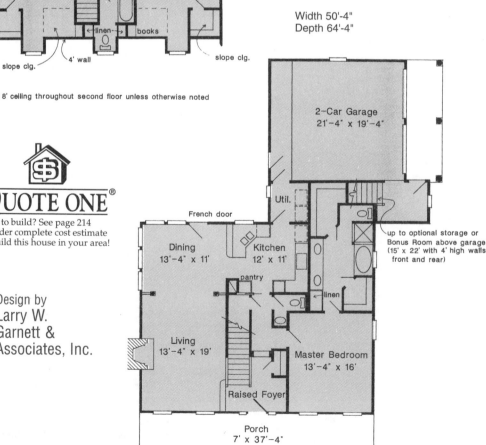

2-Car Garage
21'-4" x 19'-4"

Util.

French door

up to optional storage or Bonus Room above garage (15' x 22' with 4' high walls front and rear)

Dining
13'-4" x 11'

Kitchen
12' x 11'

pantry

linen

Living
13'-4" x 19'

Master Bedroom
13'-4" x 16'

Raised Foyer

Porch
7' x 37'-4"

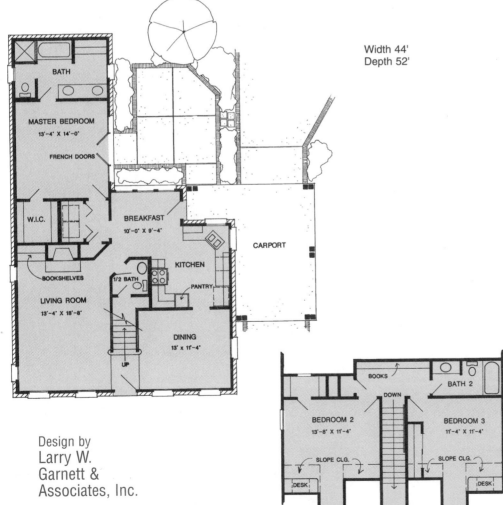

Width 44'
Depth 52'

Design by
Larry W.
Garnett &
Associates, Inc.

Design 9046

First Floor: 1,265 square feet
Second Floor: 571 square feet
Total: 1,836 square feet

◆ This quaint traditional plan
sports its architectural detail
with pride–three second-story
dormers, a covered carport
and shuttered multi-pane windows. Inside, it maintains
bragging rights to a great floor
plan as well. Note the efficient
traffic patterns established
with the placement of the living room, dining room and
kitchen/breakfast room combination. A powder room is
thoughtfully located in an out-
of-the-way corner. The master
suite is tucked to the back of
the first floor and has French
doors to the rear yard. Two
family bedrooms are found
upstairs—note the built-in
desks in each.

Design 8932

First Floor: 2,775 square feet
Second Floor: 1,082 square feet
Total: 3,857 square feet
Guest Quarters: 347 square feet

◆ This design showcases an extensive front porch and a dual-pitched hipped roof—both of which are typical features of the French Colonial style. Inside, the foyer dissolves into a dining room on one side and, on the other, a living room with a two-way fireplace and French doors to the conservatory and library. The house gourmet will relish the kitchen with its island cooktop. One of the more notable features of this house is the sunroom; it encompasses exposed brick walls, French doors to a back porch and a spiral staircase leading up to the loft. Three bedrooms define the upstairs—one has its own bath. The master bedroom, with a sitting area, library access and a large master bath, remains on the first floor for privacy. Not to be missed are the guest quarters located over the three-car garage.

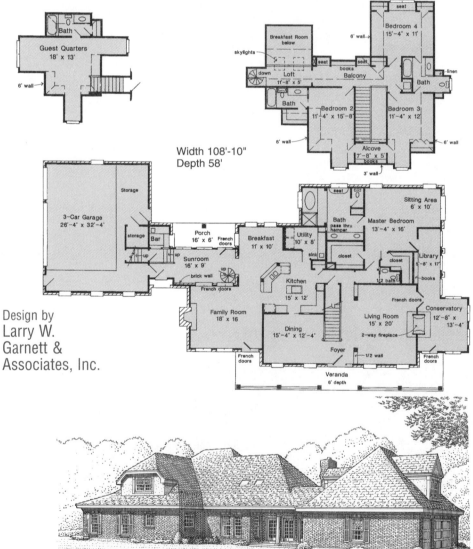

Design by
Larry W.
Garnett &
Associates, Inc.

Width 108'-10"
Depth 58'

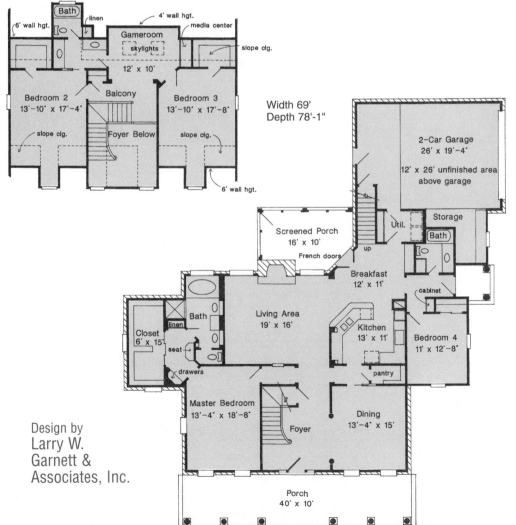

Bath
linen
6' wall hgt.
4' wall hgt.
media center
Gameroom
skylights
12' x 10'
slope clg.
Bedroom 2
13'-10" x 17'-4"
Balcony
Bedroom 3
13'-10" x 17'-8"
slope clg.
Foyer Below
slope clg.
6' wall hgt.

Width 69'
Depth 78'-1"

2-Car Garage
26' x 19'-4"
12' x 26' unfinished area above garage

Screened Porch
16' x 10'
French doors
up
Util.
Storage
Bath

Breakfast
12' x 11'
cabinet

Bath
linen
Closet
6' x 15'
seat
drawers

Living Area
19' x 16'

Kitchen
13' x 11'

Bedroom 4
11' x 12'-8"

pantry

Master Bedroom
13'-4" x 18'-8"
Foyer

Dining
13'-4" x 15'

Porch
40' x 10'

Design by
Larry W.
Garnett &
Associates, Inc.

Design 9120

First Floor: 2,109 square feet
Second Floor: 950 square feet
Total: 3,059 square feet

◆ This distinctive Greek Revival-style home works well in a 1½-story plan. The 10'-deep covered porch of this home opens to an entry foyer that connects the dining room and living room and contains the stairway to the second floor. Stairs at the breakfast room provide access to a 12'x 26' future room. The master bedroom is complemented by a bath with many amenities. Tucked away to the right of the plan is a bedroom that works well as guest quarters or could hold a home office or study. For additional sleeping space, there are two bedrooms with dormer windows and walk-in closets, plus a full bath on the second floor.

9' ceiling throughout first and second floor unless otherwise noted

Design 3614

First Floor: 2,300 square feet
Second Floor: 812 square feet
Total: 3,112 square feet

◆ If you're looking for the real McCoy—lightly influenced by classic style—you need look no further. A circle-top window and proportional balustrades provide the refined appearance on this charming farmhouse. Inside, the foyer opens to a formal living room on the right and a formal dining room on the left. The kitchen—bordered by a snack bar—unites the breakfast room with the family room which features an entertainment center and a fireplace. The first-floor master suite is filled with amenities that include a raised-hearth fireplace, a sitting room, a wall of bookshelves and a unique master bath with a relaxing whirlpool tub. Tucked behind the kitchen is a guest suite. The second-floor contains two family bedrooms and a full bath.

Design by
Home Planners

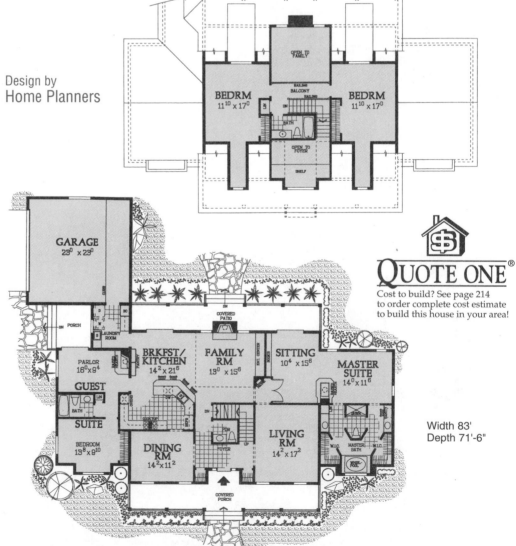

Quote One®

Cost to build? See page 214 to order complete cost estimate to build this house in your area!

Width 83'
Depth 71'-6"

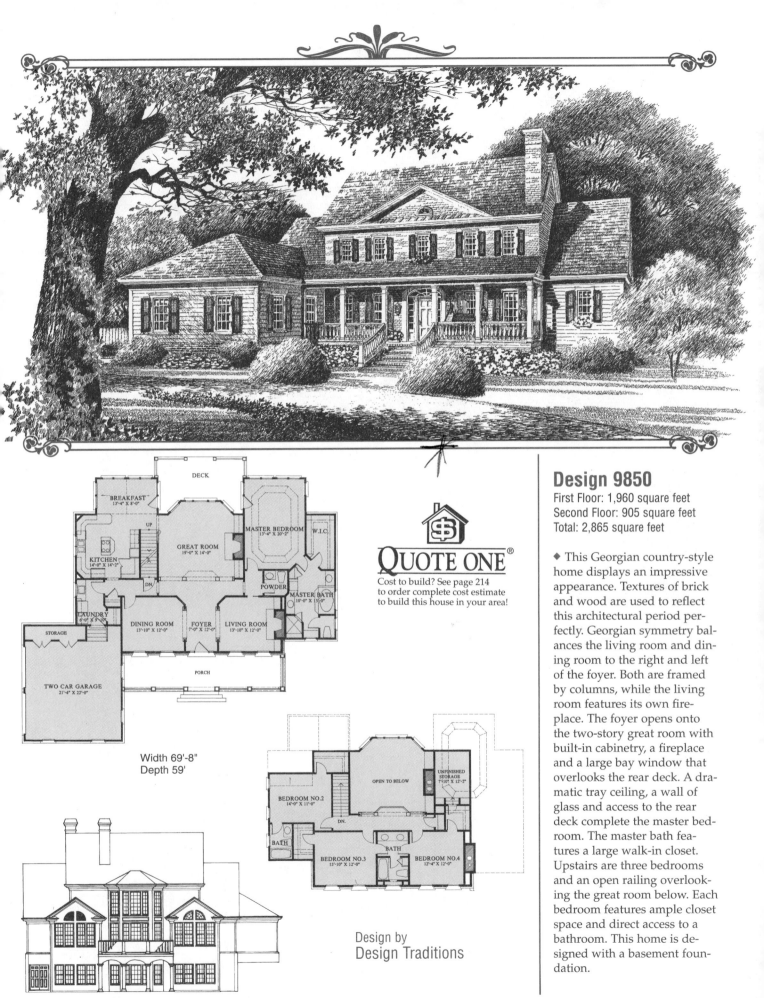

DECK

BREAKFAST
13'-4" X 8'-0"

KITCHEN
14'-0" X 14'-2"

UP

DN

GREAT ROOM
19'-0" X 14'-0"

MASTER BEDROOM
13'-4" X 20'-2"

W.I.C.

POWDER

MASTER BATH
10'-0" X 15'-0"

LAUNDRY
6'-0" X 9'-10"

STORAGE

DINING ROOM
13'-10" X 12'-0"

FOYER
7'-0" X 12'-0"

LIVING ROOM
13'-10" X 12'-0"

TWO CAR GARAGE
21'-4" X 22'-0"

PORCH

Width 69'-8"
Depth 59'

QUOTE ONE®

Cost to build? See page 214
to order complete cost estimate
to build this house in your area!

BEDROOM NO.2
14'-0" X 11'-0"

OPEN TO BELOW

UNFINISHED
STORAGE
7'-10" X 12'-2"

BATH

DN

BEDROOM NO.3
13'-10" X 12'-0"

BATH

BEDROOM NO.4
12'-4" X 12'-0"

Design by
Design Traditions

Rear Elevation

Design 9850

First Floor: 1,960 square feet
Second Floor: 905 square feet
Total: 2,865 square feet

◆ This Georgian country-style home displays an impressive appearance. Textures of brick and wood are used to reflect this architectural period perfectly. Georgian symmetry balances the living room and dining room to the right and left of the foyer. Both are framed by columns, while the living room features its own fireplace. The foyer opens onto the two-story great room with built-in cabinetry, a fireplace and a large bay window that overlooks the rear deck. A dramatic tray ceiling, a wall of glass and access to the rear deck complete the master bedroom. The master bath features a large walk-in closet. Upstairs are three bedrooms and an open railing overlooking the great room below. Each bedroom features ample closet space and direct access to a bathroom. This home is designed with a basement foundation.

Design 9977
Square Footage: 3,066

◆ Descended from the architecture that developed in America's Tidewater country, this updated adaptation retains the insouciant charm of a coastal cottage at the same time it offers an elegance that is appropriate for any setting in any climate today. Inside, the family living area is concentrated in the center of the house. Central to the social flow in the house, the great room opens to the kitchen, the breakfast room and to the rear porch that runs across the back. The left wing contains a private master suite that includes twin walk-in closets leading into a lavish master bath. Two additional bedrooms share a bath, while Bedroom 4, (located on the right side of the house) enjoys a high level of privacy that makes it an ideal guest room. This home is designed with a basement foundation.

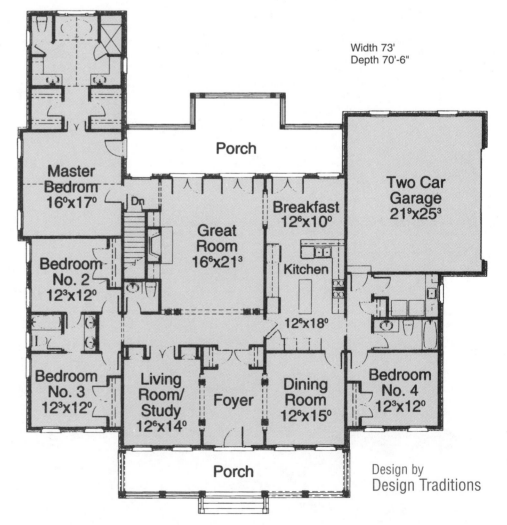

Width 73'
Depth 70'-6"

Porch

Master Bedroom
16⁰x17⁰

Dn

Great Room
16⁶x21³

Breakfast
12⁶x10⁰

Two Car Garage
21⁹x25³

Bedroom No. 2
12³x12⁰

Kitchen
12⁶x18⁰

Bedroom No. 3
12³x12⁰

Living Room/ Study
12⁶x14⁰

Foyer

Dining Room
12⁶x15⁰

Bedroom No. 4
12³x12⁰

Porch

Design by
Design Traditions

Width 74'
Depth 62'

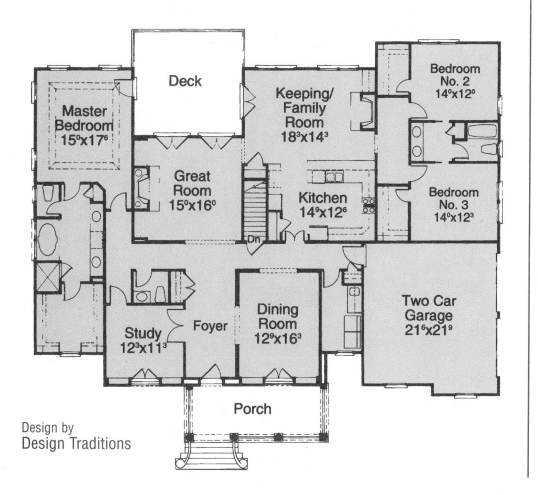

Design by
Design Traditions

Design 9969
Square Footage: 2,987

◆ Reaching back through the centuries for its inspiration, this home reflects the grandeur that was ancient Rome...as it looked to newly independent Americans in the 1700s. The entry portico provides a classic twist: the balustrade that would have marched across the roof line of a typical Revival home trims to form the balcony outside the French doors of the study. Inside, the foyer opens on the left to a quiet study, on the right to the formal dining room, and straight ahead to a welcoming great room warmed by a fireplace. The left wing is given over to a private master suite with a master bath that offers the ultimate in luxury and a large walk-in closet. On the right side of the house, two additional bedrooms share a full bath. Separating the sleeping wings is the kitchen, with its nearby keeping room/family room. This home is designed with a basement foundation.

Design 8063
Square Footage: 1,789

◆ A traditional brick and siding elevation with a lovely wraparound porch sets the stage for a plan that incorporates features demanded by today's lifestyle. The entry opens to the great room and dining room. The use of square columns to define the areas gives the plan the look and feel of a much larger home. The kitchen features loads of counter space and a large work island. The sink is angled toward the great room and features a 42" pass-through bar above. Washer, dryer and freezer space are available in the utility room along with cabinets for storage and countertops for work area. The master bedroom includes a walk-in closet with ample space for two. The master bath features all the amenities: a corner whirlpool, a shower and His and Hers vanities. Bedrooms 2 and 3 are located nearby and complete the plan. Please specify slab or crawlspace when ordering.

Quote One®
Cost to build? See page 214 to order complete cost estimate to build this house in your area!

Width 78'
Depth 47'

Design by
Larry E. Belk
Designs

Design by
Home Planners

Design 3340
Square Footage: 1,689

L

◆ A skylit covered porch extends an invitation to enjoy all seasons in comfort. The interior provides its own special appeal. Bedrooms are effectively arranged to the front of the plan, out of the traffic flow of the house. One bedroom could double nicely as a TV room or study. The adjacent master bedroom provides the ultimate in relaxation and features a large walk-in closet and a private bath. The living room/dining area features a fireplace, sliding glass doors to the skylit porch, and an open staircase with a built-in planter. The breakfast room provides a built-in desk— making it a breeze to get organized— and also accesses the rear covered porch for extended outdoor dining. An efficient U-shaped kitchen and a laundry room complete the plan.

Width 58'
Depth 52'-6"

TERRACE

COVERED PORCH
SKYLIGHT SKYLIGHT SKYLIGHT

BRKFST RM
13² x 11⁸

LIVING RM
13⁰ x 17²
SLOPED CEILING SLOPED CEILING

DINING
8⁸ x 9¹⁰
DECK

SNACK BAR
DW S

KITCHEN
13² x 9⁶
OVEN REF'G

LAUNDRY
8⁴ x 7⁸
LT W D

STORAGE
11⁰ x 8⁴

RAILING
DN

P'TRY

SLOPED CEILING
FOYER

BATH
S

WALK-IN CLOSET
LINEN

BATH

STUDY/
BEDROOM
10⁰ x 10⁴

CL CL

PORCH

GARAGE
19⁸ x 20⁴

SLOPED CEILING SLOPED CEILING

MASTER
BEDROOM
13⁴ x 13⁰

BEDROOM
13⁴ x 10⁸

SEAT

Design 9992

First Floor: 1,704 square feet
Second Floor: 1,449 square feet
Total: 3,153 square feet
Bonus Room: 455 square feet

◆ The fieldstone exterior and cupola evoke rural Southern appeal. The distinctive railed balcony, bay windows and porch arches recall Colonial detail. Inside, formal and informal spaces are separated by a graceful central stair hall that opens off the front foyer. French doors lead from the front porch into a formal dining room that links both the stair hall and the foyer. The living room, which also opens off the entrance foyer, leads to a cheerful great room that features a fireplace and built-in bookcases. An adjoining breakfast area opens onto a columned rear porch. Upstairs, a spacious master suite overlooks the rear yard. Two additional bedrooms share a convenient hall bath. A generous bonus space above the garage is also available. This home is designed with a basement foundation.

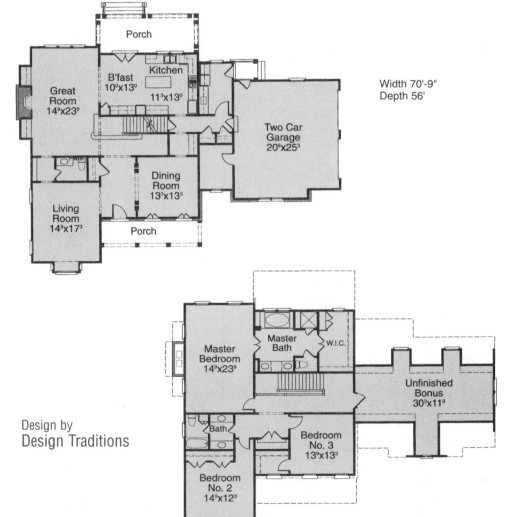

Width 70'-9"
Depth 56'

Design by
Design Traditions

Victorian Country Romance

Photo by Bob Greenspan

This home, as shown in the photograph, may differ from the actual blueprints. For more detailed information, please check the floor plans carefully.

TERRACE

VERANDA

RAILING

ROOF ABOVE

FAMILY RM
21⁰x13⁴

BREAKFAST RM
14⁰x11⁴

KITCHEN
10⁰x11⁴

PASS THRU

DINING RM
13⁰x11⁴+BAY

RANGE

DESK

PANTRY

REFG

BC

LAUNDRY
10⁰x7⁴

PDR RM

CL

PANTRY

CURB

UP

LIVING RM
16⁸x13⁴

UP

VERANDA

RAILING

GARAGE
21⁴x21⁸+STORAGE

STORAGE

UP

Width 62'-7"
Depth 54'

Design by
Home Planners

BEDROOM
11⁰x13⁰

SEAT

BATH

WHIRLPOOL

MASTER BEDROOM
13⁰x13⁰

BATH

WALK-IN CLOSET

LIN

CL

DN

CL

STUDY
9¹⁰x14⁰

BEDROOM
13⁰x10⁴

UP

Design 3309

First Floor: 1,375 square feet
Second Floor: 1,016 square feet
Total 2,391 square feet

L

QUOTE ONE®

Cost to build? See page 214 to order complete cost estimate to build this house in your area!

◆ Covered porches, front and back, are a fine preview to the livable nature of this Victorian. Living areas are defined in a family room with a fireplace, formal living and dining rooms and a kitchen with a breakfast room. Note the sliding glass doors from the breakfast room to the rear veranda. An ample laundry room, a garage with storage area and a powder room round out the first floor. Three second-floor bedrooms are joined by a study and two full baths. The master suite on this floor has two closets (one a convenient walk-in), a double vanity, a whirlpool tub and a separate shower.

75

Design 2974

First Floor: 911 square feet
Second Floor: 861 square feet
Total: 1,772 square feet
Attic: 1,131 square feet

L

◆ Victorian homes are well known for their orientation on narrow building sites. This house is 38' wide, but the livability is tremendous. From the front covered porch, the foyer directs traffic all the way to the back of the house with its open living and dining rooms. The U-shaped kitchen conveniently services both the dining room and the front breakfast room. The rear living area contains a veranda and a screened porch which both highlight the outdoor livability presented in this design. Three bedrooms account for the second floor; the third floor provides ample storage space.

ATTIC
26⁰ x 34⁰
(HEADROOM 21⁰ x 29⁹)

RAILING

DN

UPPER
BEDROOM

Width 38'
Depth 52'

Design by
Home Planners

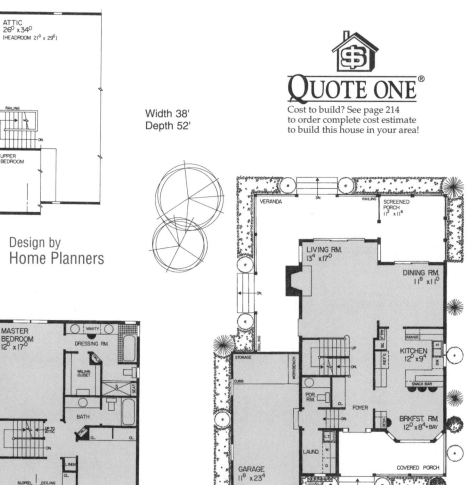

This home, as shown in the photograph, may differ from the actual blueprints. For more detailed information, please check the floor plans carefully.

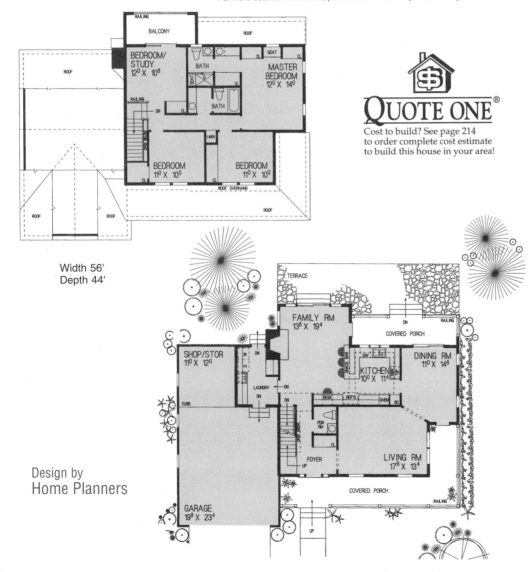

RAILING

BALCONY

ROOF

BEDROOM/
STUDY
12⁰ X 10⁸

BATH

SEAT

MASTER
BEDROOM
12⁰ X 14⁰

ROOF

RAILING

SEAT

S

CL

BATH

CL

LINEN

BEDROOM
11⁰ X 10⁰

BEDROOM
11⁰ X 10⁰

ROOF OVERHANG

ROOF

ROOF

ROOF

Width 56'
Depth 44'

TERRACE

FAMILY RM
13⁸ X 19⁴

COVERED PORCH

DN

RAILING

SHOP/STOR
11⁰ X 12⁰

DN

SNACK BAR

DW

KITCHEN
10⁰ X 11⁴

DINING RM
11⁰ X 14⁸

LAUNDRY

DN

DESK

REFG

OVEN

BC

CURB

DN

PDR
RM

CL

FOYER

UP

LIVING RM
17⁶ X 13⁴

COVERED PORCH

RAILING

UP

GARAGE
19⁸ X 23⁴

Design by
Home Planners

QUOTE ONE®
Cost to build? See page 214
to order complete cost estimate
to build this house in your area!

Design 3385
First Floor: 1,096 square feet
Second Floor: 900 square feet
Total: 1,996 square feet

L **D**

◆ Covered porches front and
rear are the first signal that
this is a fine example of Folk
Victorian styling. Comple-
menting the exterior is a grand
plan for family living. A formal living room and attached
dining room provide space for
entertaining guests. The large
family room with fireplace is a
gathering room for everyday.
Both areas have access to outdoor spaces. Four bedrooms
occupy the second floor. The
master suite features two lavatories, a window seat and
three closets. One of the family
bedrooms has its own private
balcony and could be used as
a study. Note the open staircase and linen storage.

Design 9251

First Floor: 1,653 square feet
Second Floor: 700 square feet
Total: 2,353 square feet

◆ Beautiful arches and elaborate detail give the elevation of this four-bedroom, 1½-story home an unmistakable elegance. Inside, the floor plan is equally appealing. Note the formal dining room with bay window, visible from the entrance hall. The large great room has a fireplace and a wall of windows across the back. A hearth room, with bookcase, adjoins the kitchen area with a walk-in pantry. The private, first-floor master suite features a pampering bath that contains a large whirlpool and double lavatories. Upstairs sleeping quarters share a full bath with compartmented sinks.

Design by
Design Basics, Inc.

QUOTE ONE®
Cost to build? See page 214 to order complete cost estimate to build this house in your area!

Width 54'
Depth 50'

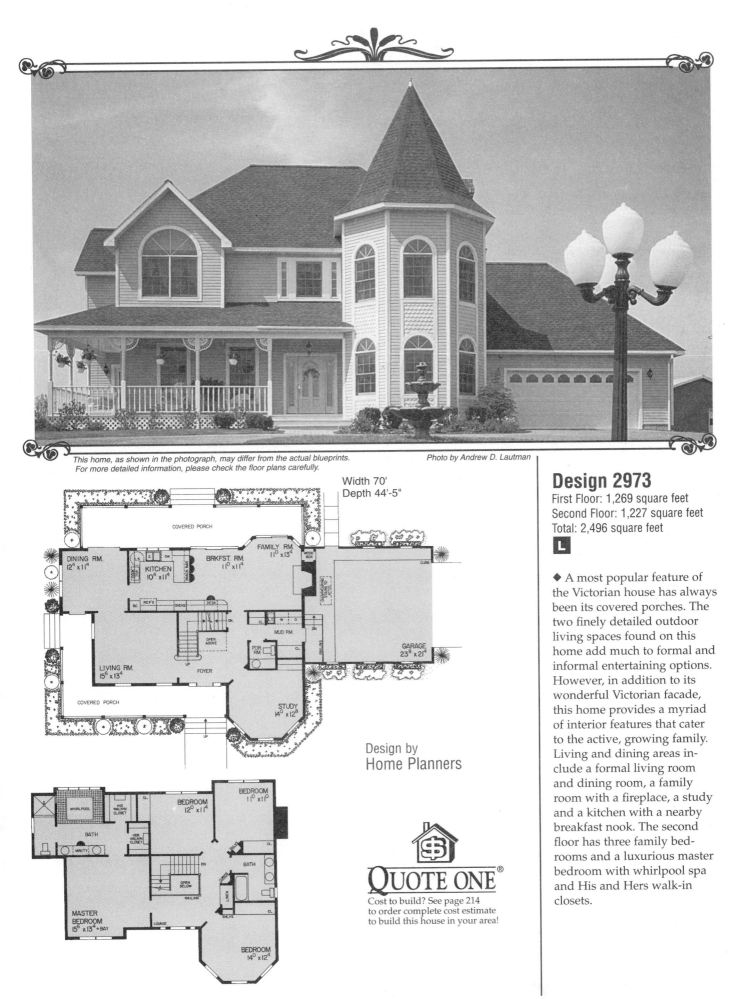

This home, as shown in the photograph, may differ from the actual blueprints. For more detailed information, please check the floor plans carefully.

Photo by Andrew D. Lautman

Width 70'
Depth 44'-5"

COVERED PORCH

DINING RM. 12⁴ x 11⁴

KITCHEN 10⁴ x 11⁴

BRKFST. RM. 11⁰ x 13⁴

FAMILY RM. 11⁰ x 13⁴

WOOD BOX

CURB

LIVING RM. 15⁶ x 13⁴

OPEN ABOVE

FOYER

MUD RM.

POR. RM.

GARAGE 23⁸ x 21⁴

COVERED PORCH

STUDY 14⁰ x 12⁸

Design by
Home Planners

WHIRLPOOL

HIS WALK-IN CLOSET

BEDROOM 12⁰ x 11⁴

BEDROOM 11⁰ x 11⁰

BATH

HER WALK-IN CLOSET

VANITY

OPEN BELOW

BATH

RAILING

LINEN

SHLVS.

MASTER BEDROOM 15⁶ x 13⁴ + BAY

LOUNGE

BEDROOM 14⁰ x 12⁴

Design 2973

First Floor: 1,269 square feet
Second Floor: 1,227 square feet
Total: 2,496 square feet

L

◆ A most popular feature of the Victorian house has always been its covered porches. The two finely detailed outdoor living spaces found on this home add much to formal and informal entertaining options. However, in addition to its wonderful Victorian facade, this home provides a myriad of interior features that cater to the active, growing family. Living and dining areas include a formal living room and dining room, a family room with a fireplace, a study and a kitchen with a nearby breakfast nook. The second floor has three family bedrooms and a luxurious master bedroom with whirlpool spa and His and Hers walk-in closets.

QUOTE ONE®

Cost to build? See page 214 to order complete cost estimate to build this house in your area!

79

Design 2970

First Floor: 1,538 square feet
Second Floor: 1,526 square feet
Third Floor: 658 square feet
Total: 3,722 square feet

L

◆ This charming Victorian features a covered outdoor living area on all four sides! It even ends at a screened porch which features a sun deck above. This interesting plan offers three floors of livability. And what livability it is! Plenty of formal and informal living facilities to go along with the potential of five bedrooms. The master suite is just fantastic. It is adjacent to a wonderful sitting room and offers a sun deck and lavish bath/personal care facilities. The third floor will make a wonderful haven for the family's student members.

Width 67'
Depth 66'

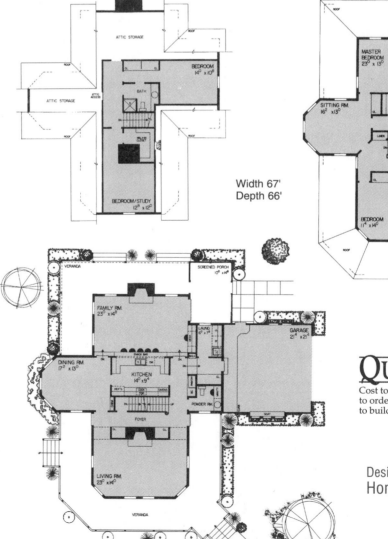

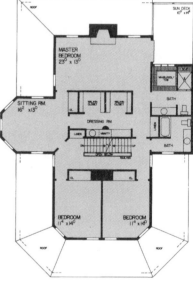

Cost to build? See page 214
to order complete cost estimate
to build this house in your area!

Design by
Home Planners

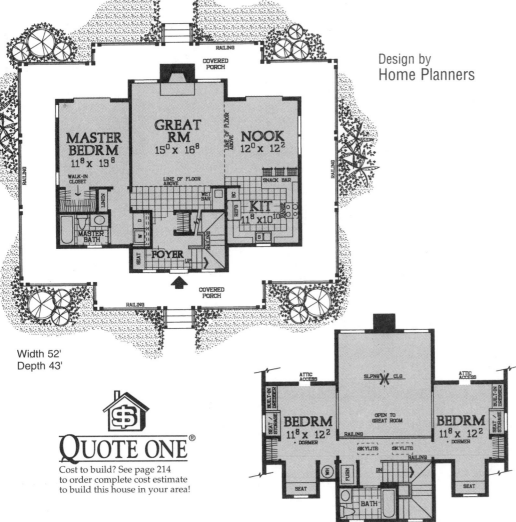

Width 52'
Depth 43'

Design by
Home Planners

Design 3674

First Floor: 1,086 square feet
Second Floor: 554 square feet
Total: 1,640 square feet

L **D**

◆ A wraparound porch, a welcoming entrance, and a thoughtful floor plan make this house a pleasure to come home to. The foyer, featuring a built-in seat with shoe storage, opens onto a large living area. Here, in the great room, a fireplace framed by unique windows provides focal interest. The adjacent nook and efficient kitchen combine with the great room to create a spacious area for formal and informal gatherings. The relaxing first-floor master suite is destined to become a favorite getaway. Skylights enhance the second floor and brighten a bridge that connects two family bedrooms to a full bath.

Design 8993

First Floor: 1,731 square feet
Second Floor: 758 square feet
Total: 2,489 square feet

◆ For the country-home enthusiast that prefers split-bedroom planning, this farmhouse dominates its class. A large Palladian window on the front lights up the central foyer. A formal dining room, defined by columns, is just to the right and connects to an island kitchen. The living room with its fireplace, and a breakfast room with porch access complete the livability. Located on the first floor for privacy, the master suite provides the ultimate in relaxation. The master bath contains an oversize walk-in closet, a skylit bath and a separate shower. Family bedrooms are found on the second floor. One features a private bath while the other two share a full bath.

Design by
Larry W.
Garnett &
Associates, Inc.

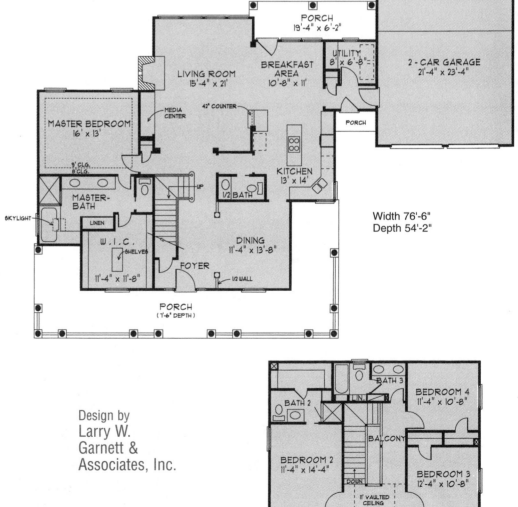

Width 76'-6"
Depth 54'-2"

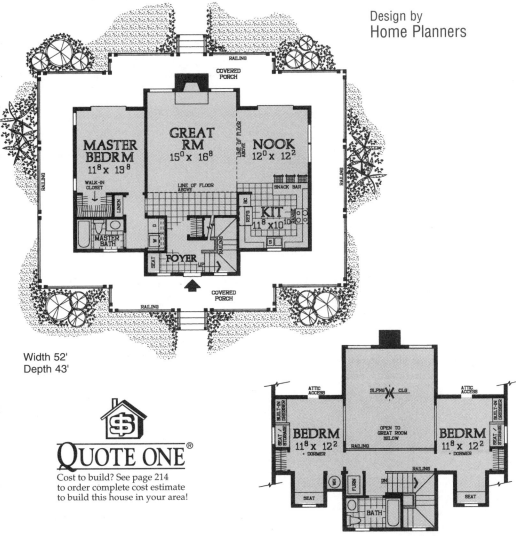

Design by
Home Planners

Width 52'
Depth 43'

Quote One®

Cost to build? See page 214
to order complete cost estimate
to build this house in your area!

Design 3673

First Floor: 1,086 square feet
Second Floor: 554 square feet
Total: 1,640 square feet

L D

◆ This country home creates an atmosphere as warm and comfortable as Grandma's feather bed. To the rear of the foyer, a two-story great room with a fireplace captures your immediate attention. An adjacent nook provides access to the covered porch via French doors, and combines with a snack bar and U-shaped kitchen for efficiency. The left wing contains a first-floor master suite designed for maximum privacy. French doors in the master bedroom extend an invitation to enjoy soft, summer breezes, while the pampering master bath provides its own soothing relaxation. The second floor contains two family bedrooms that share a full bath.

Design 3609

First Floor: 1,624 square feet
Second Floor: 596 square feet
Total: 2,220 square feet

L **D**

◆ This home's front-projecting garage allows utilization of a narrow, less expensive building site. The wraparound porch provides sheltered entrances and outdoor living access from the family kitchen. Open planning, sloping ceilings and an abundance of windows highlight the formal dining room/great room area. Notice the second bay window in the dining room. The great room has a centered fireplace as its focal point. The master bedroom has a big walk-in closet and the master bath has twin lavatories, a garden tub, a stall shower and a compartmented toilet with a linen closet. Upstairs are two bedrooms, a bath with twin lavatories, plus an outstanding computer/study area.

QUOTE ONE®

Cost to build? See page 214 to order complete cost estimate to build this house in your area!

Width 54'-4"
Depth 56'-4"

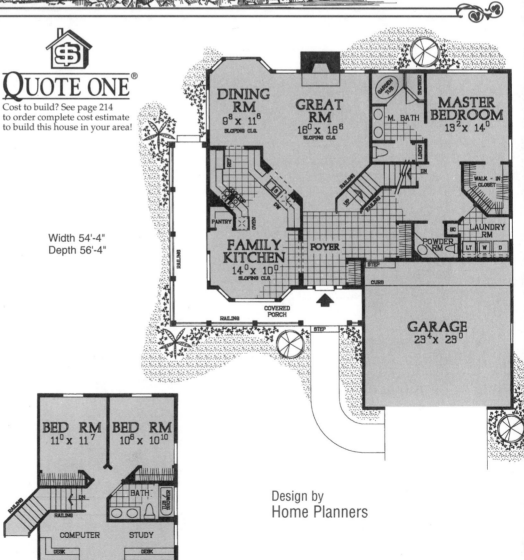

Design by
Home Planners

Design by
Home Planners

SEAT

SPA

SEAT

SUN TERRACE

VESTIBULE

BEDRM
12² x 10⁴
9'-0" CLG

BEDRM
12² x 11¹⁰
9'-0" CLG

RAILING

COVERED PATIO

MORNING
ROOM
11⁸ x 13⁶
9'-0" CLG

POWDER
RM

HVAC

WH

GARAGE
21⁸ x 20⁰

GARDEN
TUB

WALK-IN
CLOSET

MASTER
BATH

GREAT
RM
19⁰ x 13⁰
SLOPED CLG

HOME
CENTER

BROOM
CLOSET

UTILITY
SINK

KIT
11⁸ x 18⁰
9'-0" CLG

PANTRY

LAUNDRY
ROOM

W

D

MASTER
SUITE
14⁰ x 12²
SLOPED CLG

DINING
RM
11⁴ x 11⁶
SLOPED CLG

REFG

FOYER

COVERED PORCH

RAILING

Width 76'
Depth 64'

Design 3676

Square Footage: 2,090

L D

◆ Artistic angles and arches
provided in the floor plan of
this traditional design give it a
special appeal. Elegant curves
lead you from the foyer to the
private master bedroom on the
left or through a nine-foot arch
to the corner dining room on
the right. The great room features an angled fireplace with
a built-in media shelf connecting to the raised hearth. The
kitchen, in the center of the
home, provides lots of counter
space and a wonderful curved
snack bar. Its close proximity
to both the dining room and
the morning room make it
ideal. Two family bedrooms
share a full bath and easy access to the rear sun porch.

QUOTE ONE®

Cost to build? See page 214
to order complete cost estimate
to build this house in your area!

Design 9049
Square Footage: 1,891

◆ This cozy one-story Victorian provides a wealth of architectural and design details that make it a pleasure to come home to. Begin with the veranda which wraps around three sides of the home, then investigate the raised-foyer entry which introduces the intriguing floor plan. From formal dining room to kitchen/breakfast room and ample living room, amenities abound: ten- and twelve-foot ceilings, numerous built-ins, French doors, a fireplace, a wet bar, a work island in the kitchen and a bay-windowed breakfast area. The bedrooms and baths are no less well appointed: large closets, double vanities, corner windows and built-ins.

QUOTE ONE®

Cost to build? See page 214 to order complete cost estimate to build this house in your area!

Design by
Larry W.
Garnett &
Associates, Inc.

Width 52'
Depth 63'

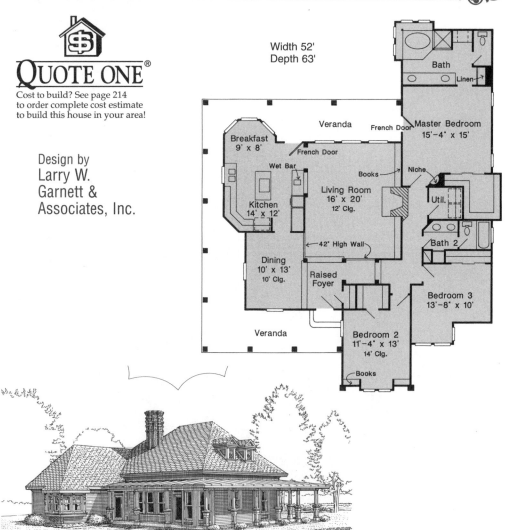

Bath

Veranda

Breakfast
9' x 8'

French Door

Master Bedroom
15'-4" x 15'

French Door

Wet Bar

Books

Niche

Living Room
16' x 20'
12' Clg.

Kitchen
14' x 12'

Util.

42" High Wall

Bath 2

Dining
10' x 13'
10' Clg.

Raised
Foyer

Bedroom 3
13'-8" x 10'

Veranda

Bedroom 2
11'-4" x 13'
14' Clg.

Books

Width 70'
Depth 58'

PORCH

UTILITY

STORAGE

DINING
12'-4" x 14'-4"

PORCH

MASTER BEDROOM
17'-4" x 16'-4"

FIREPLACE

2 - CAR GARAGE
21'-8" x 19'-4"

KITCHEN

12'-4" x 14'

PANTRY

LIVING ROOM
16' x 17'-8"

"HOME THEATER"

BOOKS

10' CEILING
9' CEILING

WALK-IN-CLOSET

MASTER
BATH

WALK-IN-CLOSET

BEDROOM 2
12' x 12'

FOYER

BATH

STUDY
11'-4" x 12'

BEDROOM 3
13'-4" x 12'
10' CEILING

PORCH

Design by
Larry W.
Garnett &
Associates, Inc.

Design 8992
Square Footage: 2,313

◆ This favorite country design
takes a turn for today with
great floor planning in a split-
bedroom plan. The covered
front porch leads to a private
study on the right and an
open living room and dining
area to the rear. A covered
porch provides a splendid setting for casual, outdoor dining. The master suite is on the
right side of the plan—located
for privacy—away from family bedrooms to the left. It contains a well-appointed bath
and two walk-in closets. The
two-car garage, with its large
storage area, connects to the
main house by way of a handy
utility room.

Design 9012

First Floor: 1,357 square feet
Second Floor: 1,079 square feet
Total: 2,436 square feet

◆ A wraparound veranda with delicate spindlework and a raised turret with leaded-glass windows recall the Queen Anne-style Victorians of the late 1880s. Double doors open from the two-story foyer to a study with built-in bookcases and a bay window. A fireplace adds warmth to the breakfast area and the island kitchen. Above the two-car garage is an optional area that is perfect for a home office or guest quarters. Upstairs, the balcony, overlooks the foyer below. An octagon-shaped ceiling and leaded-glass windows define a cozy sitting area in the master suite. A raised alcove in the master bath contains a garden tub and glass-enclosed shower. An optional exercise loft and plant shelves complete this elegant master bath. Two additional bedrooms, one with a private deck, and the other with a cathedral ceiling share a dressing area and bath.

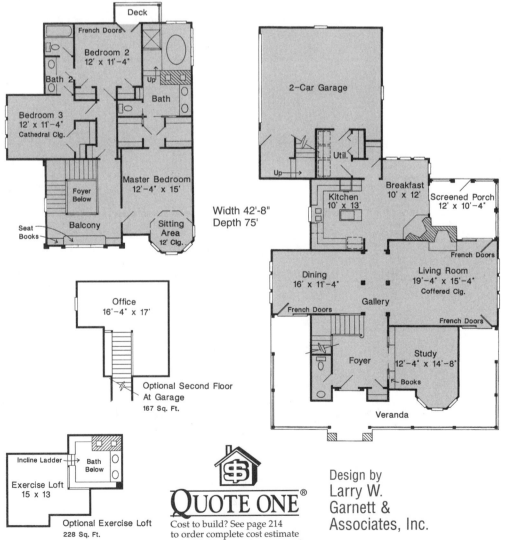

Deck

French Doors

Bedroom 2
12' x 11'-4"

Bath 2

Up

Bath

Bedroom 3
12' x 11'-4"
Cathedral Clg.

Foyer
Below

Seat
Books

Balcony

Master Bedroom
12'-4" x 15'

Sitting
Area
12' Clg.

Office
16'-4" x 17'

Optional Second Floor
At Garage
167 Sq. Ft.

Incline Ladder

Bath
Below

Exercise Loft
15 x 13

Optional Exercise Loft
228 Sq. Ft.

2-Car Garage

Util.

Up

Kitchen
10' x 13'

Breakfast
10' x 12'

Screened Porch
12' x 10'-4"

French Doors

Width 42'-8"
Depth 75'

Dining
16' x 11'-4"

Living Room
19'-4" x 15'-4"
Coffered Clg.

French Doors

Gallery

French Doors

Foyer

Study
12'-4" x 14'-8"

Books

Veranda

Quote One®

Cost to build? See page 214 to order complete cost estimate to build this house in your area!

Design by
Larry W.
Garnett &
Associates, Inc.

Bungalows—Craftsman Style

Design by
Home Planners

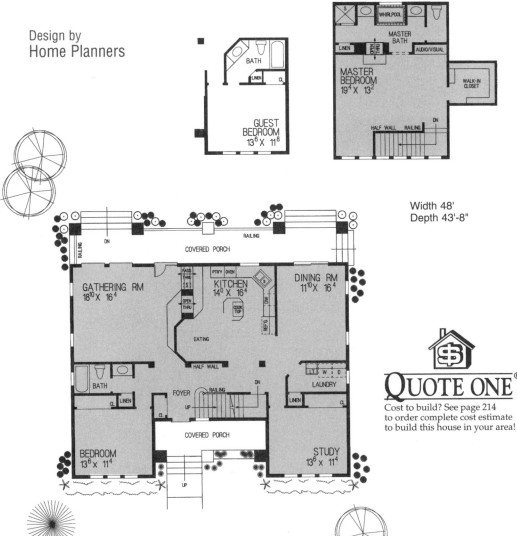

Width 48'
Depth 43'-8"

Cost to build? See page 214
to order complete cost estimate
to build this house in your area!

Design 3318

First Floor: 1,557 square feet
Second Floor: 540 square feet
Total: 2,097 square feet

L **D**

◆ Details make the difference
in this darling two-bedroom
(or three bedroom if you
choose) bungalow. From covered front porch to covered
rear porch, there's a fine floor
plan. Living areas are to the
rear: a gathering room with
through-fireplace and pass-
through counter to the kitchen
and a formal dining room
with porch access. To the front
of the plan are a family bedroom and bath and a study.
The study can also be planned
as a guest bedroom with bath.
Upstairs is the master bedroom with a through-fireplace
to the bath and a gigantic
walk-in closet.

Design 3315

First Floor: 2,918 square feet
Second Floor: 330 square feet
Total: 3,248 square feet

L

◆ Verandas at both the front and rear of this engaging bungalow provide outdoor enthusiasts with a front row seat to enjoy the changing seasons. To further entice you outdoors, the master bedroom, the breakfast room and the gathering room all have French doors that open onto the rear veranda. During frosty weather, a raised-hearth fireplace warms the combined gathering room and dining room and offers a friendly invitation. Bedrooms are efficiently separated from the living area. A romantic fireplace and a luxurious private bath enhance the master suite. Two family bedrooms share a full bath. The second floor holds a lounge that makes a great getaway for quiet contemplation or study.

Width 82'-8"
Depth 60'

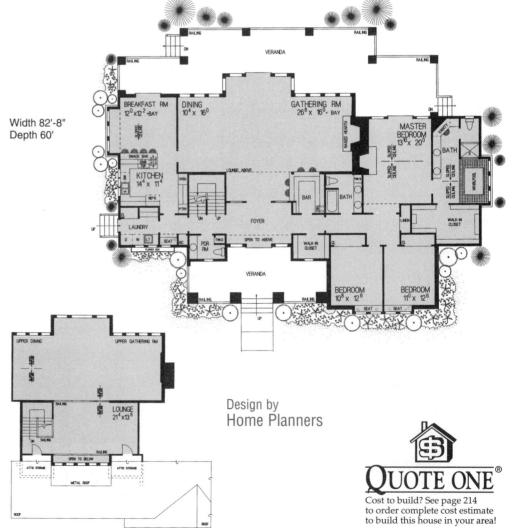

Design by
Home Planners

QUOTE ONE®

Cost to build? See page 214
to order complete cost estimate
to build this house in your area!

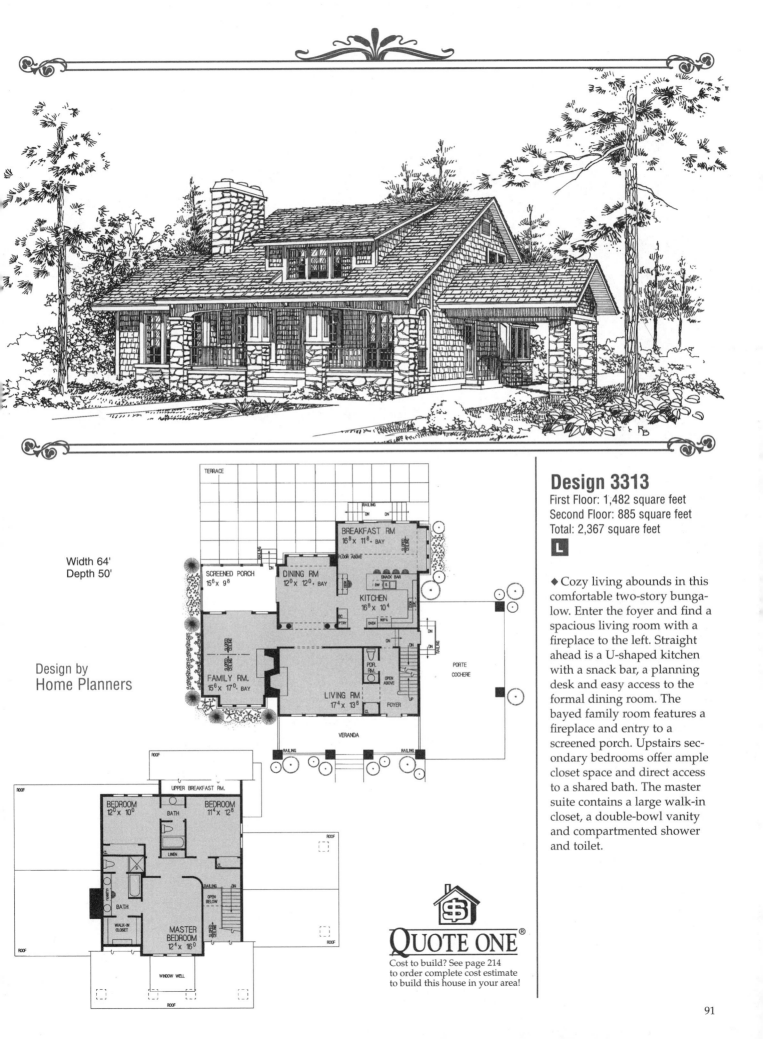

Design 3313

First Floor: 1,482 square feet
Second Floor: 885 square feet
Total: 2,367 square feet

L

◆ Cozy living abounds in this comfortable two-story bungalow. Enter the foyer and find a spacious living room with a fireplace to the left. Straight ahead is a U-shaped kitchen with a snack bar, a planning desk and easy access to the formal dining room. The bayed family room features a fireplace and entry to a screened porch. Upstairs secondary bedrooms offer ample closet space and direct access to a shared bath. The master suite contains a large walk-in closet, a double-bowl vanity and compartmented shower and toilet.

Width 64'
Depth 50'

Design by
Home Planners

QUOTE ONE®
Cost to build? See page 214
to order complete cost estimate
to build this house in your area!

Design 3316

First Floor: 1,111 square feet
Second Floor: 886 square feet
Total: 1,997 square feet

L

◆ Don't be fooled by a small-looking exterior. This plan offers three bedrooms and plenty of living space. Notice that the screened porch leads to a rear terrace with access to the breakfast room. A living room/dining room combination adds spaciousness to the floor plan. Other welcome amenities include: boxed-bay windows in the breakfast room and dining room, fireplace in the living room, planning desk and pass-through snack bar in the kitchen, whirlpool tub in the master bath and an open two-story foyer. The thoughtfully placed flower box, outside the kitchen window above the sink, adds a homespun touch to this already comfortable design.

Design by
Home Planners

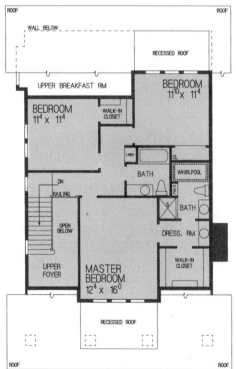

Width 34'-1"
Depth 50'

Cost to build? See page 214
to order complete cost estimate
to build this house in your area!

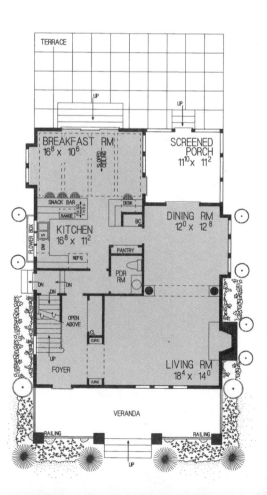

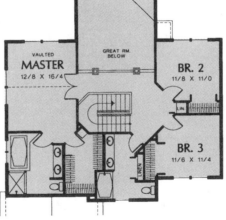

Design 9591

First Floor: 1,176 square feet
Second Floor: 994 square feet
Total: 2,170 square feet

◆ This home's covered, angled entry is elegantly echoed by an angled door to a rear covered porch, thus setting the style for this amenity-filled design. Flanking the foyer to the left is the formal dining room and to the right, through double French doors, is a cozy den. The great room opens out into the comfortable breakfast nook, giving this plan a spacious feeling. Gourmets will enjoy the large island kitchen. Upstairs, the master suite is located away from two secondary bedrooms for privacy and offers a luxurious bath and a walk-in closet.

Width 40'
Depth 64'

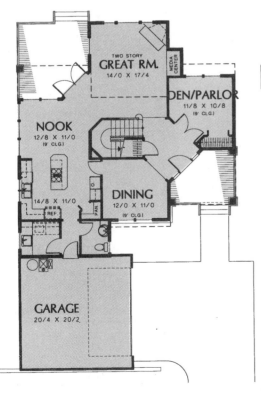

Design by
Alan Mascord
Design Associates, Inc.

Design 9535

First Floor: 1,110 square feet
Second Floor: 1,080 square feet
Total: 2,190 square feet

◆ The vaulted living room, with its fireplace and porch access, opens this design. An attached dining room makes formal meals a pleasure. In the kitchen, an island cooktop and an ample nook will satisfy the house gourmet. The family room—also with a fireplace—is open to this area. Upstairs, the vaulted master suite enjoys a private luxury bath with a spa tub. A den or fourth bedroom is accessible through double doors. Two secondary bedrooms each feature a vaulted ceiling and plenty of closet space. A full hall bath with a cheery window serves these areas well.

Cost to build? See page 214 to order complete cost estimate to build this house in your area!

Width 40'
Depth 56'-6"

Design by
Alan Mascord
Design Associates, Inc.

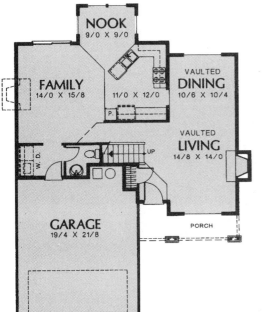

NOOK
9/0 X 9/0

FAMILY
14/0 X 15/8

VAULTED
DINING
10/6 X 10/4

11/0 X 12/0

VAULTED
LIVING
14/8 X 14/0

GARAGE
19/4 X 21/8

PORCH

Width 36'
Depth 50'

Design by
Alan Mascord
Design Associates, Inc.

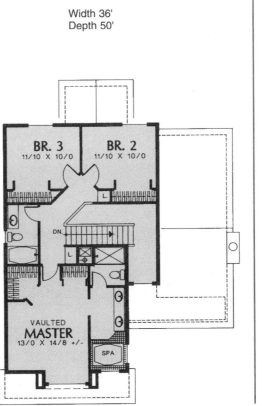

BR. 3
11/10 X 10/0

BR. 2
11/10 X 10/0

DN.

VAULTED
MASTER
13/0 X 14/8 +/-

SPA

Design 9519

First Floor: 913 square feet
Second Floor: 813 square feet
Total: 1,726 square feet

◆ Columns and pedestals
form the inviting porch on this
charming Craftsman-style
home. The decorative styling
of the pedestals is also extended to the garage and the
dormered window above.
Vaulted ceilings in the formal
living room and dining room
create a spacious, open feeling.
Completing the first floor, a
step-saving kitchen with a
bumped-out nook and a family room with a fireplace offer
the perfect space for informal
family gatherings. Upstairs,
the amenity-filled master suite
provides a welcoming retreat.
A soothing spa, dual lavs and
a compartmented toilet with a
shower complete the master
bath. Two secondary bed-
rooms share a full bath, completing the second floor.

Design 9524

First Floor: 1,032 square feet
Second Floor: 1,075 square feet
Total: 2,107 square feet

◆ This stylish country farm-house is enhanced by the classically rounded columns supporting the covered front porch. Formal living and dining rooms are found to the left of the entry. To the right rests the informal living area. A family room warmed by a cheerful fireplace shares space with the eating nook, offering access to the rear grounds. This provides a winning combination with the efficient kitchen, which features an L-shaped counter and an island cooktop. This area will quickly become a favorite place for family gatherings. The second floor is reserved for the sleeping quarters. Bedrooms 3 and 4 are separated from the master suite by Bedroom 2 which may also serve as an optional den. The master suite provides a relaxing retreat. The pampering bath features a soothing spa tub, a separate shower and a large walk-in closet.

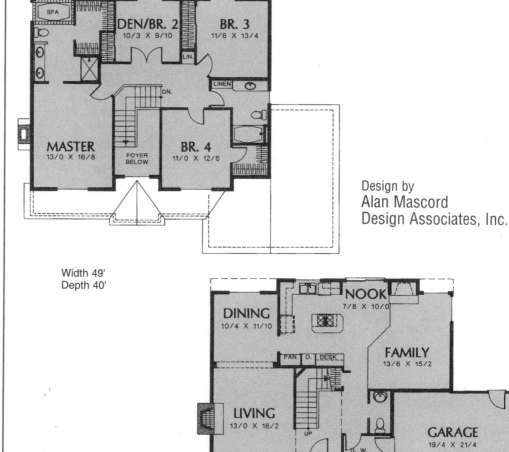

Width 49'
Depth 40'

Design by
**Alan Mascord
Design Associates, Inc.**

96

Width 47'
Depth 56'

Design by
Alan Mascord
Design Associates, Inc.

MASTER
15/0 X 16/0 +/-

BR. 2
10/0 X 13/0 +/-

BONUS RM.
11/6 X 11/0 +/-

BR. 3
11/0 X 10/4 +/-

PLANT SHELF

NOOK
11/0 X 11/0 +/-
(9' CLG)

FAMILY
17/0 X 16/0

10/0 X 13/0
MEDIA CENTER

11/6 X 13/0

PANTRY

GARAGE
20/0 X 24/8

DINING
13/0 X 10/4

BUILT-IN

DEN/
PARLOR
11/0 X 14/0

Design 9579

First Floor: 1,298 square feet
Second Floor: 1,235 square feet
Total: 2,533 square feet

◆ In the best bungalow tradition, this home offers fine livability within moderate proportions. Inside, the foyer opens onto the front parlor via angled, double doors. Built-ins enhance this room, and, if desired, allow for easy conversion to a den. An interesting window treatment brightens a formal dining room that facilitates dinner parties—large or small—with the aid of the adjacent island kitchen. A corner fireplace and a built-in media center will make the family room a favorite place for casual gatherings. Upstairs, three bedrooms and a bonus room accommodate family and guests. The master bedroom includes an elegant ceiling and double doors that open onto a glorious bath. The bonus room can be developed as additional space is needed.

$$
\boxed{\$}
$$

QUOTE ONE®

Cost to build? See page 214
to order complete cost estimate
to build this house in your area!

Design 9185
Square Footage: 1,567

◆ Square columns supported by brick pedestals and a low-pitched roof are reminiscent of the Craftsman style brought to popularity in the early 1900s. Livability is the foremost consideration in this well-designed plan. To the left of the foyer is the cozy living room, warmed by an inviting fireplace. Straight ahead, the dining room shares space with an efficient, step-saving kitchen. A French door provides access to a covered porch for outdoor meals and entertaining. To the rear of the plan rests the master suite. The master bath is highlighted by a tub and a separate shower, a double-bowl vanity, a compartmented toilet and a large walk-in closet. Two family bedrooms, a full bath and a utility room with a linen closet complete this marvelous plan.

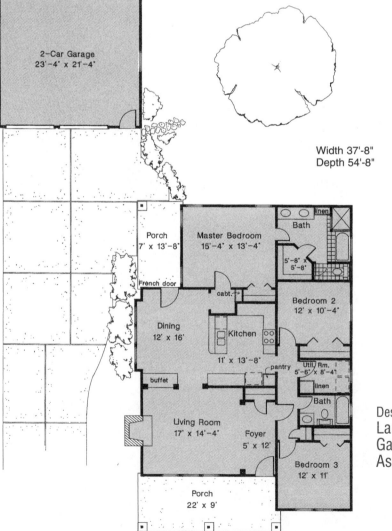

Width 37'-8"
Depth 54'-8"

2-Car Garage
23'-4" x 21'-4"

Porch
7' x 13'-8"

French door

Master Bedroom
15'-4" x 13'-4"

Bath

linen

5'-8" x
5'-8"

cabt.

Bedroom 2
12' x 10'-4"

Dining
12' x 16'

Kitchen
11' x 13'-8"

pantry

Util. Rm.
5'-6" x 8'-4"

linen

buffet

Bath

Living Room
17' x 14'-4"

Foyer
5' x 12'

Bedroom 3
12' x 11'

Porch
22' x 9'

Design by
Larry W.
Garnett &
Associates, Inc.

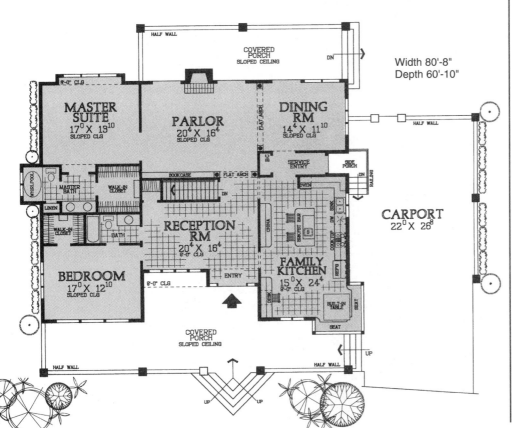

Design by
Home Planners

QUOTE ONE®

Cost to build? See page 214
to order complete cost estimate
to build this house in your area!

Width 80'-8"
Depth 60'-10"

Design 3498
Square Footage: 2,135

◆ You'll savor the timeless
style of this charming bungalow design. With pleasing proportions, it welcomes all onto
its expansive front porch—
perfect for quiet conversations.
Inside, livability excels with a
side-facing family kitchen.
Here, an interesting bumped-
out nook facilitates the placement of a built-in table and
bench seats. A formal dining
room rests to the rear of the
plan and enjoys direct access
to a back porch. The parlor,
with a central fireplace, also
has access to this outdoor living area. The master bedroom
is just a step away from the
living room. It offers large dimensions and a private bath
with a walk-in closet, dual
lavs and a bumped-out tub.
An additional bedroom may
also serve as a study.

Design 3314

Square Footage: 1,959

L

◆ Formal living areas in this plan are joined by a three-bedroom sleeping wing. One bedroom, with foyer access, could function as a study. Two verandas and a screened porch enlarge the plan and enhance indoor/outdoor livability. Special features include abundant storage space, a walk-in pantry, a built-in planning desk, a whirlpool tub and a pass-through snack bar. The breakfast room, with its wealth of windows, will be a cheerful and bright space to enjoy a cup of morning coffee.

Quote One®

Cost to build? See page 214 to order complete cost estimate to build this house in your area!

Design by
Home Planners

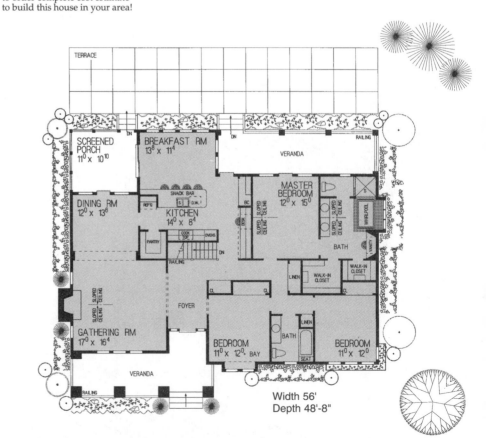

Width 56'
Depth 48'-8"

Shingled Country Character

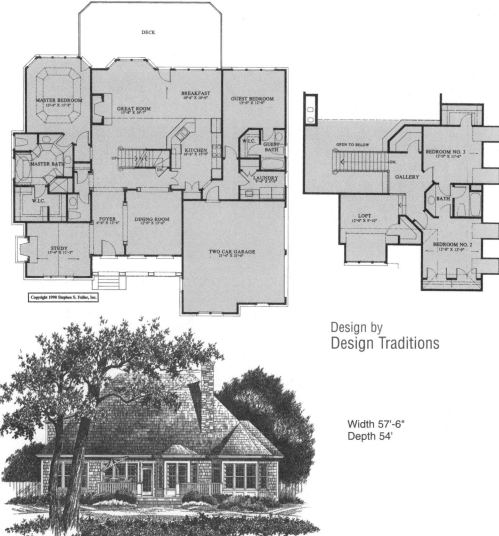

DECK

MASTER BEDROOM
13'-4" X 15'-6"

GREAT ROOM
15'-0" X 18'-7"

BREAKFAST
10'-6" X 10'-0"

GUEST BEDROOM
13'-8" X 12'-0"

MASTER BATH

KITCHEN
10'-6" X 15'-0"

W.I.C.

GUEST BATH

W.I.C.

UP

DN

LAUNDRY
9'-4" X 5'-0"

FOYER
6'-5" X 12'-6"

DINING ROOM
12'-0" X 13'-0"

STUDY
13'-4" X 11'-3"

TWO CAR GARAGE
21'-6" X 21'-4"

Copyright 1990 Stephen S. Fuller, Inc.

OPEN TO BELOW

DN.

GALLERY

BEDROOM NO. 3
12'-0" X 11'-6"

BATH

LOFT
12'-0" X 9'-10"

BEDROOM NO. 2
12'-0" X 12'-0"

Design by
Design Traditions

Width 57'-6"
Depth 54'

Design 9898

First Floor: 2,070 square feet
Second Floor: 790 square feet
Total: 2,860 square feet

◆ Wood shingles add a cozy touch on the exterior of this home; the arched covered front porch adds its own bit of warmth. Interior rooms include a great room with a bay window and a fireplace, a formal dining room and a study with another fireplace. A guest room on the first floor contains a full bath and walk-in closet. The relaxing master suite is also on the first floor and features a pampering master bath with His and Hers walk in closets, dual vanities, a separate shower and a whirlpool tub just waiting to soothe and rejuvenate. The second floor holds two additional bedrooms, a loft area and a gallery which overlooks the central hall. This home is designed with a basement foundation.

Design 9967

First Floor: 1,567 square feet
Second Floor: 1,895 square feet
Total: 3,462 square feet

◆ This home's fine proportions contain formal living areas, including a dining room and a living room. At the back of the first floor you'll find a fine kitchen that serves a breakfast nook. A great room with a fireplace and a bumped-out window make everyday living very comfortable. A rear porch allows for outdoor dining and relaxation. Upstairs, four bedrooms include a master suite with lots of notable features. A boxed ceiling, a lavish bath, a large walk-in closet and a secluded sitting room (which will also make a nice study or exercise room) assure great livability. One of the secondary bedrooms contains a full bath. This home is designed with a basement foundation.

Design by
Design Traditions

Width 63'
Depth 53'-6"

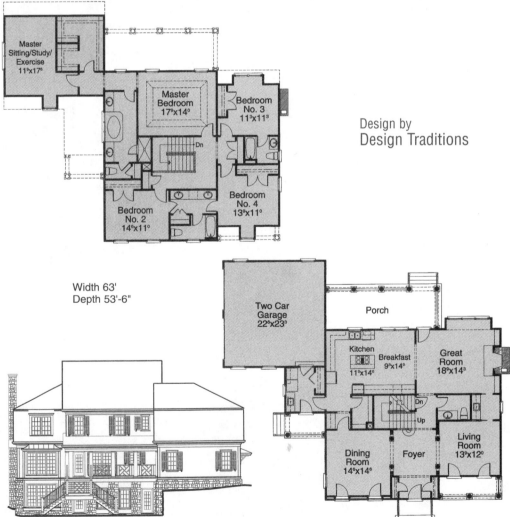

Rear Elevation

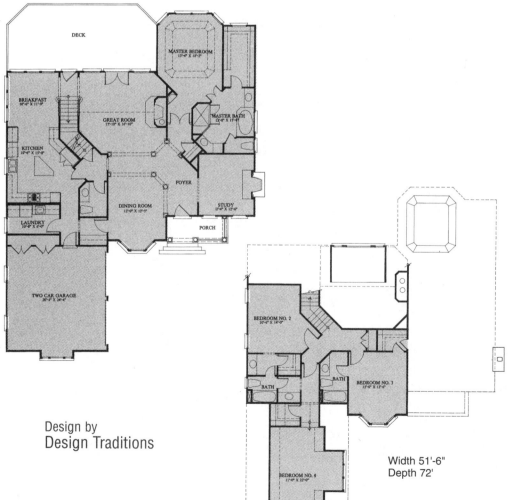

Design by
Design Traditions

Width 51'-6"
Depth 72'

Design 9908
First Floor: 1,944 square feet
Second Floor: 1,055 square feet
Total: 2,999 square feet

◆ Interesting rooflines, multi-level eaves and a two-story double-bay window create a unique cottage farmhouse appearance for this charming home. The grand foyer leads to the formal dining room and large great room, both graced with columns. The great room features a cozy fireplace and opens to the deck through French doors. The breakfast room, divided from the great room by an open staircase, shares space with an efficient L-shaped kitchen and nearby laundry room, making domestic endeavors easy to accomplish. The right wing is devoted to a sumptuous, amenity-filled master suite with convenient access to the study for after-hours research or quiet reading. The second floor contains three secondary bedrooms and two baths for family and guests. This home is designed with a basement foundation.

Design 9999

Square Footage: 2,721

◆ In this design, equally at home in the country or at the coast, classic elements play against a rustic shingle-and-stone exterior. Doric porch columns provide the elegance, while banks of cottage-style windows let in lots of natural light. The symmetrical layout of the foyer and formal dining room blend easily with the cozy great room. Here, a fireplace creates a welcome atmosphere that invites you to select a novel from one of the built-in bookcases and curl up in your favorite easy chair. The adjacent U-shaped kitchen combines with a sunny breakfast room that opens onto a rear porch, making casual meals a pleasure. Designed for privacy, the master suite occupies the right side of the house and enjoys a dramatic master bath. The left wing contains two secondary bedrooms that share a bath with compartmentalized vanity/dressing areas. This home is designed with a basement foundation.

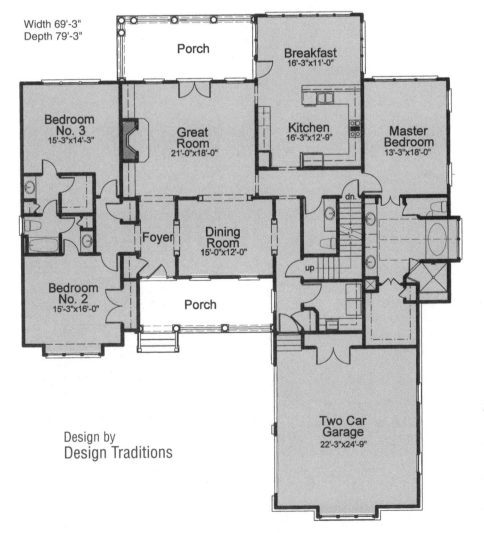

Width 69'-3"
Depth 79'-3"

Porch

Breakfast
16'-3"x11'-0"

Bedroom
No. 3
15'-3"x14'-3"

Great
Room
21'-0"x18'-0"

Kitchen
16'-3"x12'-9"

Master
Bedroom
13'-3"x18'-0"

dn.

Foyer

Dining
Room
15'-0"x12'-0"

up

Bedroom
No. 2
15'-3"x16'-0"

Porch

Design by
Design Traditions

Two Car
Garage
22'-3"x24'-9"

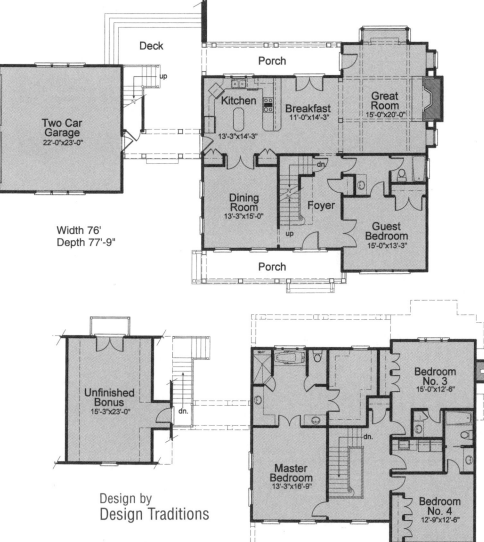

Deck

up

Porch

Kitchen
13'-3"x14'-3"

Breakfast
11'-0"x14'-3"

Great
Room
15'-0"x20'-0"

Two Car
Garage
22'-0"x23'-0"

Dining
Room
13'-3"x15'-0"

Foyer

dn

up

Guest
Bedroom
15'-0"x13'-3"

Porch

Width 76'
Depth 77'-9"

Unfinished
Bonus
15'-3"x23'-0"

dn.

Bedroom
No. 3
15'-0"x12'-6"

dn.

Master
Bedroom
13'-3"x16'-9"

Bedroom
No. 4
12'-9"x12'-6"

Design by
Design Traditions

Design 9998

First Floor: 1,578 square feet
Second Floor: 1,324 square feet
Total: 2,902 square feet

◆ The straightforward, Colonial lines of New England's early seacoast homes provide the inspiration for this two-story home. Shingles and shutters add to its cottage appeal, making it an ideal seaside or countryside residence. Inside, the foyer leads into the gracious formal dining room on the left, and a hospitable guest room on the right. At the rear of the plan, the beam-ceilinged family room with its cheery fireplace flows into a cozy breakfast area and the adjoining kitchen. The upstairs master suite includes a huge walk-in closet and a master bath designed to soothe and relax away the tensions of the day. Two family bedrooms—each with its own vanity—share a full bath. A convenient upstairs laundry room completes this delightful plan. This home is designed with a basement foundation.

Design 9557

First Floor: 1,371 square feet
Second Floor: 916 square feet
Total: 2,287 square feet

◆ The decorative pillars and the wraparound porch are just the beginning of this comfortable home. Inside, an angled, U-shaped stairway leads to the second-floor sleeping zone. On the first floor, French doors lead to a bay-windowed den that shares a see-through fireplace with the two-story family room. The large island kitchen includes a writing desk, a corner sink, a breakfast nook and access to the laundry room, the powder room and the two-car garage. The master suite provides ultimate relaxation with its French-door access, vaulted ceiling and luxurious bath. Two other bedrooms and a full bath complete the second floor.

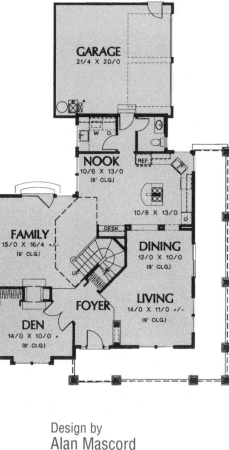

Width 43'
Depth 69'

Design by
Alan Mascord
Design Associates, Inc.

Quote One®

Cost to build? See page 214
to order complete cost estimate
to build this house in your area!

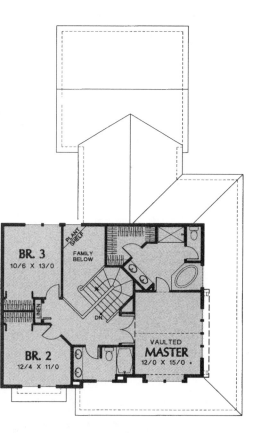

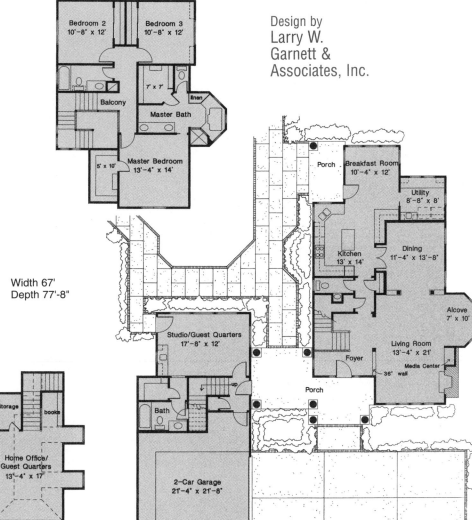

Bedroom 2
10'-8" x 12'

Bedroom 3
10'-8" x 12'

Design by
Larry W.
Garnett &
Associates, Inc.

Balcony

7' x 7'

linen

Master Bath

5' x 10'

Master Bedroom
13'-4" x 14'

Porch

Breakfast Room
10'-4" x 12'

Utility
8'-8" x 8'

Kitchen
13' x 14'

Dining
11'-4" x 13'-8"

Width 67'
Depth 77'-8"

Alcove
7' x 10'

Studio/Guest Quarters
17'-8" x 12'

Living Room
13'-4" x 21'

Bath

Foyer

Media Center
36" wall

up

Porch

Storage

books

Home Office/
Guest Quarters
13'-4" x 17'

2-Car Garage
21'-4" x 21'-8"

Design 9190

First Floor: 1,213 square feet
Second Floor: 932 square feet
Total: 2,145 square feet

◆ Step into the foyer of this delightful home and find a living room with a built-in media center and an adjacent windowed alcove. Entertaining's a cinch in the columned dining room with double doors leading to the kitchen. Here, an island work space provides an extra amount of custom feel. The breakfast room enjoys access to an airy back porch. A utility room makes chores less tedious. Upstairs, three bedrooms include a master suite with a beautiful bayed tub and shower area, two walk-in closets and twin vanities. A deluxe studio or guest suite is located off the two-car garage. A kitchenette, a full bath and a walk-in closet are found here.

Design 9587

First Floor: 822 square feet
Second Floor: 1,175 square feet
Total: 1,997 square feet

◆ The wraparound porch surrounding this shingled home provides a front row seat to enjoy the soothing sounds of the country—literally. At the entrance to the front porch, a built-in bench has been thoughtfully placed for convenience. Inside, an open floor plan makes the most of the first-floor living area. Enhanced with built-ins, a warming fireplace extends a friendly invitation into the great room. Here, a wall of windows provides plenty of natural light and unobstructed views of the backyard. A bay window fills the adjacent nook with sunlight and brightens the adjoining U-shaped kitchen. Located near the garage for convenience, a laundry room and powder room complete the first floor. The second floor contains a restful master suite, two family bedrooms that share a full bath, and a game room.

Width 47'
Depth 48'

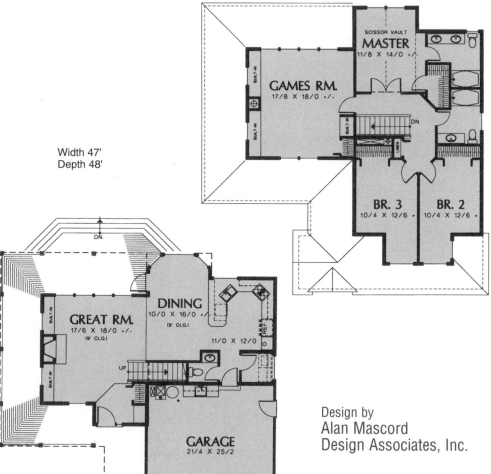

Design by
Alan Mascord
Design Associates, Inc.

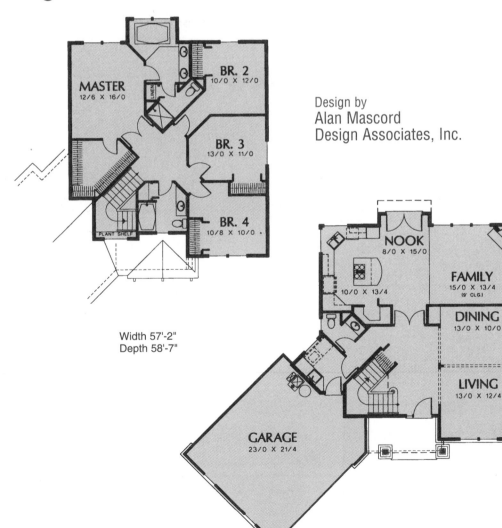

Design by
Alan Mascord
Design Associates, Inc.

Width 57'-2"
Depth 58'-7"

Design 9590

First Floor: 1,205 square feet
Second Floor: 1,123 square feet
Total: 2,328 square feet

◆ A covered porch, multi-paned windows and shingle-and-stone siding combine to give this home plenty of curb appeal. Inside, the foyer is flanked by the formal living room and an angled staircase. The formal dining room shares space with the living room and the kitchen is accessible through double doors. A large family room is graced by a fireplace and opens off a cozy eating nook. The second level presents many attractive angles. The master suite has a spacious walk-in closet and a sumptuous bath complete with a garden tub and separate shower. Three bedrooms share a full hall bath.

Design 9195

First Floor: 1,872 square feet
Second Floor: 724 square feet
Total: 2,596 square feet

◆ Open floor planning is the key to the spacious combination of formal and informal areas. Blended for convenience is the formal dining room, a gallery, a living room with a fireplace and a home theater, a breakfast area with porch access and an efficient L-shaped kitchen. Guest quarters tucked behind the two-car garage provide an extra measure of privacy and access to the covered porch. Completing the first floor is a private master suite. Pamper yourself in the relaxing master bath which is highlighted by a separate tub and shower, a double vanity and a huge walk-in closet. Upstairs, Bedrooms 2 and 3 share a full bath. A loft provides built-in space for books, a desk and additional storage.

MASTER BEDROOM 14'-4" x 16'
1/2 BATH
"HOME THEATER"
LIVING ROOM 15' x 19'
BREAKFAST AREA 10'-6" x 10'-4"
GALLERY
PORCH 10'-6" x 15'-6"
MASTER BATH
LINEN
FOYER
DINING 13'-4" x 11'
KITCHEN 10'-6" x 12'-4"
WALK-IN-CLOSET 14'-4" x 5'-4"
BOOKS
PORCH
GUEST QUARTERS 11'-4" x 14'-8"
UTILITY
BATH 2
2-CAR GARAGE 23'-4" x 21'-4"

Width 63'-8"
Depth 69'-2"

BALCONY
DOWN
BOOKS
BEDROOM 2 15'-4" x 12'-4"
LOFT
BOOKS
DESK
STORAGE
BEDROOM 3 13' x 12'-4"

Design by
Larry W. Garnett & Associates, Inc.

110

Design 9183

First Floor: 2,138 square feet
Second Floor: 842 square feet
Total: 2,980 square feet

◆ This plan abounds with all
the amenities, starting with a
columned foyer that leads to a
spacious dining room and an
even bigger family room. A
study located at the front of
the house will convert to the
ideal guest room with its
walk-in closet and nearby full
bath. In the kitchen, an island
cooktop sets the pace—along
with an immense walk-in
pantry. Off the breakfast area,
a screened porch wraps
around to the back of the
house and even gains access to
a wash room that connects to
the garage. A utility room enjoys its own sunny spot as
well as a helpful countertop.
Three bedrooms include a
first-floor master suite with
two walk-in closets and a
fabulous private bath. The
family bedrooms on the second floor each feature walk-in
closets and their own full
bathrooms. A gameroom on
this floor further enhances the
plan.

Width 69'-8"
Depth 65'

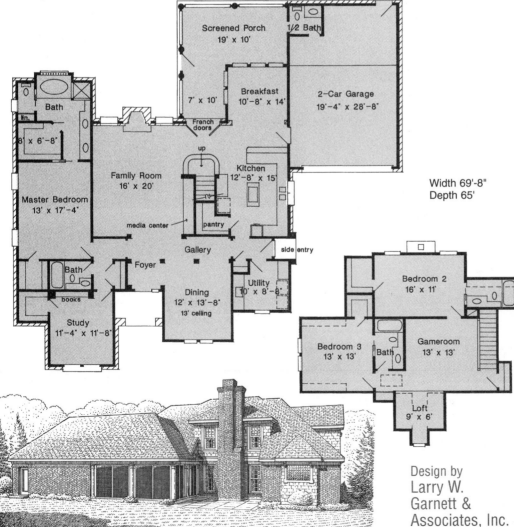

Design by
Larry W.
Garnett &
Associates, Inc.

Design 8981

Square Footage: 1,703
Bonus Room: 280 square feet

◆ This quaint cottage features a shingled exterior reminiscent of the homes often found in coastal areas. A living room is located to the left of the foyer, creating special interest with a bay window and a warmly welcoming fireplace. The efficient U-shaped kitchen and dining room combine to make meal preparation a breeze. On the right side of the plan rests the sleeping wing. The pleasant master suite sports double-bowl vanities, a separate tub and shower and a large walk-in closet. Two additional bedrooms share a full bath. For future use, a bonus room is conveniently located over the garage.

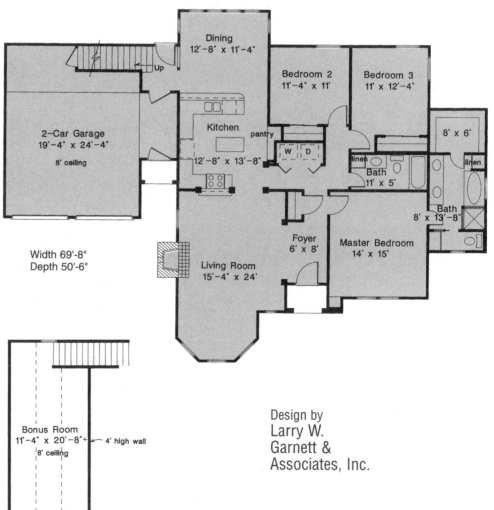

Width 69'-8"
Depth 50'-6"

Dining
12'-8" x 11'-4"

Bedroom 2
11'-4" x 11'

Bedroom 3
11' x 12'-4"

2-Car Garage
19'-4" x 24'-4"
8' ceiling

Kitchen
12'-8" x 13'-8"

pantry

8' x 6'

W D

linen   linen

Bath
11' x 5'

Bath
8' x 13'-8"

Foyer
6' x 8'

Master Bedroom
14' x 15'

Living Room
15'-4" x 24'

Bonus Room
11'-4" x 20'-8"+   ← 4' high wall
8' ceiling

Design by
Larry W.
Garnett &
Associates, Inc.

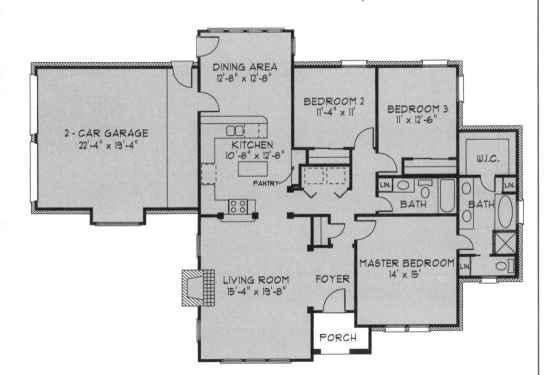

Width 68'-4"
Depth 46'

DINING AREA
12'-8" x 12'-8"

2 - CAR GARAGE
22'-4" x 19'-4"

KITCHEN
10'-8" x 12'-8"

PANTRY

BEDROOM 2
11'-4" x 11'

BEDROOM 3
11' x 12'-6"

W.I.C.

LIN.

LIN.

BATH

BATH

LIVING ROOM
15'-4" x 19'-8"

FOYER

MASTER BEDROOM
14' x 15'

LIN.

PORCH

Design by
Larry W.
Garnett &
Associates, Inc.

Design 8984
Square Footage: 1,667

◆ Winsome details on the facade of this cozy three-bedroom home add a great deal of cottage character. To the left of the foyer, the large living room extends an open invitation to relax, enjoy a crackling fire and a good book, or intimate conversation. Located nearby, the step-saving island kitchen is designed for efficiency and combines easily with the dining area for formal and informal meals. The sleeping accommodations offer a master bedroom, and two family bedrooms that share a full hall bath. The master suite includes a private bath that features twin vanities, a garden tub, a separate shower, two linen closets and a large walk-in closet. A centrally located washer and dryer make wash days a breeze.

Design 8076

Square Footage: 2,733

◆ The favorite gathering place of this beautiful home is certain to be its sun-filled breakfast and keeping room complemented by the full kitchen. Thoughtful placement of the kitchen provides easy service to both formal and informal eating areas. A large living room enjoys two sets of double French doors that open to outdoor living areas. French doors open onto the spacious master suite and its elegant master bath. Here, a soothing whirlpool tub takes center-stage. Three other bedrooms, or two bedrooms and a study, are positioned at the opposite end of the house for privacy. Bedrooms 2 and 3 have their own walk-in closets. Please specify slab or crawlspace foundation when ordering.

Width 88'
Depth 54'-2"

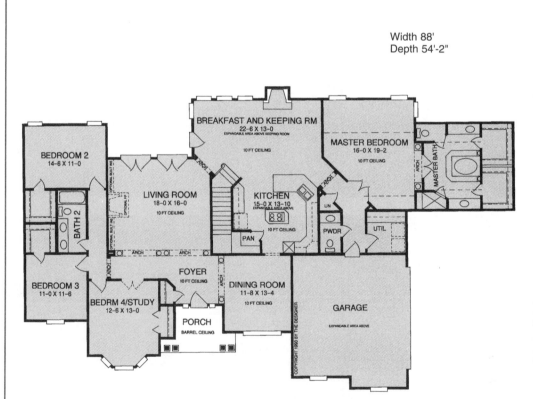

Design by
Larry E. Belk
Designs

113

Rustic Country Reflections

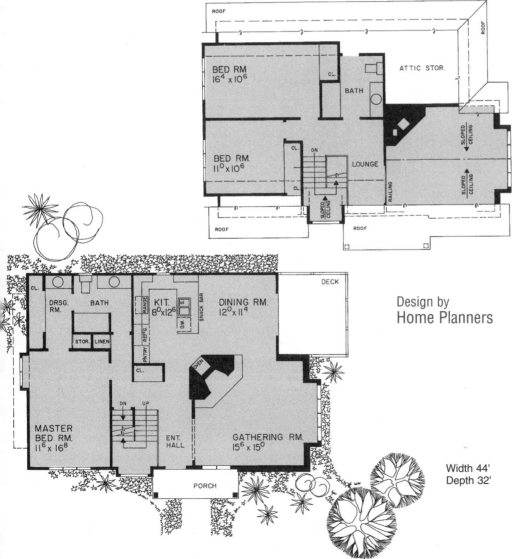

ROOF

BED RM. 16⁴ x 10⁶

ATTIC STOR.

BATH

BED RM. 11⁰ x 10⁶

CL.

DN

LOUNGE

SLOPED CEILING

RAILING

SLOPED CEILING

ROOF

ROOF

CL.

DRSG. RM.

BATH

KIT. 8⁰ x 12⁶

DINING RM. 12⁰ x 11⁴

DECK

STOR. LINEN

CL.

RANGE

REFG.

DW.

PNTRY

SNACK BAR

DN UP

MASTER BED RM. 11⁶ x 16⁸

ENT. HALL

GATHERING RM. 15⁶ x 15⁰

PORCH

Design by
Home Planners

Width 44'
Depth 32'

Design 2488

First Floor: 1,113 square feet
Second Floor: 543 square feet
Total: 1,656 square feet

D

◆ A cozy cottage tailor-made for a country lifestyle! This winsome design performs equally well serving active families as a leisure-time retreat or a retirement cottage that provides a quiet haven. As a year-round home, the upstairs with its two sizable bedrooms, full bath and lounge area overlooking the gathering room comfortably holds family and guests. The second floor may also be used to accommodate a home office, a study, a sewing room, a music area or a hobby room. No matter what the lifestyle, this design functions well.

Design 2776

First Floor: 1,134 square feet
Second Floor: 874 square feet
Total: 2,008 square feet

L **D**

◆ This board-and-batten farm-house design has all of the country charm of New England. The large covered front porch surely will be appreciated during the beautiful warm weather months. Immediately off the front entrance is the delightful corner living room. The dining room with a bay window will be easily served by the U-shaped kitchen. Informal family living enjoyment will be obtained in the family room which features a raised-hearth fireplace, sliding glass doors to the rear terrace and easy access to the work center. The second floor houses all of the sleeping facilities. There is a master bedroom with a private bath and a walk-in closet. Two secondary bedrooms share a full bath.

Width 61'-4"
Depth 38'

Design by
Home Planners

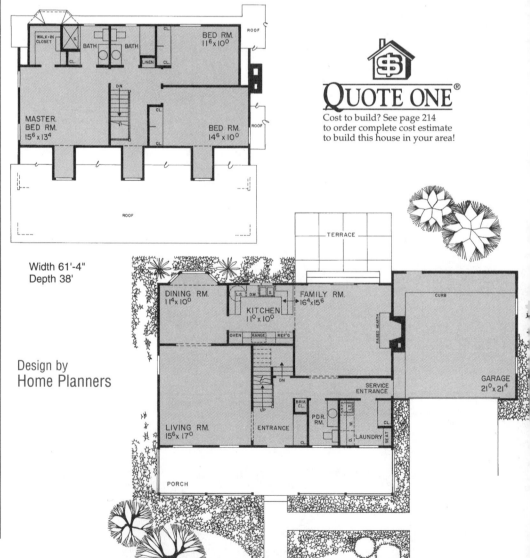

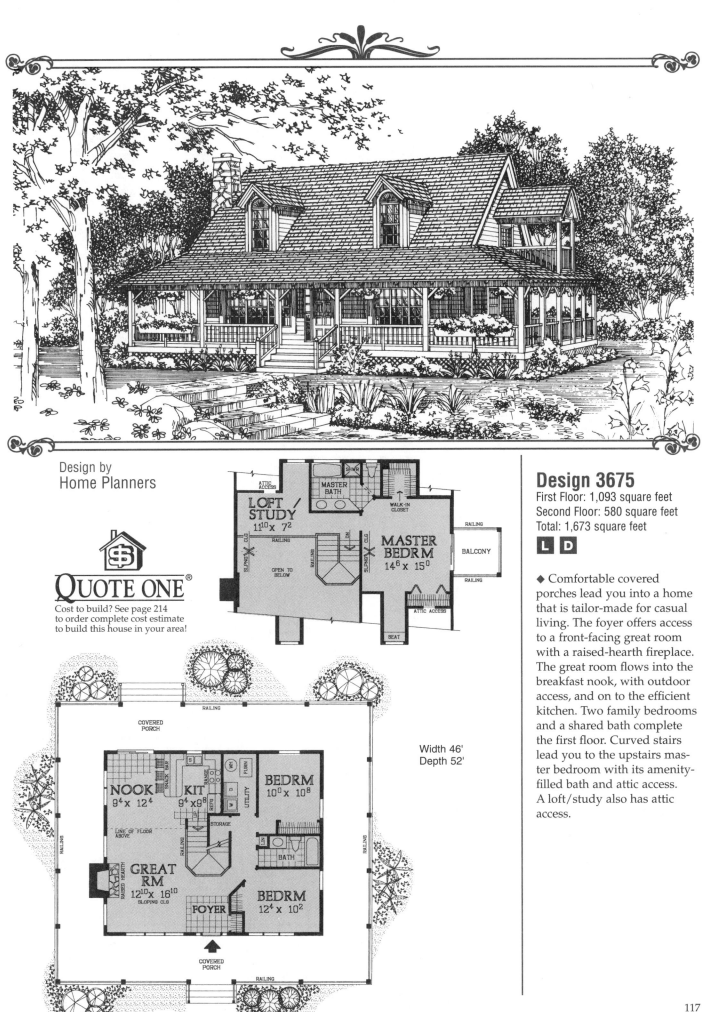

Design by
Home Planners

QUOTE ONE®

Cost to build? See page 214
to order complete cost estimate
to build this house in your area!

ATTIC ACCESS

MASTER BATH

SHWR

LOFT / STUDY
11¹⁰ x 7²

WALK-IN CLOSET

RAILING

OPEN TO BELOW

MASTER BEDRM
14⁶ x 15⁰

BALCONY

RAILING

ATTIC ACCESS

SEAT

COVERED PORCH

RAILING

NOOK
9⁴ x 12⁴

KIT
9⁴ x 9⁸

SNACK BAR

RANGE

FURN

BEDRM
10⁰ x 10⁸

UTILITY

REFRIG

W

LINE OF FLOOR ABOVE

STORAGE

RAILING

BATH

GREAT RM
12¹⁰ x 16¹⁰
SLOPING CLG

RAISED HEARTH

FOYER

BEDRM
12⁴ x 10²

RAILING

RAILING

COVERED PORCH

RAILING

Width 46'
Depth 52'

Design 3675

First Floor: 1,093 square feet
Second Floor: 580 square feet
Total: 1,673 square feet

L **D**

◆ Comfortable covered porches lead you into a home that is tailor-made for casual living. The foyer offers access to a front-facing great room with a raised-hearth fireplace. The great room flows into the breakfast nook, with outdoor access, and on to the efficient kitchen. Two family bedrooms and a shared bath complete the first floor. Curved stairs lead you to the upstairs master bedroom with its amenity-filled bath and attic access. A loft/study also has attic access.

Design 9663

First Floor: 1,002 square feet
Second Floor: 336 square feet
Total: 1,338 square feet

◆ A mountain retreat, this rustic home features covered porches front and rear. Open living is enjoyed in a great room and kitchen/dining room combination. The cathedral ceiling gives an open, inviting sense of space. Two bedrooms and a full bath on the first level are complemented by a master suite on the second level which includes a walk-in closet and deluxe bath. There is also attic storage on the second level. Please specify basement or crawlspace foundation when ordering.

Design by
Donald A.
Gardner,
Architects, Inc.

Width 36'-8"
Depth 44'-8"

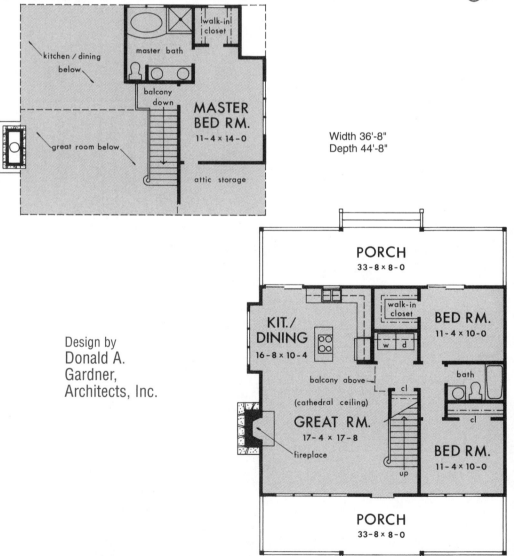

Design 9666

First Floor: 1,027 square feet
Second Floor: 580 square feet
Total: 1,607 square feet

◆ This economical, rustic three-bedroom plan sports a relaxing country image with both front and back covered porches. The openness of the great room to kitchen/dining areas and loft/study area is reinforced with a shared cathedral ceiling. The first level allows for two bedrooms, a full bath and a utility area. The master suite on the second level has a walk-in closet and a master bath with whirlpool tub, shower and double-bowl vanity.

LOFT/ STUDY 11-4 × 13-8

STO. 3-4 × 6-4

walk-in closet

master bath

railing

down

MASTER BED RM. 12-0 × 14-0

great room below

Width 37'-4"
Depth 44'-8"

Design by
Donald A. Gardner, Architects, Inc.

PORCH 34-4 × 8-0

KIT./DINING 18-0 × 11-8

bath

BED RM. 12-0 × 10-0

cl

w/d

cl

loft above

GREAT RM. 17-4 × 16-4

fireplace

up

cl

BED RM. 12-0 × 12-4

PORCH 34-4 × 8-0

Design 9759

First Floor: 1,100 square feet
Second Floor: 584 square feet
Total: 1,684 square feet

◆ A relaxing country image projects from the front and rear covered porches of this rustic three-bedroom home. Open planning extends to the great room, the dining room and the efficient kitchen. A shared cathedral ceiling creates an impressive space. Completing the first floor are two family bedrooms, a full bath and a handy utility area. The second floor contains the master suite featuring a spacious walk-in closet and a master bath with a whirlpool tub and a separate corner shower. A generous loft/study overlooks the great room below.

Quote One®

Cost to build? See page 214 to order complete cost estimate to build this house in your area!

Width 36'-8"
Depth 45'

Design by
Donald A.
Gardner,
Architects, Inc.

STORAGE

BATH · SEAT

LINEN · DRESSING

STORAGE

SEAT

BEDROOM
12⁴ x 12⁸

DOWN

OPEN
BELOW

MASTER
BEDROOM
19¹⁰ x 12⁸

RAISED HEARTH

STOR. · STOR. · STOR.

Width 40'
Depth 32'

COVERED PORCH

W/D · REFG. · SINK · D.W.

SEAT

KITCHEN
13⁶ x 9⁰

DINING
RM
10⁰ x 9⁰

RANGE · PASS THRU

PDR

BRM.
CL.

FURN

W.H.

GARAGE
12⁸ x 22⁸

FOYER

LIVING ROOM
14⁶ x 13⁸

SLATE HEARTH

UP

HALF
WALL

COVERED PORCH

Design by
Home Planners

Design 3474

First Floor: 663 square feet
Second Floor: 624 square feet
Total: 1,287 square feet

L

◆ This rustic cabin is a delight. A spacious living room with a beam ceiling and warming fireplace greets you as you enter the foyer from the inviting covered porch. The adjoining dining room offers a picturesque window seat and convenience to the large kitchen with its window sink, pass-through to the living room and access to the powder room and rear covered porch. A roomy master bedroom, featuring a fireplace and a walk-in closet with a seat, and a second bedroom complete the second floor. An abundance of upstairs storage space is available also.

Design 7292

First Floor: 1,210 square feet
Second Floor: 405 square feet
Total: 1,615 square feet

◆ An interesting front porch furnishes the exterior of this delightful home with a country mile of charm. Inside, an expansive great room, enhanced by a warming fireplace, is sure to be the focus of this efficient three bedroom plan. The kitchen will please even the fussiest of gourmets with its large pantry, abundance of counter space and corner snack bar. Connecting the kitchen and great room is a sun-filled breakfast room with a bumped-out bay and access to the rear yard. Located on the first floor for privacy, the master suite supplies the perfect retreat to relax and pamper yourself. On the second floor, two comfortable family bedrooms share a full hall bath with twin lavatories.

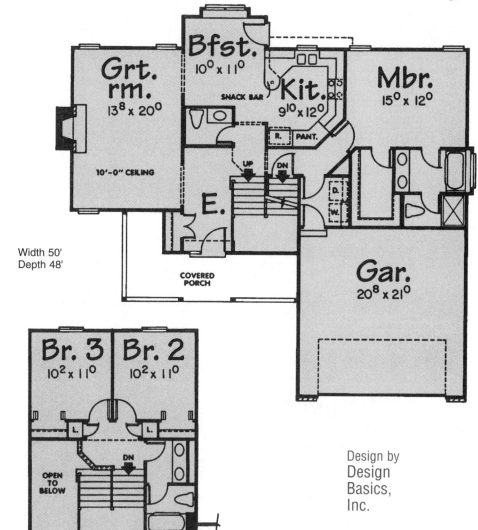

Width 50'
Depth 48'

Design by
Design
Basics,
Inc.

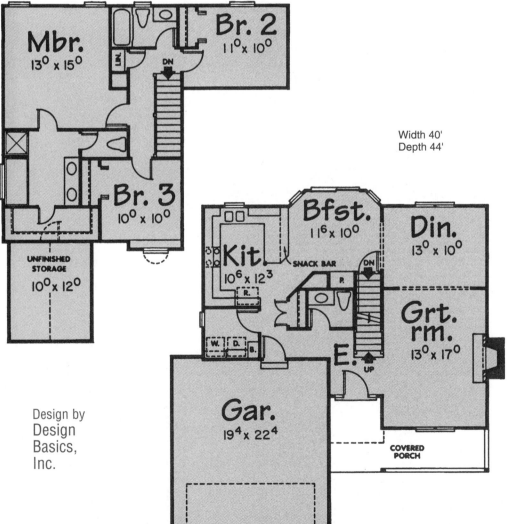

Mbr.
13⁰ x 15⁰

Br. 2
11⁰ x 10⁰

LIN.

DN

Br. 3
10⁰ x 10⁰

UNFINISHED STORAGE
10⁰ x 12⁰

Width 40'
Depth 44'

Bfst.
11⁶ x 10⁰

Kit.
10⁶ x 12³

SNACK BAR

Din.
13⁰ x 10⁰

DN

Grt. rm.
13⁰ x 17⁰

W. D.

E.

UP

Gar.
19⁴ x 22⁴

COVERED PORCH

Design by
Design Basics, Inc.

Design 7291

First Floor: 862 square feet
Second Floor: 780 square feet
Total: 1,642 square feet

◆ A wide, gabled porch provides this home with its country identity and comfortable welcome. Inside, the foyer opens on the right to a great room and formal dining room that flow together to create a wonderful space for entertaining. The step-saving kitchen connects to a sunny, bay-windowed breakfast nook that provides direct access to the backyard. A convenient laundry room and a powder room complete the first floor. Upstairs, two family bedrooms share a hall bath and a linen closet. Designed for ultimate relaxation, the master suite features a private bath with a compartmented toilet, a double-bowl vanity and a large walk-in closet with access to lots of unfinished storage space.

Design 9619

Square Footage: 2,021

◆ Multi-pane windows, dormers, bay windows and a delightful covered porch provide a neighborly welcome into this delightful country cottage. The great room contains a fireplace, a cathedral ceiling and sliding glass doors with an arched window above to allow for natural illumination. A sunroom with a hot tub leads to an adjacent deck. This space can also be reached from the master bath. The generous master suite is filled with amenities that include a walk-in closet and a spacious bath with a double-bowl vanity, a shower and a garden tub. Two additional bedrooms are located at the other end of the house for privacy. The garage is connected to the house by a breezeway. Please specify basement or crawlspace foundation when ordering.

Width 67'-6"
Depth 67'4"

Design by
Donald A.
Gardner,
Architects, Inc.

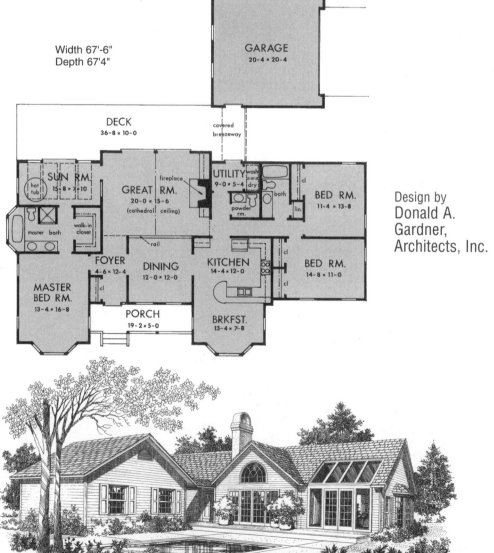

GARAGE 20-4 × 20-4

DECK 36-8 × 10-0

covered breezeway

SUN RM. 15-8 × 7-10

hot tub

GREAT RM. 20-0 × 15-6 (cathedral ceiling)

fireplace

UTILITY 9-0 × 5-4

wash dry

bath

powder rm.

lin.

cl

BED RM. 11-4 × 13-8

master bath

walk-in closet

rail

FOYER 4-6 × 12-4

DINING 12-0 × 12-0

KITCHEN 14-4 × 12-0

cl

BED RM. 14-8 × 11-0

MASTER BED RM. 13-4 × 16-8

cl

PORCH 19-2 × 5-0

BRKFST. 13-4 × 7-8

Floor Plan

Width 72'-8"
Depth 54'-4"

DECK
27-2 × 10-0

seat

down

SUN RM.
18-0 × 7-6

BRKFST.
8-6 × 10-10

MASTER
BED RM.
13-4 × 17-8

master
bath

walk-in
closet

storage

pantry

BED RM.
11-4 × 12-0

fireplace

GREAT RM.
18-0 × 16-2
(cathedral ceiling)

KITCHEN
12-0 × 10-0

cl

dry

wash

GARAGE
19-6 × 21-0

cl

bath

lin.

cl

FOYER
11-8 × 5-6

DINING
12-0 × 12-0

storage

cl

STUDY/
BED RM.
11-4 × 12-0

PORCH
16-0 × 5-2

Design by
Donald A.
Gardner,
Architects, Inc.

Design 9602
Square Footage: 1,899

◆ Dormers, a covered porch and two bumped-out windows with shed roofs at the dining room and study provide a warm country reception for the front exterior to this home. The great room has built-in cabinets, a warming fireplace, and bookshelves, and has direct access to the sunroom through two sliding glass doors. The convenient kitchen features a center island cooktop and provides service to both the formal dining room and the breakfast area. It is connected to the great room by a pass-through. Overlooking the private rear deck is the sumptuous master suite with a double-bowl vanity, a shower and a garden tub. Two other bedrooms are located at the other end of the house for privacy (the front bedroom could double as a study).

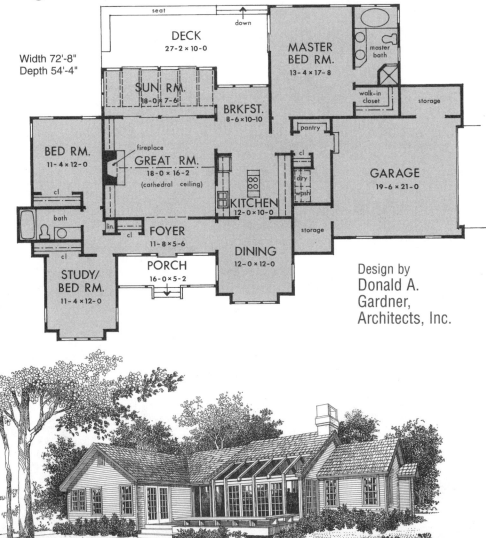

Design 9622
Square Footage: 1,842

◆ What visual excitement is created in this country ranch with the use of a combination of exterior building materials and shapes! The angular nature of the plan allows for flexibility in design—lengthen the great room or family room, or both, to suit individual space needs. Cathedral ceilings grace both rooms and a fireplace embellishes the great room with warmth. An amenity-filled master bedroom features a cathedral ceiling, a private deck and a master bath with whirlpool tub. Two family bedrooms share a full bath. An expansive deck area with hot tub wraps around interior family gathering areas for enhanced outdoor living. Please specify basement or crawl-space foundation when ordering.

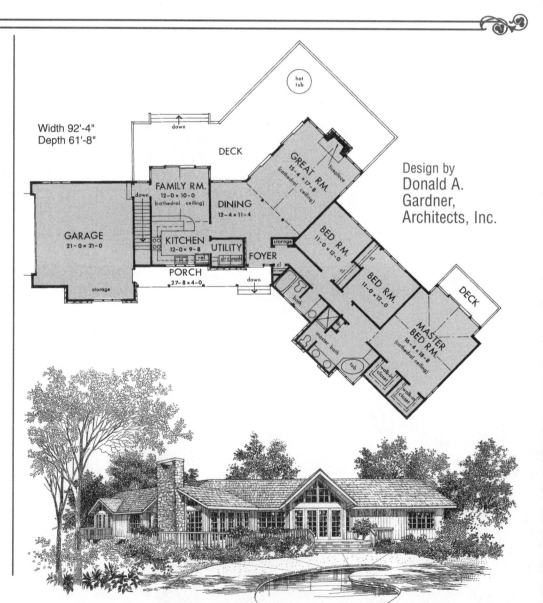

Width 92'-4"
Depth 61'-8"

Design by
Donald A.
Gardner,
Architects, Inc.

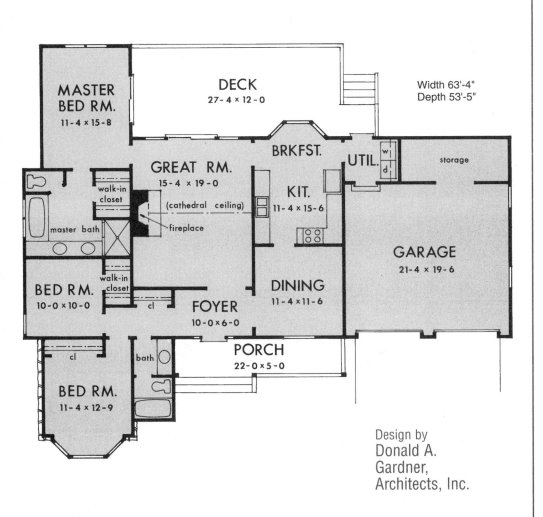

Design 9679
Square Footage: 1,512

◆ A multi-pane bay window, dormers, a cupola, a covered porch and a variety of building materials all combine to dress up this intriguing country cottage. The generous entry foyer leads to a formal dining room and an impressive great room with a cathedral ceiling and a fireplace. The kitchen includes a breakfast area with a bay window overlooking the deck. The great room and master bedroom also access the deck. An amenity-filled master suite is highlighted by a master bath that includes a double-bowl vanity, a shower and a garden tub. Two additional bedrooms are located at the front of the house for privacy and share a full bath.

Design by
Donald A.
Gardner,
Architects, Inc.

Design 3355

Square Footage: 1,387

L **D**

◆ Though modest in size, this fetching one-story home offers a great deal of livability with three bedrooms (or two with study) and a spacious gathering room with a fireplace and a sloped ceiling. The galley kitchen, designed to save steps, provides a pass-through snack bar and has a planning desk and attached breakfast room. In addition to two secondary bedrooms with a full bath, there's a private master bedroom that enjoys views and access to the backyard. The master bath features a large dressing area, a corner vanity and a raised whirlpool tub. Indoor/outdoor living relationships are strengthened by easy access from the dining room, study/bedroom and master bedroom to the rear terrace.

Width 54'
Depth 52'

Design by
Home Planners

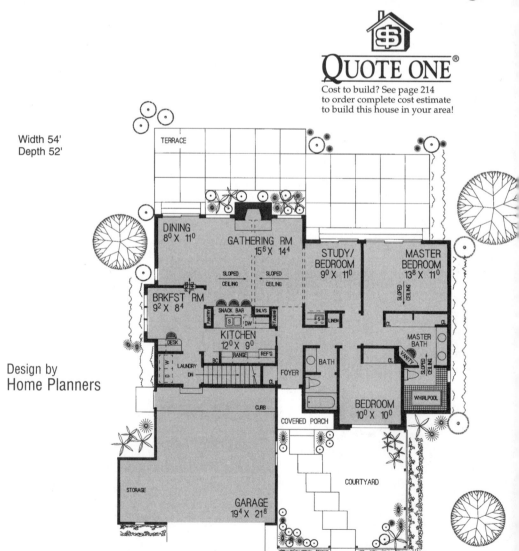

Southern Originals

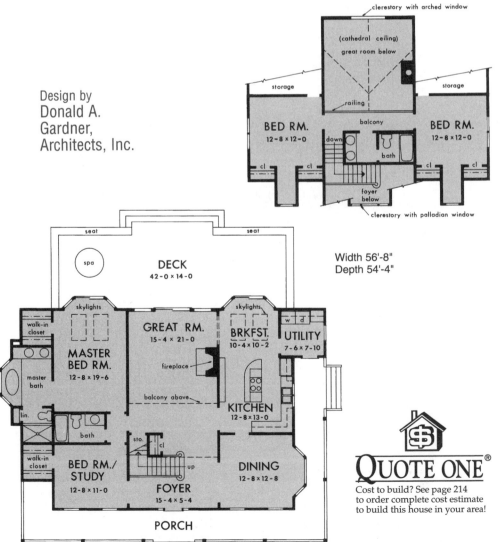

clerestory with arched window

(cathedral ceiling)

great room below

storage

storage

railing

BED RM.
12-8 × 12-0

balcony

BED RM.
12-8 × 12-0

down

bath

cl

cl

cl

cl

foyer
below

clerestory with palladian window

Design by
Donald A.
Gardner,
Architects, Inc.

Width 56'-8"
Depth 54'-4"

seat

seat

spa

DECK
42-0 × 14-0

skylights

skylights

walk-in
closet

GREAT RM.
15-4 × 21-0

BRKFST.
10-4 × 10-2

w | d

UTILITY
7-6 × 7-10

MASTER
BED RM.
12-8 × 19-6

fireplace

master
bath

balcony above

lin.

KITCHEN
12-8 × 13-0

bath

walk-in
closet

sto.

cl

BED RM./
STUDY
12-8 × 11-0

up

DINING
12-8 × 12-8

FOYER
15-4 × 5-4

PORCH

Design 9632

First Floor: 1,756 square feet
Second Floor: 565 square feet
Total: 2,321 square feet

◆ A wraparound covered porch at the front and sides of this house and an open deck at the back provide plenty of outside living area. The spacious great room features a fireplace, cathedral ceiling and clerestory with an arched window. The island kitchen has an attached, skylit breakfast room complete with a bay window. The first-floor master bedroom contains a generous closet and a master bath with garden tub, double-bowl vanity and shower. The second floor sports two bedrooms and a full bath with double-bowl vanity. An elegant balcony overlooks the great room. Please specify basement or crawlspace foundation when ordering.

QUOTE ONE®

Cost to build? See page 214
to order complete cost estimate
to build this house in your area!

Design 9707

First Floor: 1,632 square feet
Second Floor: 669 square feet
Total: 2,301 square feet
Bonus Room: 528 square feet

◆ This open country plan boasts front and rear covered porches and a bonus room for future expansion. The entrance foyer with sloped ceiling has a Palladian window clerestory to allow natural light in. The spacious great room has a fireplace, cathedral ceiling and clerestory with arched windows. The second-floor balcony overlooks the great room. A U-shaped kitchen provides the ideal layout for food preparation. For flexibility, access is provided to the bonus room from both the first and second floors. The first-floor master bedroom features a bath with dual lavatories, a separate tub and shower and a walk-in closet. Two large bedrooms and a full bath are located on the second floor.

Design by
Donald A.
Gardner
Architects, Inc.

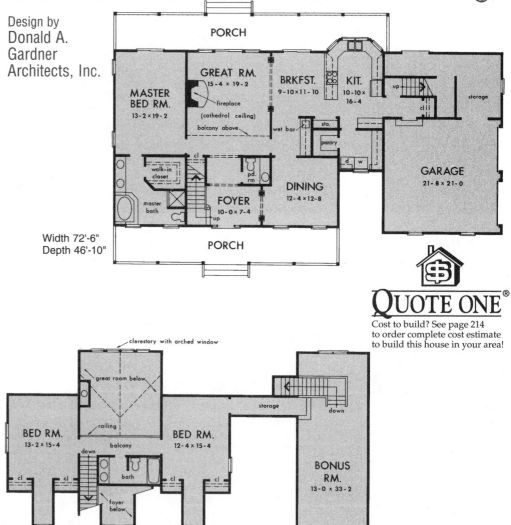

Cost to build? See page 214 to order complete cost estimate to build this house in your area!

130

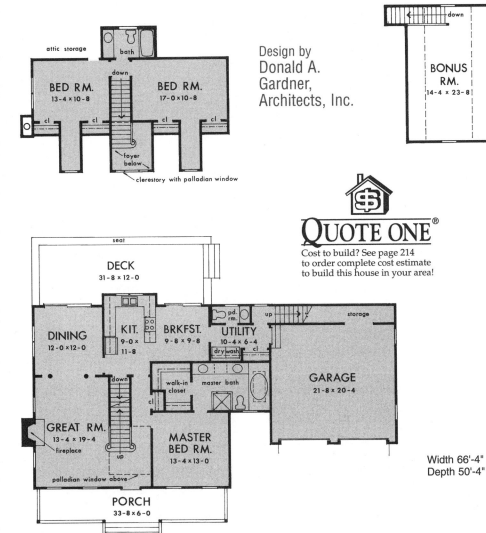

attic storage

bath

BED RM.
13-4 x 10-8

BED RM.
17-0 x 10-8

down

cl   cl   cl   cl

foyer below

clerestory with palladian window

Design by
Donald A.
Gardner,
Architects, Inc.

down

BONUS RM.
14-4 x 23-8

QUOTE ONE®

Cost to build? See page 214
to order complete cost estimate
to build this house in your area!

seat

DECK
31-8 x 12-0

DINING
12-0 x 12-0

KIT.
9-0 x 11-8

BRKFST.
9-8 x 9-8

UTILITY
10-4 x 6-4

pd. rm.

up

storage

dry wash   cl

down

walk-in closet

master bath

cl

GARAGE
21-8 x 20-4

GREAT RM.
13-4 x 19-4

fireplace

up

MASTER
BED RM.
13-4 x 13-0

palladian window above

PORCH
33-8 x 6-0

Width 66'-4"
Depth 50'-4"

Design 9606

First Floor: 1,289 square feet
Second Floor: 542 square feet
Total: 1,831 square feet
Bonus Room: 393 square feet

◆ This cozy country cottage is perfect for the growing family—offering both an unfinished basement option and a bonus room. Enter through the two-story foyer with a Palladian window in a clerestory dormer above. The master suite is on the first floor for privacy and accessibility. Its accompanying bath boasts a whirlpool tub with a skylight above and a double-bowl vanity. The second floor contains two bedrooms, a full bath and plenty of storage. Note that all first-floor rooms except the kitchen and utility room boast nine-foot ceilings. Please specify basement or crawlspace foundation when ordering.

Design 9822

First Floor: 1,944 square feet
Second Floor: 954 square feet
Total: 2,898 square feet

◆ This story-and-a-half home combines warm informal materials with a modern livable floor plan to create a true Southern classic. The dining room, study and great room work together to create one large, exciting space. Just beyond the open rail, the breakfast room is lined with windows. Plenty of counter space and storage make the kitchen truly usable. The master suite, with its tray ceiling and decorative wall niche, is a gracious and private owners' retreat. Upstairs, two additional bedrooms each have their own vanity within a shared bath while the third bedroom or guest room has its own bath and walk-in closet. This home is designed with a basement foundation.

Width 51'-6"
Depth 73'

Design by
Design Traditions

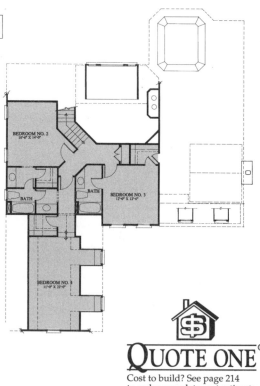

Rear Elevation

Quote One®
Cost to build? See page 214
to order complete cost estimate
to build this house in your area!

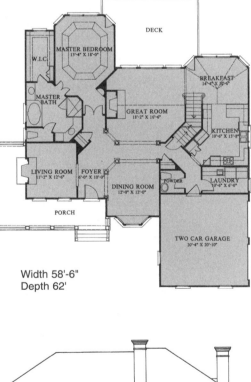

Design by
Design Traditions

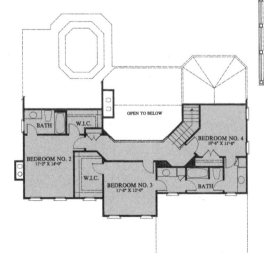

Width 58'-6"
Depth 62'

Rear Elevation

Design 9852
First Floor: 1,840 square feet
Second Floor: 950 square feet
Total: 2,790 square feet

◆ The appearance of this Early
American home brings the
past to mind with its wraparound porch and flower-box
detailing. The uniquely-
shaped foyer leads to the dining room accented by columns.
Nearby, columns frame the
great room as well, while a
ribbon of windows creates a
wall of glass at the back of the
house from the great room to
the breakfast area. Left of the
foyer lies the living room with
a warming fireplace. The master suite begins with double
doors that open to a large living space with a bay window.
The spacious master bath and
walk-in closet complete the
suite. Stairs to the second level
lead from the breakfast area to
an open landing overlooking
the great room. Three additional bedrooms with large
walk-in closets and a variety
of bath arrangements com-
plete this level. This home is
designed with a basement
foundation.

Design 9993

First Floor: 1,634 square feet
Second Floor: 1,598 square feet
Total: 3,232 square feet
Bonus Room: 273 square feet

◆ Only a sloping pediment above double front windows adorns this simple, country-style house, where a side-entry garage looks like a rambling addition. The wide porch signals a welcome that continues throughout the house. A front study doubles as a guest room with an adjacent full bath. A large dining room is ideal for entertaining and a sun-filled breakfast room off a spacious kitchen provides comfortable space for casual family meals. The open, contemporary interior plan flows from a stair hall at the heart of the house. On the private second floor, the master bedroom includes a luxurious bath; two other bedrooms share a bath with dual vanities. An extra room over the kitchen makes a perfect children's play area. This home is designed with a basement foundation.

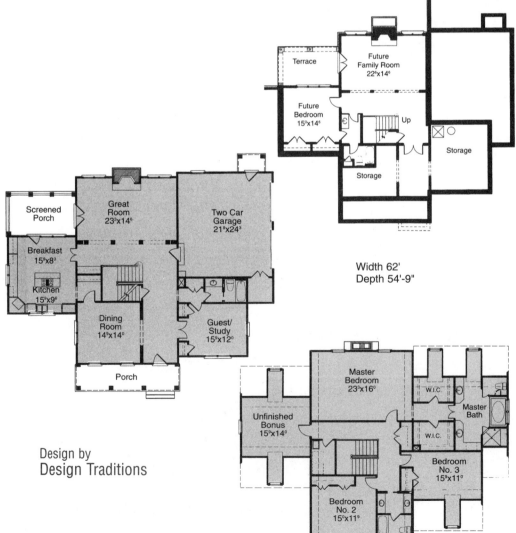

Width 62'
Depth 54'-9"

Design by
Design Traditions

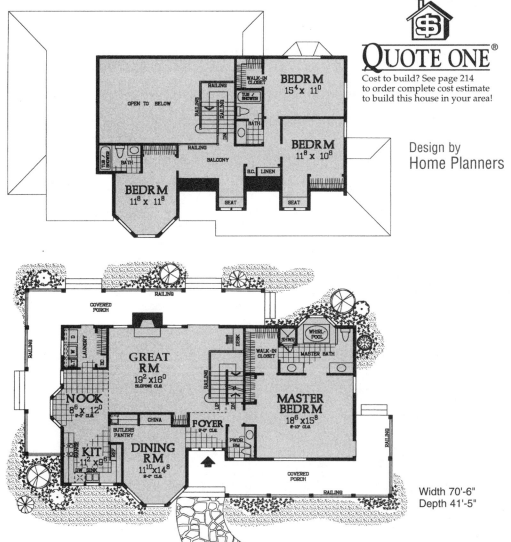

Quote One®

Cost to build? See page 214
to order complete cost estimate
to build this house in your area!

Design by
Home Planners

Design 3605

First Floor: 1,622 square feet
Second Floor: 900 square feet
Total: 2,522 square feet

L **D**

◆ Dormered windows, a covered porch and an abundance of country charm combine to create a welcoming facade to this comfortable two-story home. Living centers around a two-story great room, which offers a warming fireplace, a built-in desk and access to the rear covered porch. The U-shaped kitchen efficiently serves a bay-windowed dining room and a sunny nook with yet a second bay window. Secluded on the first floor for privacy, the master bedroom has many amenities, including two closets and a deluxe bath with a whirlpool, a separate shower and twin vanities. On the second floor, two family bedrooms share a hall bath while a third bedroom has its own full bath and could be used as a guest suite.

Width 70'-6"
Depth 41'-5"

Design 8996

First Floor: 1,748 square feet
Second Floor: 880 square feet
Total: 2,628 square feet

◆ Three dormers and a wrap-around porch give this farmhouse plenty of down-home charm. Inside, a large formal dining room is just steps away from the efficient kitchen. At the rear of the plan, the living room is graced by a fireplace and a French door to the covered porch. A nearby breakfast area is easily served by the snack bar off the kitchen. Secluded on the first floor for privacy, the master bedroom offers many amenities including two walk-in closets, a built-in bookcase and a skylit bath. Upstairs, two bedrooms share a full hall bath while a third bedroom has its own bath. A cozy study area with built-ins completes this level.

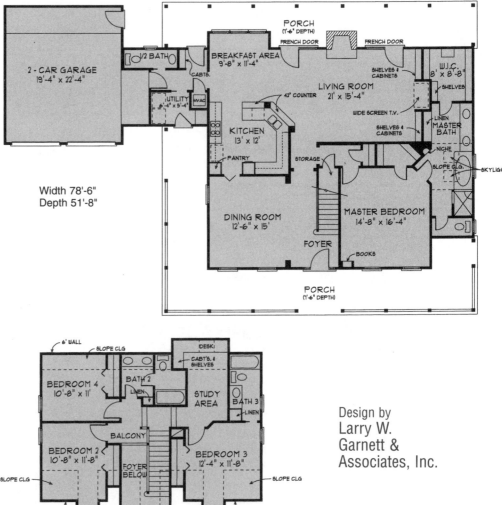

Width 78'-6"
Depth 51'-8"

Design by
Larry W.
Garnett &
Associates, Inc.

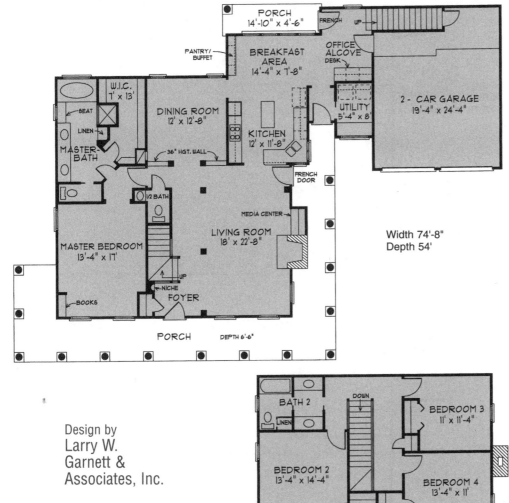

PORCH
14'-10" x 4'-6"

PANTRY/
BUFFET

BREAKFAST
AREA
14'-4" x 7'-8"

FRENCH

UP

OFFICE
ALCOVE
DESK

2 - CAR GARAGE
19'-4" x 24'-4"

UTILITY
5'-4" x 8'

W.I.C.
7' x 13'

SEAT

LINEN

MASTER
BATH

DINING ROOM
12' x 12'-8"

KITCHEN
12' x 11'-8"

36" HGT. WALL

FRENCH
DOOR

1/2 BATH

MEDIA CENTER

MASTER BEDROOM
13'-4" x 17'

LIVING ROOM
18' x 22'-8"

Width 74'-8"
Depth 54'

BOOKS

UP

NICHE

FOYER

PORCH   DEPTH 6'-6"

Design by
Larry W.
Garnett &
Associates, Inc.

BATH 2

LINEN

DOWN

BEDROOM 3
11' x 11'-4"

BEDROOM 2
13'-4" x 14'-4"

BEDROOM 4
13'-4" x 11'

Design 9194

First Floor: 1,629 square feet
Second Floor: 795 square feet
Total: 2,424 square feet

◆ The sturdy pillars lining the front porch of this farmhouse give it a unique, stately appearance. They continue within as columns define the large living room with its fireplace and media center. Another set of columns and a half-wall provide entry into the formal dining room. Adjacent to the kitchen is a breakfast area that features a writing desk, a pantry/buffet and access to the back porch, the side porch, the utility area, the garage and the bonus room above. The left wing of the house is reserved for the master suite. It includes a built-in bookcase, a huge walk-in closet and a fine bath. Three bedrooms and a full bath with dual vanities reside upstairs.

Design 9196

First Floor: 1,525 square feet
Second Floor: 795 square feet
Total: 2,320 square feet

◆ An L-shaped covered porch provides a happy marriage of indoor/outdoor relationships. The foyer opens onto a living room that presents opportunities to curl up in front of the fire with a good book, use state of-the art electronics housed in the built-in media center and access the porch through a French door. A kitchen designed for efficiency combines with the breakfast area for informal meals and serves the nearby dining room for formal occasions. Located on the first floor for privacy, the master suite provides a relaxing retreat. A built-in bookcase stores your favorite novels and a spacious master bath features a whirlpool tub and a separate shower. Three bedrooms and a full bath complete the second floor.

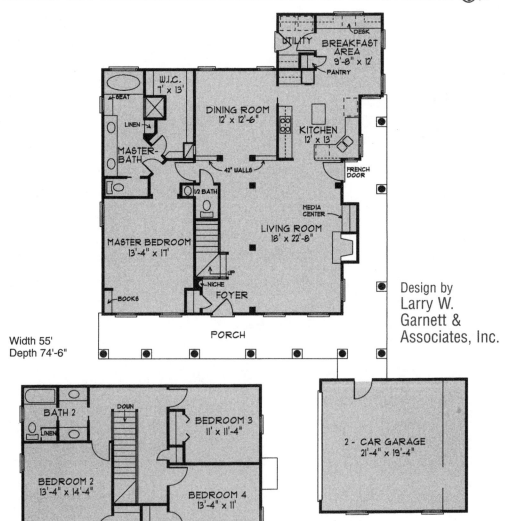

Width 55'
Depth 74'-6"

Design by
Larry W.
Garnett &
Associates, Inc.

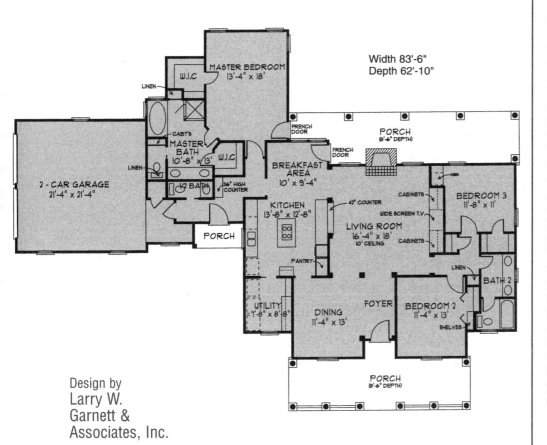

Width 83'-6"
Depth 62'-10"

MASTER BEDROOM
13'-4" x 18'

LINEN

W.I.C

CAB'T'S

MASTER BATH
10'-8" x 13'

LINEN

W.I.C

1/2 BATH

36" HIGH COUNTER

2 - CAR GARAGE
21'-4" x 21'-4"

PORCH

FRENCH DOOR

PORCH
(8'-6" DEPTH)

FRENCH DOOR

BREAKFAST AREA
10' x 9'-4"

KITCHEN
13'-8" x 12'-8"

42" COUNTER

CABINETS

WIDE SCREEN T.V.

LIVING ROOM
16'-4" x 18'
10' CEILING

CABINETS

BEDROOM 3
11'-8" x 11'

DESK

PANTRY

LINEN

UTILITY
7'-8" x 8'-8"

DINING
11'-4" x 13'

FOYER

BEDROOM 2
11'-4" x 13'

BATH 2

SHELVES

PORCH
(8'-6" DEPTH)

Design by
Larry W.
Garnett &
Associates, Inc.

Design 8998
Square Footage: 1,980

◆ Encompassing just one floor, this farmhouse plan provides excellent livability. From the large covered porch, the foyer opens to a dining room on the left and a center living room with space for a wide-screen TV flanked by cabinets and a fireplace with a scenic view on each side. The large kitchen sports an island cooktop and easy accessibility to the rear breakfast area, the utility room, and the dining room. While the family bedrooms reside on the right side of the plan and share a full bath with twin vanities, the master bedroom takes advantage of its secluded rear location. It features twin walk-in closets and vanities, a windowed corner tub, a separate shower and private access to the rear covered porch.

Design 8994
Square Footage: 1,672

◆ The columns that adorn this delightful farmhouse evoke the true Southern spirit that speaks of gracious hospitality. From the foyer, open planning lends a feeling of spaciousness to the living room, dining room and adjacent kitchen. A warm reception is provided by a living room that features a center fireplace flanked by media centers and window seats. Access to the rear yard from the dining room provides indoor and outdoor options for enjoying meals. The left wing of the house contains the sleeping facilities. Here, two secondary bedrooms share a full bath. A laundry room and an office alcove separate the master bedroom from Bedrooms 2 and 3. Located to the rear of the plan, the master suite provides a restful getaway that features a walk-in closet and a relaxing bath that awaits to soothe and pamper.

Design by
Larry W.
Garnett &
Associates, Inc.

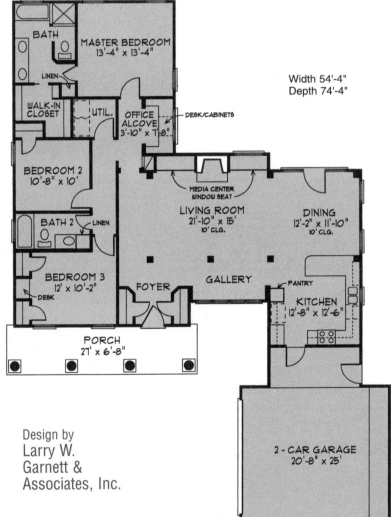

Width 54'-4"
Depth 74'-4"

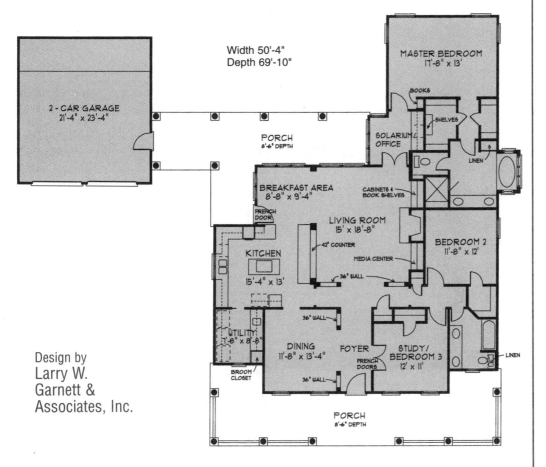

Width 50'-4"
Depth 69'-10"

2 - CAR GARAGE
21'-4" x 23'-4"

PORCH
8'-6" DEPTH

MASTER BEDROOM
17'-8" x 13'

BOOKS

SHELVES

SOLARIUM/
OFFICE

LINEN

BREAKFAST AREA
8'-8" x 9'-4"

CABINETS &
BOOK SHELVES

FRENCH
DOOR

LIVING ROOM
15' x 18'-8"

42" COUNTER

BEDROOM 2
11'-8" x 12'

KITCHEN
15'-4" x 13'

MEDIA CENTER

36" WALL

36" WALL

UTILITY
7'-8" x 8'-8"

36" WALL

DINING
11'-8" x 13'-4"

FOYER

STUDY/
BEDROOM 3
12' x 11'

LINEN

BROOM
CLOSET

FRENCH
DOORS

36" WALL

PORCH
8'-6" DEPTH

Design by
Larry W.
Garnett &
Associates, Inc.

Design 8997

Square Footage: 2,077

◆ This is not just an average farmhouse plan. It was designed to delight and cater to those looking for special details. The full front porch greets all comers and leads to a center-hall foyer. On the left is a formal dining room accented by half-walls. On the right is a study or bedroom that is accessed through French doors. The main living area has a fireplace, built-in bookshelves and cabinets and a media center. It is open to the breakfast area and island kitchen. The master suite features a small solarium/office. A pampering bath containing two large walk-in closets, a bumped-out tub, a shower and dual vanities enhance the master suite. An additional family bedroom also has a walk-in closet. The two-car garage is detached but is reached by the rear covered porch.

Design 9748

Square Footage: 1,737

◆ Inviting porches are just the beginning of this lovely country home. To the left of the foyer, a columned entry supplies a classic touch to a spacious great room that features a cathedral ceiling, built-in bookshelves and a fireplace that invites you to share its warmth. An octagonal dining room with a tray ceiling provides a perfect setting for formal occasions. The adjacent kitchen is designed to easily serve both formal and informal areas. It includes an island cooktop and a built-in pantry, with the sunny breakfast area just a step away. The master bedroom, separated from two family bedrooms by the walk-in closet and utility room, offers privacy and comfort.

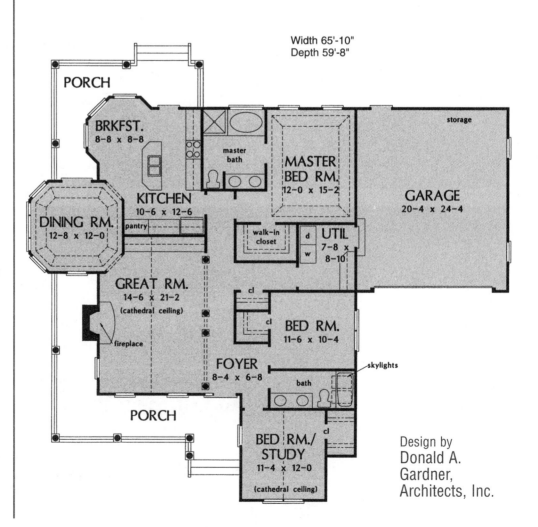

Width 65'-10"
Depth 59'-8"

PORCH

BRKFST.
8-8 x 8-8

master bath

MASTER BED RM.
12-0 x 15-2

storage

GARAGE
20-4 x 24-4

KITCHEN
10-6 x 12-6

pantry

DINING RM.
12-8 x 12-0

walk-in closet

UTIL
7-8 x 8-10

d
w

GREAT RM.
14-6 x 21-2
(cathedral ceiling)

fireplace

cl

cl

cl

BED RM.
11-6 x 10-4

FOYER
8-4 x 6-8

skylights

bath

PORCH

BED RM./ STUDY
11-4 x 12-0
(cathedral ceiling)

Design by
Donald A.
Gardner,
Architects, Inc.

142

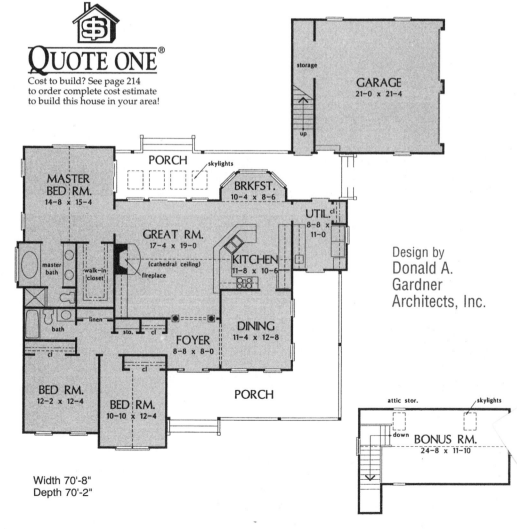

GARAGE
21-0 x 21-4

storage

up

PORCH

skylights

MASTER
BED RM.
14-8 x 15-4

BRKFST.
10-4 x 8-6

UTIL.
8-8 x
11-0

cl

master
bath

walk-in
closet

GREAT RM.
17-4 x 19-0

(cathedral ceiling)
fireplace

KITCHEN
11-8 x 10-6

linen

bath

sto.

cl

FOYER
8-8 x 8-0

DINING
11-4 x 12-8

cl

BED RM.
12-2 x 12-4

BED RM.
10-10 x 12-4

cl

PORCH

Design by
Donald A.
Gardner
Architects, Inc.

attic stor.

skylights

down

BONUS RM.
24-8 x 11-10

Width 70'-8"
Depth 70'-2"

Design 9764
Square Footage: 1,815

◆ Dormers, arched windows
and covered porches lend this
home its country appeal. Inside, the foyer opens to the
dining room on the right and
leads through a columned entrance to the great room and
its warming fireplace. Access
is provided to the covered,
skylit rear porch for outdoor
livability. The open kitchen
easily serves the great room,
the bayed breakfast area and
the dining room. A cathedral
ceiling graces the master bedroom with its walk-in closet
and private bath with a dual
vanity and a whirlpool
Two additional bed
share a full bath
garage with
room is
ere

Design 9742

Square Footage: 1,954
Bonus Room: 436 square feet

◆ This beautiful brick country home has all the amenities needed for today's active family. Covered front and back porches along with a rear deck provide plenty of room for outdoor enjoyment. Inside, the focus is on the large great room with its cathedral ceiling and welcoming fireplace. To the right, columns separate the kitchen and breakfast area while keeping this area open. Resident gourmets will certainly appreciate the convenience of the kitchen with its center island and additional eating space. The master bedroom provides a splendid private retreat, featuring a cathedral ceiling and a large walk-in closet. A double-bowl vanity, a separate shower and a relaxing skylit whirlpool tub highlight the luxurious master bath. At the opposite end of the home, two additional bedrooms share a full bath. A bonus room above the garage allows for additional

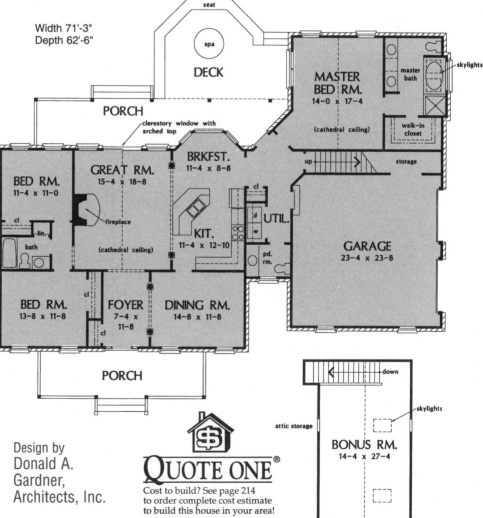

Width 71'-3"
Depth 62'-6"

Design by
Donald A.
Gardner,
Architects, Inc.

Quote One®
Cost to build? See page 214
to order complete cost estimate
to build this house in your area!

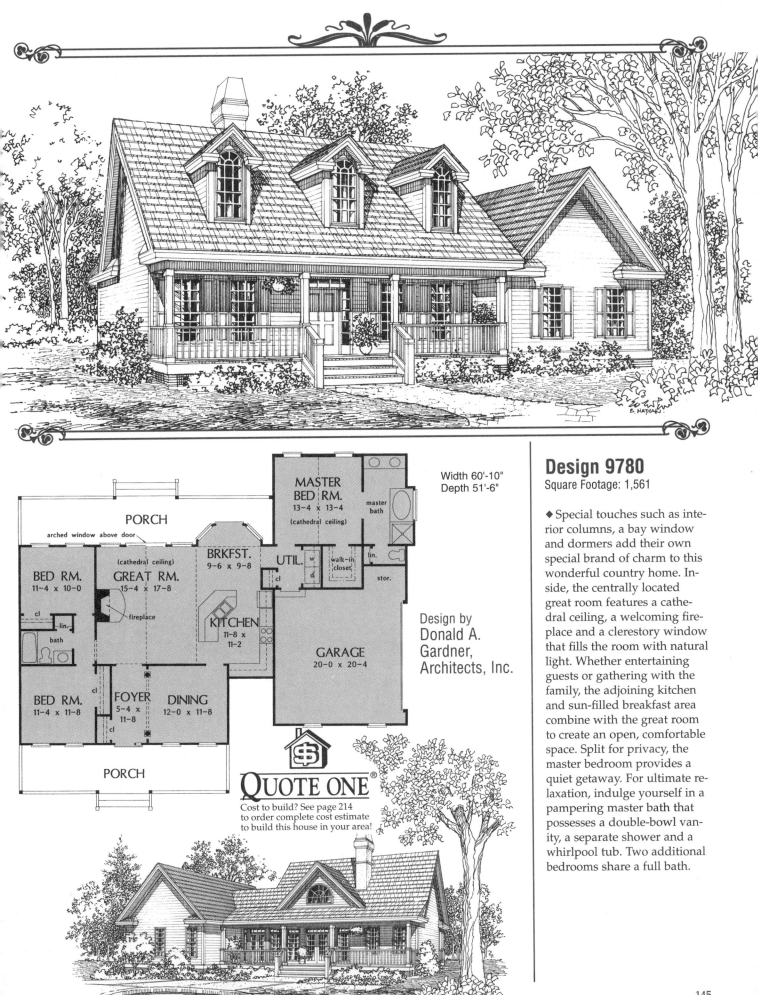

Width 60'-10"
Depth 51'-6"

Design 9780
Square Footage: 1,561

◆ Special touches such as interior columns, a bay window and dormers add their own special brand of charm to this wonderful country home. Inside, the centrally located great room features a cathedral ceiling, a welcoming fireplace and a clerestory window that fills the room with natural light. Whether entertaining guests or gathering with the family, the adjoining kitchen and sun-filled breakfast area combine with the great room to create an open, comfortable space. Split for privacy, the master bedroom provides a quiet getaway. For ultimate relaxation, indulge yourself in a pampering master bath that possesses a double-bowl vanity, a separate shower and a whirlpool tub. Two additional bedrooms share a full bath.

Design by
Donald A.
Gardner,
Architects, Inc.

Quote One®
Cost to build? See page 214
to order complete cost estimate
to build this house in your area!

Floor plan labels

PORCH

arched window above door

BED RM.
11-4 x 10-0

GREAT RM.
15-4 x 17-8
(cathedral ceiling)

fireplace

BRKFST.
9-6 x 9-8

UTIL.

KITCHEN
11-8 x
11-2

MASTER
BED RM.
13-4 x 13-4
(cathedral ceiling)

master
bath

w   d

walk-in
closet

lin.

stor.

BED RM.
11-4 x 11-8

FOYER
5-4 x
11-8

DINING
12-0 x 11-8

GARAGE
20-0 x 20-4

cl

lin.

bath

PORCH

145

Design 9779

Square Footage: 1,632

◆ This country home has a big heart in a cozy package. Inside, interior columns, a bay window and dormers add elegance. The central great room features a cathedral ceiling and a fireplace. A clerestory window splashes the room with natural light. The open kitchen easily services the breakfast area and the nearby dining room. The private master suite, with a tray ceiling and a walk-in closet, boasts amenities found in much larger homes. The bath features skylights over the whirlpool tub. Two additional bedrooms share a bath. The front bedroom features a walk-in closet and also doubles as a study.

Design by
Donald A.
Gardner,
Architects, Inc.

PORCH

MASTER BED RM.
13-4 x 16-4

skylight

master bath

walk-in closet

lin.

storage

BRKFST.
10-4 x 8-8

cl

w
d

UTIL.

BED RM.
11-4 x 11-0

GREAT RM.
15-4 x 18-6
(cathedral ceiling)

fireplace

cl
lin.

bath

walk-in closet

KIT.
11-4 x 12-10

GARAGE
21-0 x 21-8

storage

BED RM./
STUDY
11-0 x 11-8

FOYER
6-0 x 8-4

DINING
11-0 x 11-8

storage

(optional door location)

PORCH

Width 62'-4"
Depth 55'-2"

QUOTE ONE®

Cost to build? See page 214 to order complete cost estimate to build this house in your area!

146

Design 9782
Square Footage: 2,192

◆ Exciting volumes and nine-foot ceilings add elegance to a comfortable, open plan while secluded bedrooms are pleasant retreats in this home. Sunlight fills the airy foyer from a vaulted dormer and streams into the great room. A formal dining room, delineated from the foyer by columns, features a tray ceiling. Hosts whose guests always end up in the kitchen will enjoy entertaining here with only columns to separate them from the great room. Secondary bedrooms share a full bath complete with a linen closet. The front bedroom doubles as a study for extra flexibility and is accented by a tray ceiling. The master suite is highlighted by a tray ceiling and a spacious master bath with a walk-in closet.

attic storage

down

BONUS RM.
14-4 x 21-8

skylights

Width 74'-10"
Depth 55'-8"

lin.

skylight

master bath

MASTER BED RM.
14-0 x 17-4

walk-in closet

sto.

up

GARAGE
23-0 x 25-8

storage

UTIL.

d w

pd. rm.

KIT.
11-8 x 12-8

BRKFST.
11-8 x 9-0

(cathedral ceiling)

PORCH

GREAT RM.
16-4 x 18-8

fireplace

opening above

opening above

DINING
14-8 x 11-8

FOYER
6-4 x 11-8

vaulted ceiling

BED RM./ STUDY
14-8 x 11-8

PORCH

BED RM.
12-0 x 11-0

cl

BED RM.
10-10 x 11-0

cl

lin.

bath

walk-in closet

Design by
Donald A. Gardner, Architects, Inc.

© The Sater Group, Inc.

Design 6654

First Floor: 1,342 square feet
Second Floor: 511 square feet
Total: 1,853 square feet

◆ With influences from homes of the Caribbean as well as Tidewater homes of the South, this home is a perfect seaside residence or primary residence. The main living area is comprised of a grand room with a fireplace and access to a deck. The dining space also accesses this deck plus another that it shares with a secondary bedroom. An L-shaped kitchen with a prep island is open to the living areas. Two bedrooms on this level share a full bath. The master suite dominates the upper level. It has its own balcony and a rewarding bath with dual vanities and whirlpool tub.

Design by
The Sater
Design Collection

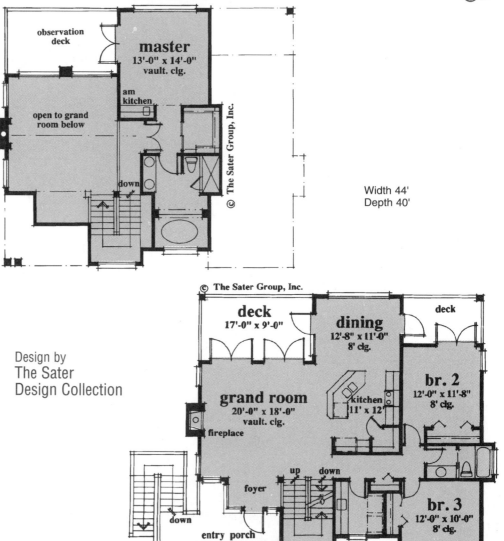

Width 44'
Depth 40'

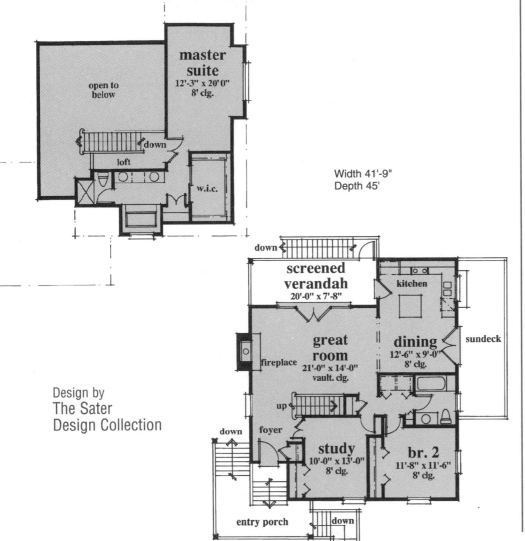

master suite
12'-3" x 20'0"
8' clg.

open to below

down

loft

w.i.c.

Design by
**The Sater
Design Collection**

Width 41'-9"
Depth 45'

down

screened
verandah
20'-0" x 7'-8"

kitchen

great
room
21'-0" x 14'-0"
vault. clg.

dining
12'-6" x 9'-0"
8' clg.

fireplace

sundeck

up

down

foyer

study
10'-0" x 13'-0"
8' clg.

br. 2
11'-8" x 11'-6"
8' clg.

entry porch

down

Design 6616
First Floor: 1,136 square feet
Second Floor: 636 square feet
Total: 1,772 square feet

◆ This two-story home's pleasing exterior is complemented by its warm character and decorative "widow's walk." The covered entry—with its dramatic transom window—leads to a spacious great room highlighted by a warming fireplace. To the right, the dining room and kitchen combine to provide a delightful place for mealtimes inside or out, with access to a side deck through double doors. Two bedrooms and a full bath complete the first floor. The luxurious master suite is located on the second floor for privacy and features an oversized walk-in closet and a separate dressing area. The pampering master bath enjoys a relaxing whirlpool tub, a double-bowl vanity and a compartmented toilet.

COPYRIGHT LARRY E. BELK

Design 8114

First Floor: 1,785 square feet
Second Floor: 830 square feet
Total: 2,615 square feet
Bonus Room: 280 square feet

◆ Looking to the past for style, the character of this winning plan is vintage Americana. A huge great room opens through classic arches to the island kitchen and the breakfast room. A corner sink in the kitchen gives the cook a view to the outside and brings in sunlight. Nearby, a small side porch provides a charming entry. The master suite is found on the first floor for privacy and features a luxury bath with separate vanities, His and Hers walk-in closets and a corner tub. The three bedrooms upstairs feature dormer windows and share a full bath. An additional 280-square foot area is available above the garage. Please specify crawlspace or slab foundation when ordering.

Design by
Larry E. Belk
Designs

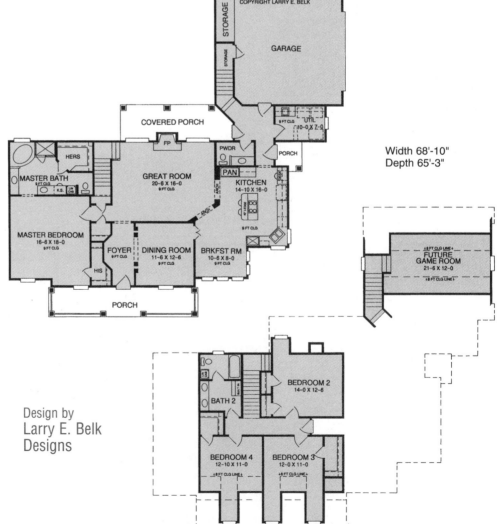

Width 68'-10"
Depth 65'-3"

Midwestern Masterpieces

Design by
Design Basics, Inc.

QUOTE ONE®
Cost to build? See page 214 to order complete cost estimate to build this house in your area!

Design 9310
First Floor: 1,505 square feet
Second Floor: 610 square feet
Total: 2,115 square feet

◆ Many windows, lap siding and a covered porch give this elevation a welcoming country flair. The formal dining room with hutch space is conveniently located near the island kitchen. A main-floor laundry room with a sink is discreetly located next to the bright breakfast area with desk and pantry. Highlighting the spacious great room are a raised-hearth fireplace, a cathedral ceiling and trapezoid windows. Special features in the master suite include a large dressing area with a double vanity, a skylight, a step-up corner whirlpool and a generous walk-in closet. Upstairs, the three secondary bedrooms are well separated from the master bedroom and share a hall bath.

Br.3
11³ x 12⁰

Br.2
12⁴ x 11¹

Br.4
10⁸ x 12⁵

DN

OPEN TO BELOW

PLANT SHELF

10'-0" CLG.

Width 64'
Depth 52'

TRAPS

TRANSOMS

TRANSOMS

Grt. rm.
15³ x 22⁰

CATHEDRAL CEILING

Mbr.
13⁰ x 16⁰

10'-0" CLG.

SKYLIGHT

Bfst.
11⁴ x 14⁰

Kit.
9⁰ x 14⁰

DESK

P.

W. D.

SNACK BAR

HUTCH

DN

UP

Din.
14⁰ x 11⁵

WHIRL-POOL

Gar.
30⁷ x 22⁷

COVERED PORCH

© design basics inc.

151

Design 3325

First Floor: 1,595 square feet
Second Floor: 1,112 square feet
Total: 2,707 square feet

L D

◆Horizontal clapboard siding and finely detailed window treatments set the tone for this delightful family farmhouse. For informal occasions, a spacious family room and breakfast room extend a wealth of livability. The U-shaped kitchen utilizes a work island supplemented by plenty of cabinet, cupboard and counter space. The sleeping accommodations of this plan include a master bedroom suite with a walk-in closet in addition to a long wardrobe closet. The master bath has a tub plus a stall shower and twin lavatories. The rear bedroom will make a fine study, guest room or fourth bedroom.

Design by
Home Planners

Width 63'-6"
Depth 48'

QUOTE ONE®

Cost to build? See page 214
to order complete cost estimate
to build this house in your area!

Design by
Home Planners

Width 66'
Depth 47'-6"

QUOTE ONE®

Cost to build? See page 214
to order complete cost estimate
to build this house in your area!

Design 3324

First Floor: 1,762 square feet
Second Floor: 1,311 square feet
Total: 3,073 square feet

L **D**

◆ This home provides a perfect opportunity to share the comforts of traditional family living with in-home office space. The versatile plan allows for a well-positioned study off the foyer and a combination guest room/office near the laundry room. The large kitchen presents many possibilities for dining pleasures—a cozy meal in the breakfast nook; light eating and conversation at the bar; and evening meals in the dining room. The master bedroom provides spacious comfort with His and Hers walk-in closets and an impressive dressing area. The two family bedrooms share a large bathroom with plenty of linen space.

Design 7250

First Floor: 904 square feet
Second Floor: 796 square feet
Total: 1,700 square feet

◆ French doors to the kitchen and a U-shaped stairway highlight the entry of this traditional country elevation. Large cased openings define both the great room and the dining room without restricting any space. The U-shaped kitchen and the adjoining breakfast area provide functional access to the utility room, the garage, the powder room and the side and rear yards. A workbench and extra storage space are available in the garage. Secondary bedrooms share a generous compartmented bath that includes two sinks. The stately master suite features dual walk-in closets, a nine-foot box ceiling and a whirlpool tub.

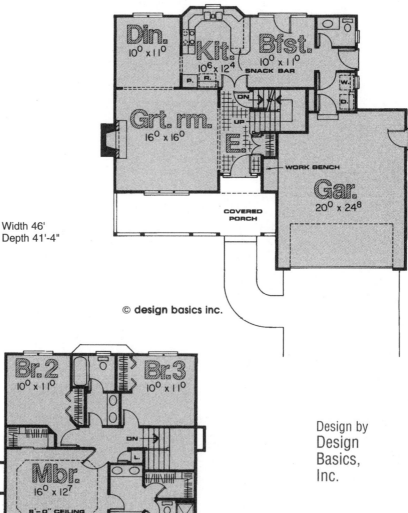

Width 46'
Depth 41'-4"

© design basics inc.

Design by
Design Basics, Inc.

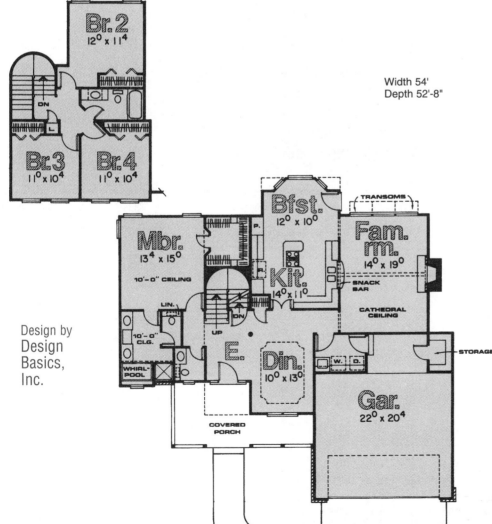

Br. 2
12⁰ x 11⁴

Br. 3
11⁰ x 10⁴

Br. 4
11⁰ x 10⁴

Width 54'
Depth 52'-8"

Design by
Design
Basics,
Inc.

Mbr.
13⁴ x 15⁰

10'-0" CEILING

LIN.

10'-0"
CLG.

WHIRL-
POOL

Bfst.
12⁰ x 10⁰

TRANSOMS

Kit.
14⁰ x 11⁰

**Fam.
rm.**
14⁰ x 19⁰

SNACK
BAR

CATHEDRAL
CEILING

UP   DN

E.

Din.
10⁰ x 13⁰

W. D.

STORAGE

Gar.
22⁰ x 20⁴

COVERED
PORCH

Design 7288

First Floor: 1,400 square feet
Second Floor: 584 square feet
Total: 1,984 square feet

◆ The wrapping covered front
porch of this home leads to an
oak foyer showcasing an elegant U-shaped staircase. The
formal dining room to the
right is enhanced by intricate
ceiling detail. Double French
doors lead into an island
kitchen with an attached bay-
windowed breakfast nook.
With a cathedral ceiling, transom windows and a warming
fireplace, the family room is
sure to please. Located on the
first floor for privacy, the
deluxe master suite offers a
large walk-in closet and a
sumptuous bath complete
with a whirlpool tub, separate
shower and twin vanities. Upstairs, three family bedrooms
share a full hall bath.

© design basics inc.

Design 9298

First Floor: 1,881 square feet
Second Floor: 814 square feet
Total: 2,695 square feet

◆ Oval windows and an appealing covered porch lend character to this 1½-story home. Inside, a volume entry views the formal living and dining rooms. Three large windows and a raised-hearth fireplace flanked by bookcases highlight a volume great room. An island kitchen with a huge pantry and two Lazy Susans serves a captivating gazebo dinette. In the master suite, a cathedral ceiling, corner whirlpool and roomy dressing area deserve careful study. A gallery wall for displaying family mementos and prized heirlooms graces the upstairs corridor. Each secondary bedroom has convenient access to the bathrooms. This home's charm and blend of popular amenities will fit your lifestyle!

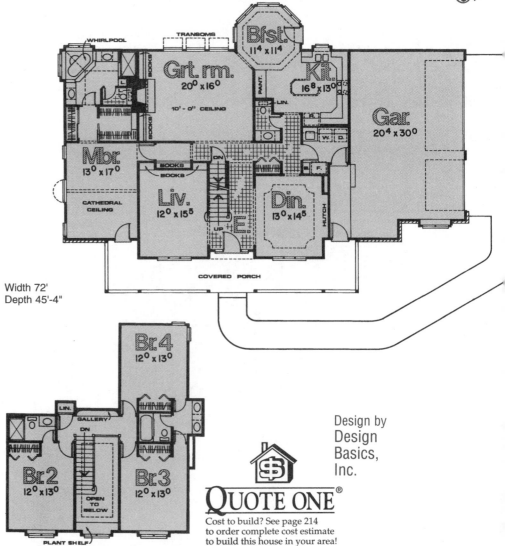

Width 72'
Depth 45'-4"

Design by
Design Basics, Inc.

Quote One®
Cost to build? See page 214 to order complete cost estimate to build this house in your area!

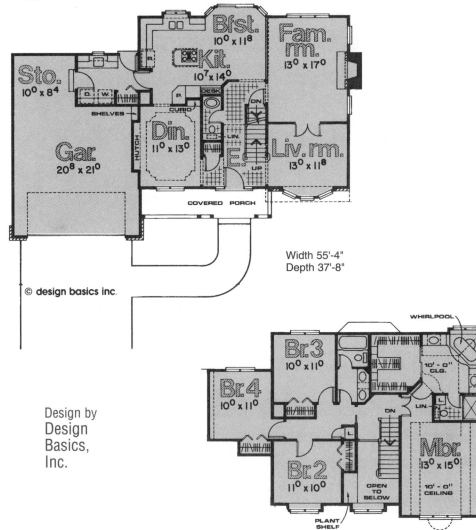

Sto.
10⁰ x 8⁴

Gar.
20⁸ x 21⁰

Bfst.
10⁰ x 11⁸

Kit.
10⁷ x 14⁰

Fam. rm.
13⁰ x 17⁰

SHELVES

HUTCH

Din.
11⁰ x 13⁰

CURIO

DESK

P.

LIN.

DN

UP

Liv. rm.
13⁰ x 11⁸

COVERED PORCH

Width 55'-4"
Depth 37'-8"

© design basics inc.

Design by
Design
Basics,
Inc.

WHIRLPOOL

Br. 3
10⁰ x 11⁰

Br. 4
10⁰ x 11⁰

10'-0"
CLG.

LIN.

DN

Mbr.
13⁰ x 15⁰

Br. 2
11⁰ x 10⁰

OPEN
TO
BELOW

10'-0"
CEILING

PLANT
SHELF

Design 7261

First Floor: 1,093 square feet
Second Floor: 1,038 square feet
Total: 2,131 square feet

◆ This beautifully proportioned design is complemented by a large covered porch framed with a wood railing. The living room is enhanced by a bay window and French doors leading to the family room with its central fireplace. The dining room is accented by a built-in curio cabinet and is just steps away from the open island kitchen and the breakfast bay area. The four-bedroom sleeping zone is located on the second floor. Bedroom 2 features a box-bay window. The master bedroom contains a distinctive vaulted ceiling, plus a luxurious bath with a corner whirlpool tub and a massive walk-in closet.

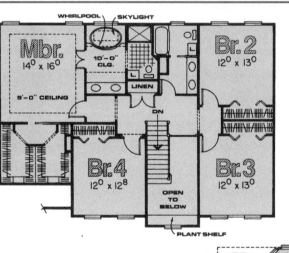

WHIRLPOOL — SKYLIGHT

Mbr.
14⁰ x 16⁰

10'-0"
CLG.

Br. 2
12⁰ x 13⁰

9'-0" CEILING

LINEN

L

DN

Br. 4
12⁰ x 12⁸

Br. 3
12⁰ x 13⁰

OPEN
TO
BELOW

PLANT SHELF

Design 7286

First Floor: 1,366 square feet
Second Floor: 1,278 square feet
Total: 2,644 square feet

◆ A covered porch and a front door with sidelites create an inviting facade to this four-bedroom house. Inside, the formal dining room and formal living room flank a two-story foyer. The rear of the home holds the informal areas. A large kitchen with cook-top island opens to a bay-windowed breakfast area which shares a through-fireplace with the bay-windowed family room complete with built-ins. Upstairs is the sleeping zone. Three family bedrooms share a full hall bath with twin vanities. A sumptuous master suite offers an abundance of closet space with twin walk-ins and presents an elegant bath designed to pamper.

Design by
Design
Basics,
Inc.

Width 54'-8"
Depth 42'

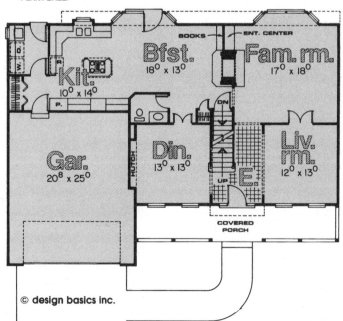

BOOKS

ENT. CENTER

Bfst.
18⁰ x 13⁰

Fam. rm.
17⁰ x 18⁰

Kit.
10⁰ x 14⁰

P.

Gar.
20⁸ x 25⁰

HUTCH

DN

Din.
13⁰ x 13⁰

Liv.
rm.
12⁰ x 13⁰

UP

COVERED
PORCH

© design basics inc.

158

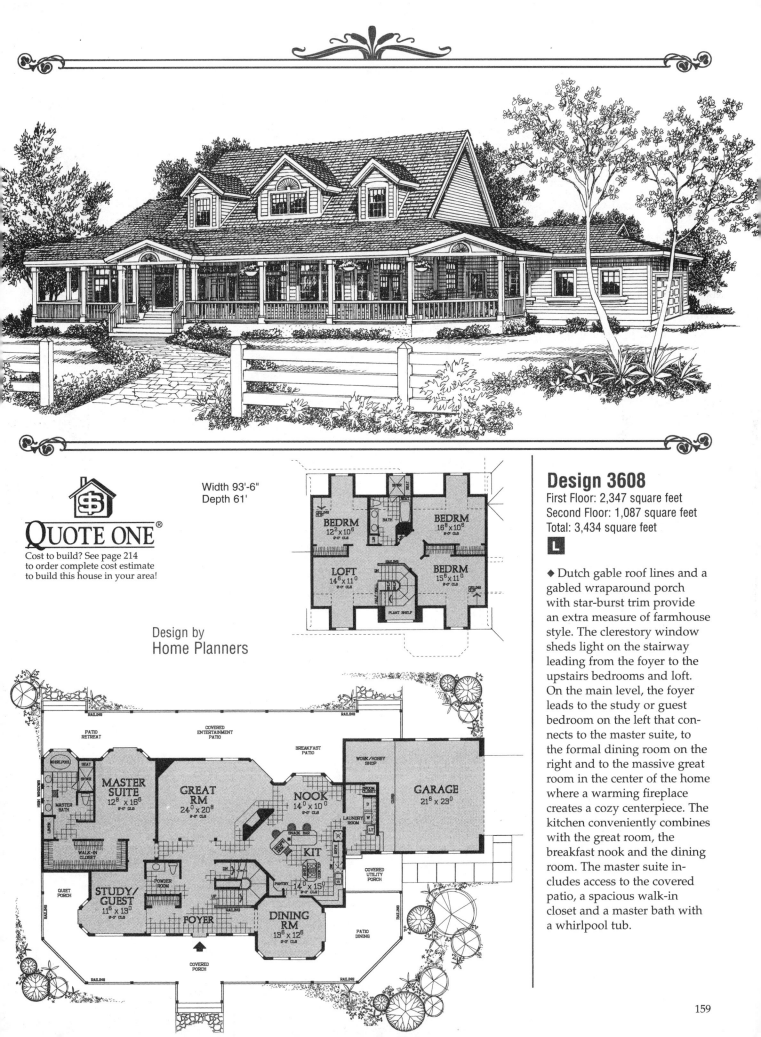

Width 93'-6"
Depth 61'

Design by
Home Planners

BEDRM
12² x 10⁶

BEDRM
16⁸ x 10⁶

LOFT
14⁶ x 11⁰

BEDRM
15⁸ x 11⁰

BATH

Design 3608

First Floor: 2,347 square feet
Second Floor: 1,087 square feet
Total: 3,434 square feet

L

◆ Dutch gable roof lines and a
gabled wraparound porch
with star-burst trim provide
an extra measure of farmhouse
style. The clerestory window
sheds light on the stairway
leading from the foyer to the
upstairs bedrooms and loft.
On the main level, the foyer
leads to the study or guest
bedroom on the left that connects to the master suite, to
the formal dining room on the
right and to the massive great
room in the center of the home
where a warming fireplace
creates a cozy centerpiece. The
kitchen conveniently combines
with the great room, the
breakfast nook and the dining
room. The master suite includes access to the covered
patio, a spacious walk-in
closet and a master bath with
a whirlpool tub.

PATIO
RETREAT

COVERED
ENTERTAINMENT
PATIO

BREAKFAST
PATIO

WORK/HOBBY
SHOP

MASTER
SUITE
12⁸ x 16⁸

GREAT
RM
24⁰ x 20⁸

NOOK
14⁰ x 10⁰

GARAGE
21⁸ x 29⁰

MASTER
BATH

LAUNDRY
ROOM

WALK-IN
CLOSET

KIT

COVERED
UTILITY
PORCH

QUIET
PORCH

POWDER
ROOM

PANTRY

14⁰ x 15⁰

STUDY/
GUEST
11⁸ x 19⁰

FOYER

DINING
RM
13⁸ x 12⁸

PATIO
DINING

COVERED
PORCH

Design 3654

First Floor: 1,378 square feet
Second Floor: 912 square feet
Total: 2,290 square feet

L

◆ Though giving all the appearance of a traditional farmhouse on the exterior, this classic design has some interesting floor plan features that make it stand out. The formal living room sits just off the main foyer and is defined by lovely columns and access to the front porch. The family room and angled kitchen are connected to the formal dining room but express their boundaries by a snack-bar counter and three-sided fireplace. The master suite is on the first floor and is introduced by a hall niche. Its accompanying bath has a large walk-in closet, a whirlpool tub and a compartmented toilet. Upstairs, three bedrooms share a large bath with a separate tub and shower. A loft area that allows room for studying or games, and a laundry room that accommodates family members complete the second floor.

QUOTE ONE®

Cost to build? See page 214 to order complete cost estimate to build this house in your area!

Design by
Home Planners, Inc.

Width 74'
Depth 46'

Design 3733

First Floor: 1,300 square feet
Second Floor: 1,251 square feet
Total: 2,551 square feet

L **D**

◆ This stately two-story farm-house is perfect for a relatively narrow site with its optional, attached two-car garage. The covered front porch with columns and railings provides a sheltered front entrance. Straight ahead from the foyer is the hub of the family's in-formal living activities. Here is a spacious area with open planning, which stretches across the rear of the house. The morning/breakfast room has a bay window, which looks out onto the rear terrace. The U-shaped corner kitchen will be a delight in which to function. It has a wide counter snack bar, built-in cooking units, a pantry and a view of the terrace. For the develop-ment of additional recreational space and bulk storage facili-ties, there is the full basement. There are four sizable bed-rooms and two full baths, each with double lavatories.

Width 44'
Depth 38'

Quote One®

Cost to build? See page 214 to order complete cost estimate to build this house in your area!

Design by
Home Planners

MASTER BATH
LIN.
WAL.
LINEN
WALK-IN CLOSET
LAUNDRY
BEDRM 12¹⁰ x 12²
MASTER SUITE 13⁸ x 18⁸
LINEN
BATH
BEDRM 11⁸ x 11⁶
BEDRM 13⁰ x 12⁸
ROOF OF PORCH BELOW

ENTERTAINMENT TERRACE
KIT 14⁰ x 11⁸
SNACK BAR
BREAKFAST-MORNING 13⁰ x 11⁸
FAMILY RM 14⁰ x 16⁸
DW
COOK TOP
REF.
PANTRY
OVEN
DN
POWDER RM
DINING RM 13⁸ x 11⁸
RAILING
UP
LIVING RM 13⁰ x 16⁰
FOYER
COVERED PORCH
RAILING

ENTERTAINMENT TERRACE
GARAGE 19⁸ x 21⁴
KIT 14⁰ x 11⁸
DW
COOK TOP
REF.
PANTRY
DINING RM 13⁸ x 11⁸
COVERED PORCH
RAILING

Optional Garage

Design 3462

First Floor: 1,395 square feet
Second Floor: 813 square feet
Total: 2,208 square feet

L

◆ Horizontal siding with corner boards, muntin windows and a raised veranda enhance the appeal of this country home. Twin carriage lamps flank the sheltered entrance. Inside, the central foyer delights with its two sets of columns at the openings to the formal living and dining rooms. In the L-shaped kitchen, an adjacent snack bar offers everyday ease. Open to the kitchen, the great room boasts a centered fireplace, a high ceiling and access to the veranda. Sleeping accommodations start off with the master bedroom; a connecting bath will be a favorite spot. Upstairs, the bedrooms share a full bath with twin lavatories.

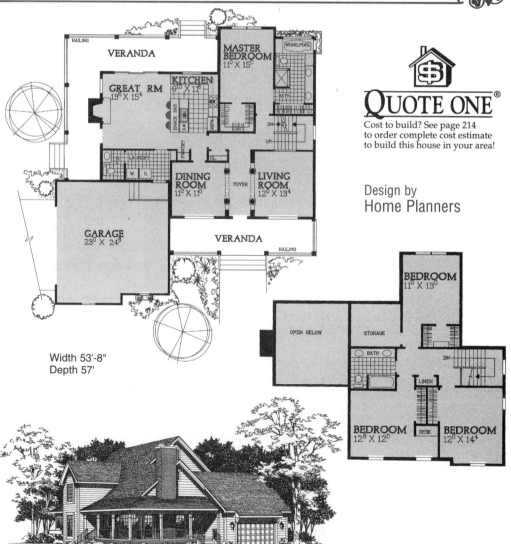

Width 53'-8"
Depth 57'

Quote One®

Cost to build? See page 214 to order complete cost estimate to build this house in your area!

Design by
Home Planners

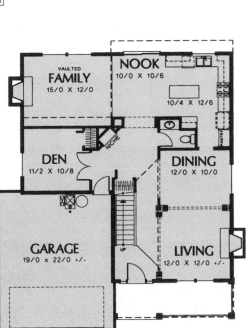

Width 40'
Depth 49'

Design by
Alan Mascord
Design Associates, Inc.

Design 9592

First Floor: 1,168 square feet
Second Floor: 1,157 square feet
Total: 2,325 square feet

◆ A covered front porch and multi-pane windows combine to present the pleasing facade on this three-bedroom home. The two-story foyer leads directly to the formal, columned living and dining rooms, with a fireplace gracing the living room. To the left of the foyer, double doors lead to a cozy den. A large family room with a second fireplace opens to the breakfast nook and the L-shaped kitchen. Upstairs, two family bedrooms share a full hall bath and access to a large bonus room that can be developed at a later date. The master suite is entered through double doors and offers a walk-in closet and a pampering bath.

Design 7297

First Floor: 925 square feet
Second Floor: 960 square feet
Total: 1,885 square feet

◆ A covered porch wraps this home's exterior in country comfort. Inside, a second-floor balcony overlooks a spacious entry highlighted by a plant shelf. Open directly to the right of the entry, a formal dining room sets a festive stage for special occasions and holidays. An adjacent kitchen serves the formal and informal areas with equal ease. Unobstructed views of the backyard and a welcoming fireplace enhance the spacious family room found at the rear of the plan. A laundry room and a powder room complete the first floor. Upstairs, three family bedrooms—two with angled entries—share a full hall bath. The master suite is filled with amenities that include two walk-in closets, a double-bowl vanity, a compartmented toilet and a separate shower.

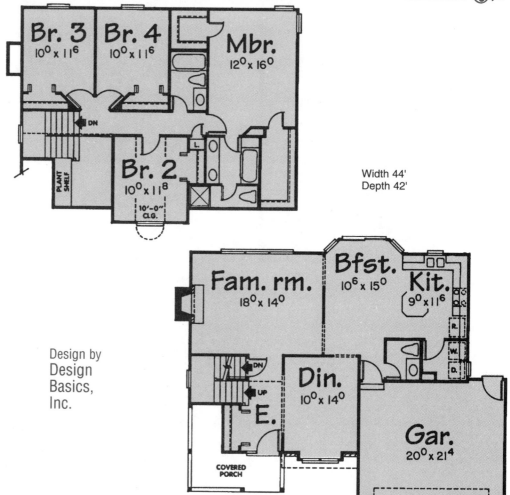

Width 44'
Depth 42'

Design by
Design
Basics,
Inc.

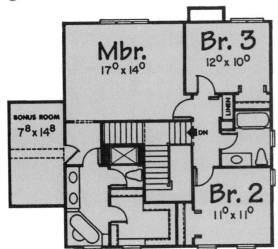

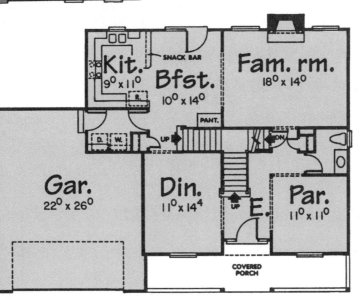

Width 52'
Depth 38'

Design by
Design
Basics,
Inc.

Design 7290

First Floor: 1,111 square feet
Second Floor: 886 square feet
Total: 1,997 square feet

◆ Old-fashioned country splendor graces the facade of this charming farmhouse. Inside, an elegant parlor—open to the entry—invites guests to relax and feel at home. Open planning at the rear of this home combines the kitchen, breakfast room and family room to create a spacious, yet connected feeling. Nearby, the dining room sets a congenial mood for festive and formal occasions. Upstairs, the luxurious master suite provides the ultimate getaway, featuring a relaxing bath with a huge walk-in closet, a corner tub and a separate shower. Also accessible from the master bedroom is a small bonus room that can be used as an exercise room, office or deluxe storage. Two secondary bedrooms, a full hall bath and a large linen closet complete the second floor.

Design 9218

First Floor: 1,098 square feet
Second Floor: 1,095 square feet
Total: 2,193 square feet

◆ This attractive two-story home makes for comfortable, easy family living. To the left of the foyer, efficient room arrangements place the formal living areas together—a nice arrangement for entertaining. Nearby is the spacious kitchen with a work island, a pantry, a planning desk and a bay-windowed breakfast area. One step down is the beam-ceilinged family room with a fireplace and access to the outdoors. The four-bedroom upstairs features an elegant master suite with a vaulted ceiling, a walk in closet and an opulent bath with a corner tub. The laundry room is also found on this level.

Design by
Design Basics, Inc.

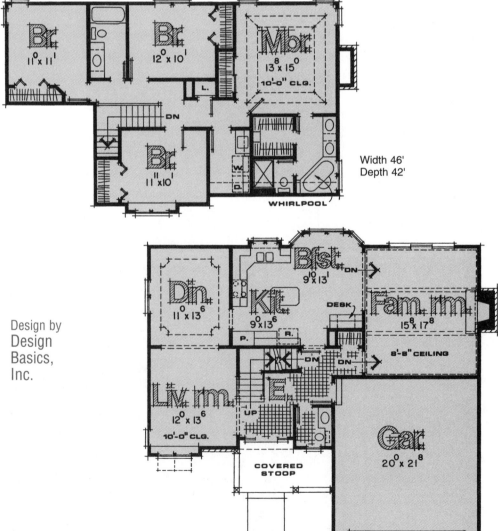

Width 46'
Depth 42'

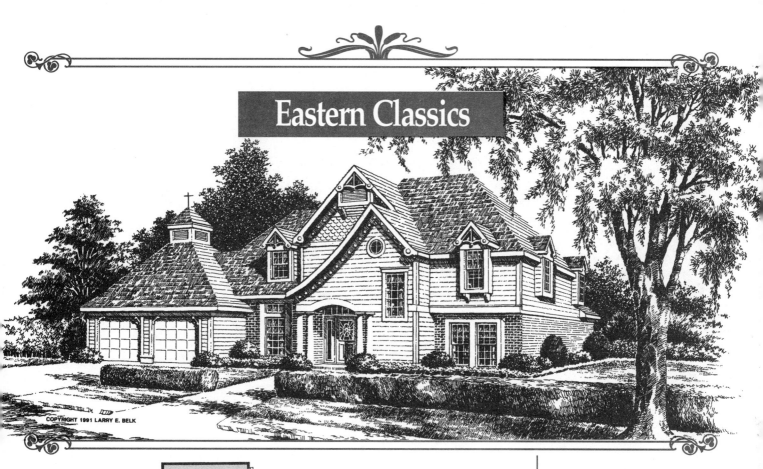

Eastern Classics

BEDROOM 4
13'-6" X 10'-0"

FUTURE GAME ROOM
17'-0" X 16'-6"

FUTURE CLOSET

CLO. CLO.

LIN.

BATH 3

CLO. CLO.

BEDROOM 3
13'-4" X 11'-6"

Design by
Larry E. Belk
Designs

Width 64'-10"
Depth 59'-8"

BREAKFAST
11'-8" X 13'-0"
10' COFFERED CLG.

PORCH

MASTER BEDROOM
13'-4" X 16'-3"
10' COFFERED CLG.

KITCHEN
13'-10" X 13'-0"
10' CLG.

MASTER BATH

W.I.C.

LIVING ROOM
17'-6" X 19'-0"
10' COFFERED CLG.

PAN.

LIN.

UTILITY ROOM

BATH 2

STORAGE

CLO.

DINING ROOM
11'-8" X 13'-6"
10' CLG.

FOYER
17' CLG.

CLO.

BEDROOM 2
13'-6" X 11'-6"

GARAGE
21'-6" X 20'-0"
10' CLG.

UP

PORCH

Design 8011
First Floor: 1,934 square feet
Second Floor: 528 square feet
Total: 2,462 square feet

◆ This charming cottage-style home features sweeping rooflines and an undeniably exquisite exterior. Inside, a two-story foyer opens through a large arch to the living room with a ten-foot coffered ceiling. Another arch defines the dining room. A see-through fireplace is located between the living room and the breakfast area which features a bay window and a coffered ceiling. A large kitchen, a utility room and a walk-in pantry complete the area. The master bedroom, with ten-foot ceiling, a sitting area and a luxury master bath, is located on the opposite side of the home. Bedroom 2 and Bath 2 are located nearby. Bedrooms 3 and 4 are located upstairs with an expandable game room.

Design 8959

First Floor: 1,051 square feet
Second Floor: 631 square feet
Total: 1,682 square feet

◆ This charming farmhouse, with its wide, wraparound veranda supplies all the space needed for whittling and listening to cricket songs. Once inside, the charm continues with a foyer that opens to a bay-windowed living room with a fireplace and a media center. The thoughtfully designed kitchen furnishes a step-saving layout and a nearby formal dining room opens to the veranda through a French door. Privacy is paramount in the master bedroom located at the rear of the first floor. A large walk-in closet, dual vanities, a separate tub and shower and a compartmented toilet are contained in the private bath. The second floor holds two secondary bedrooms, a full bath, a sunroom, a built-in bookcase and a large storage space.

Design by
Larry W.
Garnett &
Associates, Inc.

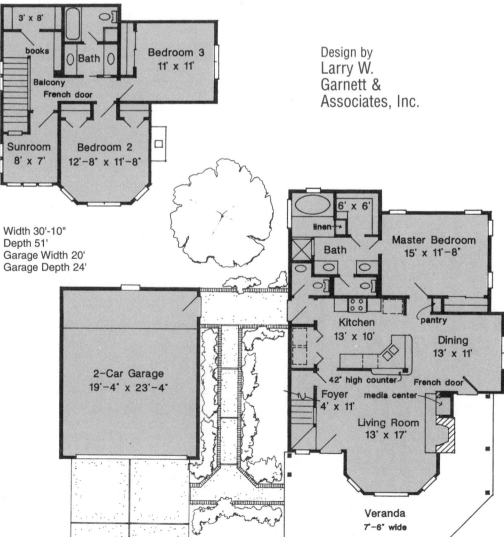

3' x 8'

books

Bath

Bedroom 3
11' x 11'

Balcony
French door

Sunroom
8' x 7'

Bedroom 2
12'-8" x 11'-8"

Width 30'-10"
Depth 51'
Garage Width 20'
Garage Depth 24'

6' x 6'

linen

Bath

Master Bedroom
15' x 11'-8"

pantry

Kitchen
13' x 10'

Dining
13' x 11'

2-Car Garage
19'-4" x 23'-4"

42" high counter

French door

Foyer
4' x 11'

media center

Living Room
13' x 17'

Veranda
7'-6" wide

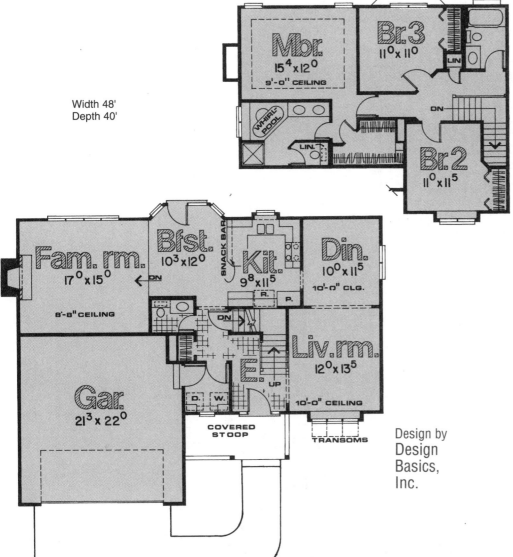

Width 48'
Depth 40'

Mbr.
15⁴ x 12⁰
9'-0" CEILING

Br.3
11⁰ x 11⁰

WHIRL-POOL

LIN.

LIN.

DN

Br.2
11⁰ x 11⁵

Fam. rm.
17⁰ x 15⁰
8'-8" CEILING

DN

Bfst.
10³ x 12⁰

SNACK BAR

Kit.
9⁸ x 11⁵

Din.
10⁰ x 11⁵
10'-0" CLG.

R.

P.

DN

UP

Liv. rm.
12⁰ x 13⁵
10'-0" CEILING

Gar.
21³ x 22⁰

D.   W.

COVERED
STOOP

TRANSOMS

Design by
Design
Basics,
Inc.

Design 9282

First Floor: 1,042 square feet
Second Floor: 803 square feet
Total: 1,845 square feet

◆ At 1,845 square feet, this classic two-story home is perfect for a variety of lifestyles. Upon entry from the covered front porch, the thoughtful floor plan is immediately evident. To the right of the entry is a formal volume living room with ten-foot ceiling. Nearby is the formal dining room with a bright window. Serving the dining room and bright bayed dinette, the kitchen features a pantry, Lazy Susan and window sink. Off the breakfast area, step down into the family room with a handsome fireplace and wall of windows. Upstairs, two secondary bedrooms share a hall bath. The private master bedroom has a boxed ceiling, walk-in closet and a pampering dressing area with double vanity and whirlpool.

Design 9593

First Floor: 968 square feet
Second Floor: 837 square feet
Total: 1,805 square feet

◆ Stone piers add character to the charming covered porch that welcomes you into this three-bedroom home. Inside, a columned hallway provides a graceful entrance into the formal living and dining rooms from the two-story foyer. An L-shaped kitchen located nearby conveniently serves both the formal dining room and the casual bay-windowed breakfast nook. Board games, good books and lively conversation are just a few of the family pursuits that will be enjoyed in a comfortable family room warmed by the glow of the fireplace. Upstairs, two fine, secondary bedrooms share a full hall bath. Double doors provide entry into a luxurious master suite designed to transport you into a world of relaxation. A walk-in closet and a soothing master bath complete this quiet retreat. Laundry facilities handily accommodate the family and complete the second floor.

Width 40'
Depth 46'

Design by
**Alan Mascord
Design Associates, Inc.**

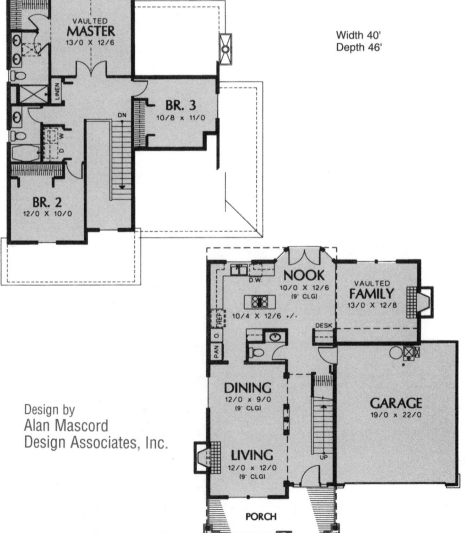

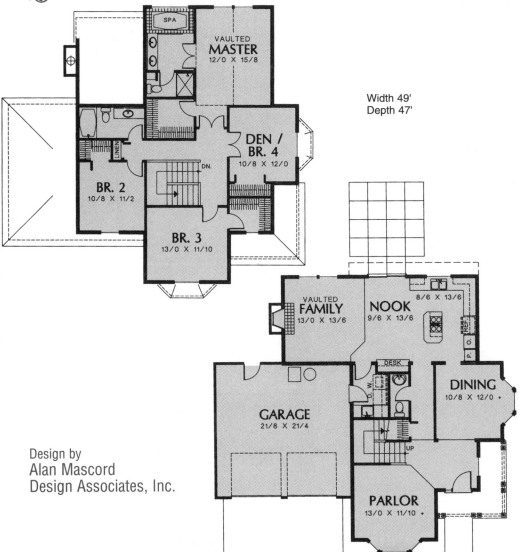

VAULTED MASTER
12/0 X 15/8

SPA

DEN / BR. 4
10/8 X 12/0

BR. 2
10/8 X 11/2

DN.

LINEN

BR. 3
13/0 X 11/10

VAULTED FAMILY
13/0 X 13/6

NOOK
9/6 X 13/6

8/6 X 13/6

REF.

P. O.

DESK

D. W.

GARAGE
21/8 X 21/4

DINING
10/8 X 12/0 +

UP

PARLOR
13/0 X 11/10 +

Design by
Alan Mascord
Design Associates, Inc.

Width 49'
Depth 47'

Design 9475

First Floor: 1,085 square feet
Second Floor: 1,110 square feet
Total: 2,195 square feet

◆ Farmhouse design is popular throughout the country—this plan is an outstanding example. The corner entry leads to a formal parlor on the left and dining room on the right—each sports a bay window. To the rear of the first floor you will find the casual living area which encompasses a family room with a vaulted ceiling and cheerful fireplace, and an L-shaped island kitchen with a sunny nook and built-in planning desk. A nearby powder room and laundry facilities complete this floor. Upstairs are four bedrooms (or three and a den). The master bedroom has a vaulted ceiling and lovely private bath.

Design 9644

First Floor: 943 square feet
Second Floor: 840 square feet
Total: 1,783 square feet
Bonus Room: 323 square feet

◆ Roundtop windows and an inviting covered porch offer an irresistible appeal for this three-bedroom plan. A two-story foyer provides a spacious feeling to this well-organized open layout. Round columns between the great room and kitchen add to the impressive quality of the plan. Enjoy casual meals from the bay-windowed breakfast nook that overlooks an expansive deck which promotes casual outdoor living to its fullest. The master suite with walk-in closet and complete master bath is on the second floor along with two additional bedrooms and a full bath. The bonus room over the garage offers room for expansion.

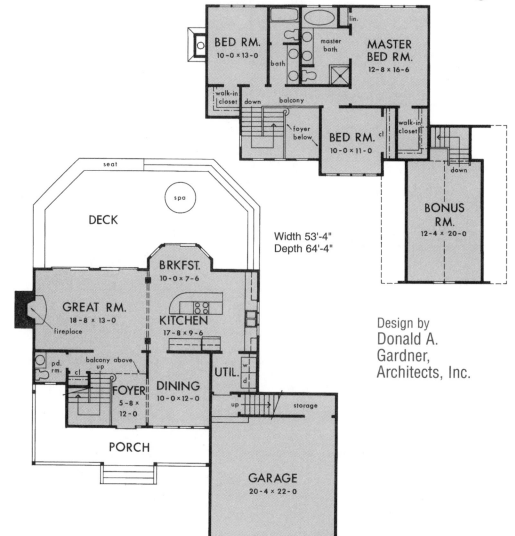

Width 53'-4"
Depth 64'-4"

Design by
Donald A. Gardner, Architects, Inc.

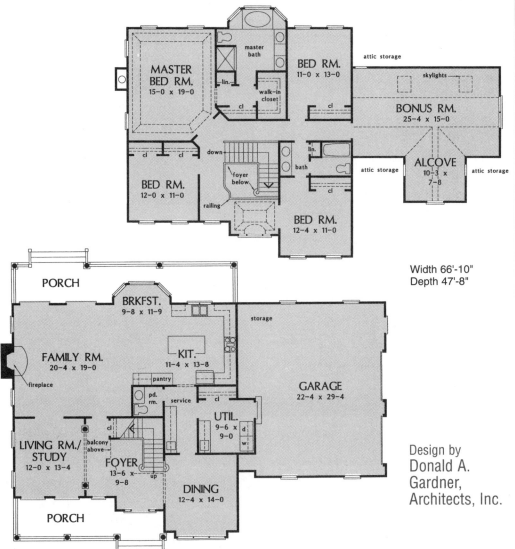

Design 9798

First Floor: 1,483 square feet
Second Floor: 1,349 square feet
Total: 2,832 square feet

◆ With two covered porches to encourage outdoor living, multi-pane windows and an open layout, this farmhouse has plenty to offer. Columns define the living room/study area. The great room is graced by a fireplace and has access to the rear porch. An adjacent sunny, bayed breakfast room is convenient to the U-shaped island kitchen. A formal dining room is nearby for ease in serving elegant meals. Four bedrooms upstairs include a deluxe master suite with a detailed ceiling, a luxurious bath with a tub surrounded by a bay window, and a walk-in closet. Three secondary bedrooms share a full hall bath and offer plenty of storage space. A large bonus room with skylights can be developed at a later date.

Width 66'-10"
Depth 47'-8"

Design by
Donald A.
Gardner,
Architects, Inc.

Design 9784

First Floor: 1,385 square feet
Second Floor: 1,008 square feet
Total: 2,393 square feet

◆ In this traditional country home, a two-story great room accesses a porch and deck through French doors. Nine-foot ceilings throughout the first floor add extra volume and elegance. The great room is open to the kitchen. Here, a conveniently angled peninsula and a breakfast room with a bay window complement work space. For added flexibility, a separate formal living room can double as a casual study. It features accent columns and French doors leading to the front porch. Upstairs, the roomy master suite features a sitting area, a spacious walk-in closet and a bath complete with a garden tub. An ample bonus room is highlighted by skylights and a vaulted ceiling.

Design by
Donald A. Gardner, Architects, Inc.

Width 67'-10"
Depth 52'-4"

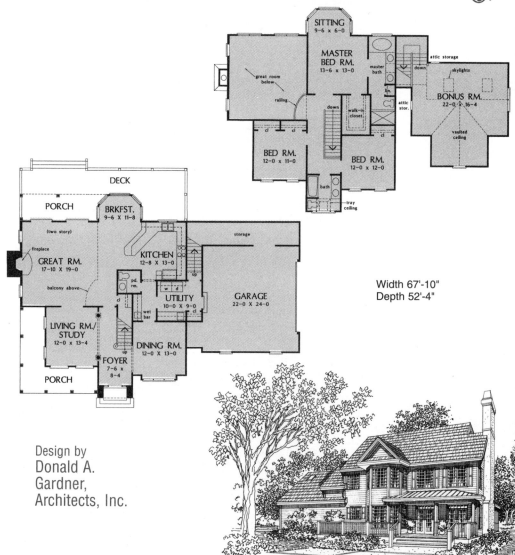

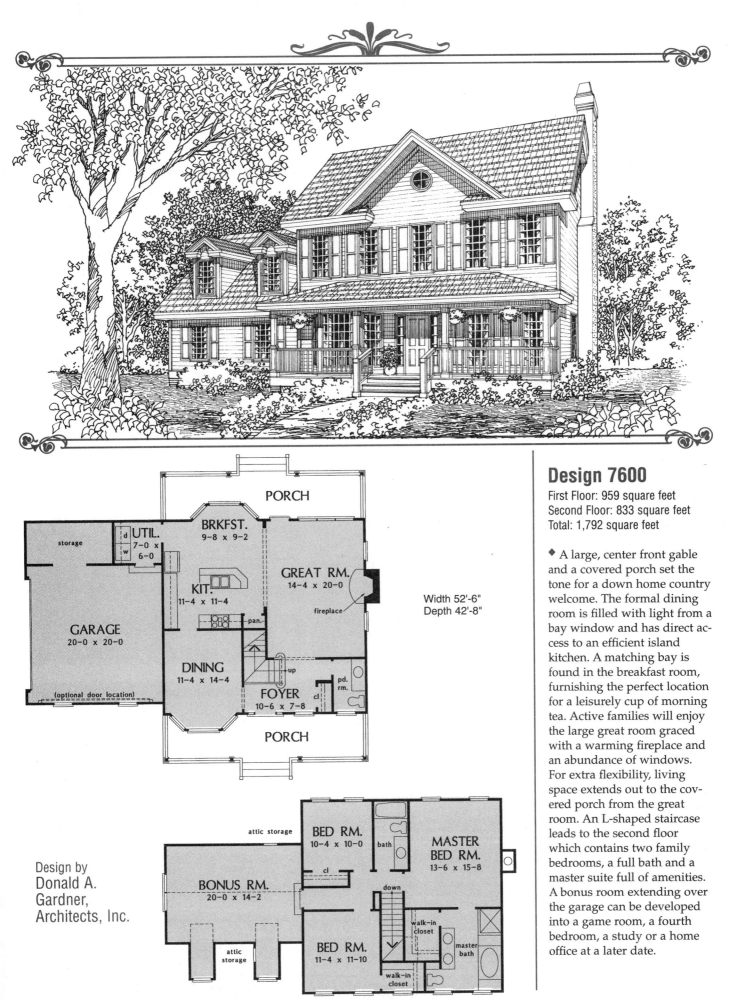

Design 7600

First Floor: 959 square feet
Second Floor: 833 square feet
Total: 1,792 square feet

◆ A large, center front gable and a covered porch set the tone for a down home country welcome. The formal dining room is filled with light from a bay window and has direct access to an efficient island kitchen. A matching bay is found in the breakfast room, furnishing the perfect location for a leisurely cup of morning tea. Active families will enjoy the large great room graced with a warming fireplace and an abundance of windows. For extra flexibility, living space extends out to the covered porch from the great room. An L-shaped staircase leads to the second floor which contains two family bedrooms, a full bath and a master suite full of amenities. A bonus room extending over the garage can be developed into a game room, a fourth bedroom, a study or a home office at a later date.

Width 52'-6"
Depth 42'-8"

PORCH

BRKFST.
9-8 x 9-2

UTIL.
7-0 x
6-0

storage

KIT.
11-4 x 11-4

GREAT RM.
14-4 x 20-0

fireplace

pan.

GARAGE
20-0 x 20-0

(optional door location)

DINING
11-4 x 14-4

up

pd. rm.

cl

FOYER
10-6 x 7-8

PORCH

attic storage

BED RM.
10-4 x 10-0

bath

cl

MASTER BED RM.
13-6 x 15-8

BONUS RM.
20-0 x 14-2

down

walk-in closet

attic storage

BED RM.
11-4 x 11-10

master bath

walk-in closet

Design by
Donald A.
Gardner,
Architects, Inc.

175

Design 9789

First Floor: 1,313 square feet
Second Floor: 525 square feet
Total: 1,838 square feet

◆ Vaulted ceilings and daylit dormers will welcome your family home to open, contemporary living with comfortable country style. An airy foyer, emphasized by a grand staircase, flows into a great room differentiated from the dining room by accent columns. The breakfast room and the dining room are conveniently located adjacent to the kitchen and expand entertaining space to the deck. Split for privacy, the master suite is highlighted by a vaulted ceiling. A garden tub with a double window enhances a relaxing master bath that includes a spacious walk-in closet. Upstairs, two secondary bedrooms—both with walk-in closets—share a bath with a double-bowl vanity. A bonus room may be developed as additional space is needed.

Design by
Donald A.
Gardner,
Architects, Inc.

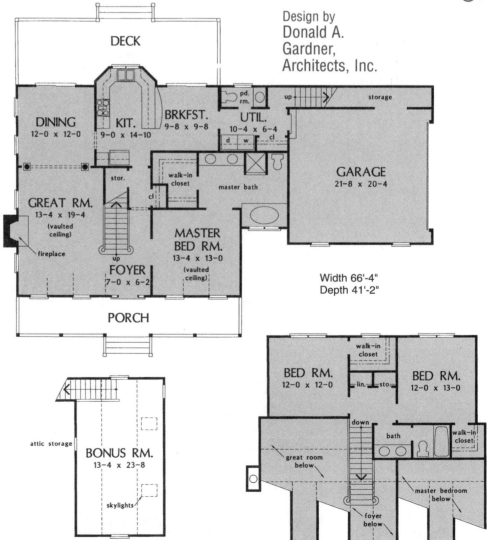

Width 66'-4"
Depth 41'-2"

Design by
Home Planners

Width 64'
Depth 44'

Design 3461
First Floor: 1,391 square feet
Second Floor: 611 square feet
Total: 2,002 square feet

L

◆ Muntin windows, shutters
and flower boxes add exterior
appeal to this well-designed
family farmhouse. The high
ceiling, open staircase and
wide, columned opening to
the living room all lend them-
selves to an impressive entry
foyer. In the living room, a
long expanse of windows and
two, long blank walls for effective furniture placement set
the pace. Informal living takes
off in the open kitchen and
family room. An island cooktop will be a favorite feature,
as will be the fireplace. On t
way to the garage, with i
workshop area, is the l
room and its handy
Sleeping accomm
defined by the
room where
provides
nook.
larg
t

Design 9778
Square Footage: 1,655

◆ A covered front porch,
dormers and arched windows
welcome you to this modified
version of one of our most
popular country home plans.
Interior columns dramatically
open the foyer and the kitchen
to the spacious great room.
The drama is heightened by
the great room's cathedral ceiling and centered fireplace. The
kitchen, with its preparation
island, easily serves the breakfast area and the formal dining
room. The master suite has a

Design by
Donald A.
Gardner
Architects, Inc.

the
ts
laundry
closet.
odations are
master bed-
a bay window
a perfect sitting
the master bath has a
walk-in closet, a vanity,
in lavatories, a stall shower
and a whirlpool tub. Three
bedrooms reside upstairs.

177

DECK

spa

MASTER
BED RM.
13-4 x 14-8

skylights

master
bath

fireplace

BRKFST.
11-4 x 8-0

GREAT RM.
15-4 x 19-8
(cathedral ceiling)

w
d

walk-in
closet

storage

lin.

BED RM.
12-4

KIT.
11-4 x 10-4

lin.

cl

FOYER
8-2 x 6-2

cl

GARAGE
20-0 x 19-8

RM./
TUDY
x 11-4

PORCH

DINING RM.
11-4 x 12-4

(optional door location)

Width 61'
Depth 53'-8"

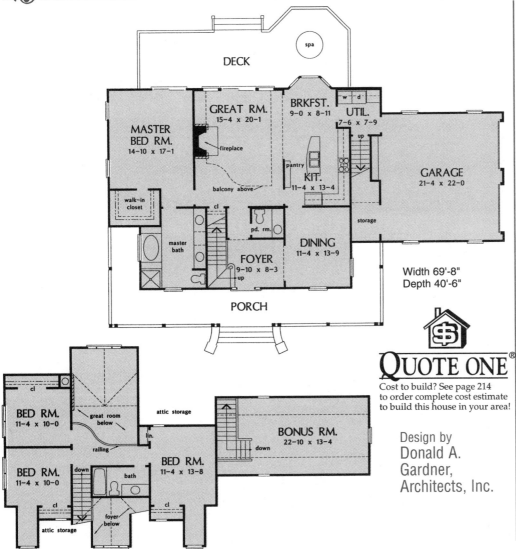

DECK

spa

GREAT RM.
15-4 x 20-1

BRKFST.
9-0 x 8-11

UTIL.
7-6 x 7-9

w | d

MASTER
BED RM.
14-10 x 17-1

fireplace

balcony above

pantry

KIT.
11-4 x 13-4

up

GARAGE
21-4 x 22-0

walk-in
closet

cl

pd. rm.

storage

master
bath

DINING
11-4 x 13-9

FOYER
9-10 x 8-3

up

PORCH

Width 69'-8"
Depth 40'-6"

BED RM.
11-4 x 10-0

cl

great room
below

attic storage

railing

lin.

down

BONUS RM.
22-10 x 13-4

BED RM.
11-4 x 10-0

down

bath

BED RM.
11-4 x 13-8

cl

cl

attic storage

foyer
below

Design 9773

First Floor: 1,499 square feet
Second Floor: 665 square feet
Total: 2,164 square feet

◆ The warm, down-home appeal of this country house is as apparent inside as it is out. A wraparound front porch and a rear deck with a spa provide plenty of space to enjoy the surrounding scenery. Inside, a two-story foyer and a great room give the home an open feel. The great room leads to a breakfast area and an efficient kitchen with an island work area and a large pantry. The master bedroom is situated on the left side of the house for privacy. It features deck access, a large walk-in closet and a bath that includes dual vanities, a whirlpool tub and a separate shower. Three bedrooms, a full bath and bonus space are located upstairs.

Quote One®

Cost to build? See page 214 to order complete cost estimate to build this house in your area!

Design by
Donald A.
Gardner,
Architects, Inc.

Design 9186

First Floor: 1,340 square feet
Second Floor: 514 square feet
Total: 1,854 square feet

◆ This quaint brick home excels in livability. The front porch gives way to a multi-faceted living area emphasized by a fireplace. The kitchen serves this area through a pass-through, making entertaining a breeze. Defined by columns, the dining room presents a simply elegant atmosphere for meals. The rear of the house is made up of the master bedroom suite. A full private bath with dual lavatories, a compartmented toilet and a separate tub and shower enhance this retreat. Upstairs, two bedrooms each sport walk-in closets and share a full bath. A detached two-car garage rests to the rear of the plan.

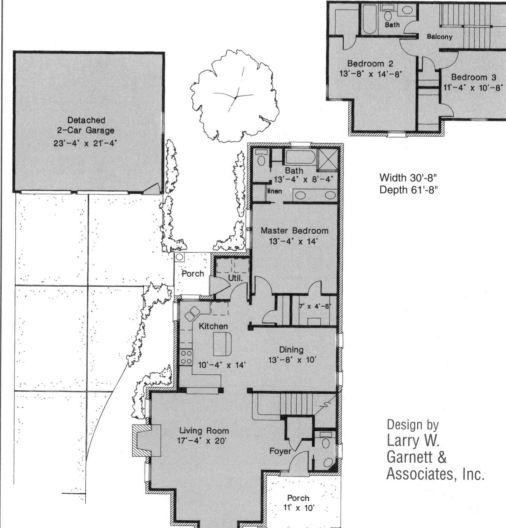

Width 30'-8"
Depth 61'-8"

Design by
Larry W.
Garnett &
Associates, Inc.

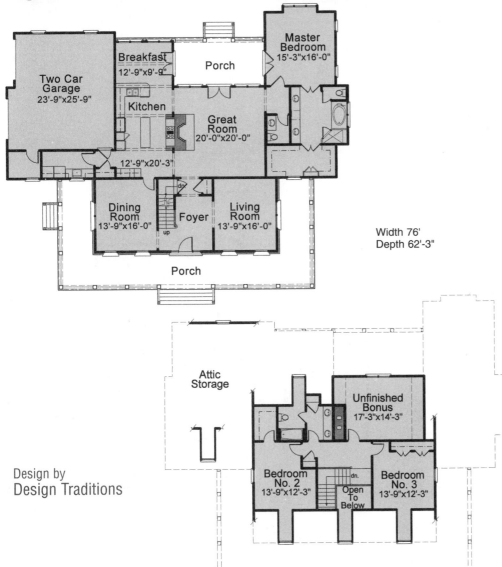

Two Car Garage
23'-9"x25'-9"

Breakfast
12'-9"x9'-9"

Porch

Master Bedroom
15'-3"x16'-0"

Kitchen

Great Room
20'-0"x20'-0"

12'-9"x20'-3"

Dining Room
13'-9"x16'-0"

Foyer

Living Room
13'-9"x16'-0"

Porch

Width 76'
Depth 62'-3"

Attic Storage

Unfinished Bonus
17'-3"x14'-3"

Bedroom No. 2
13'-9"x12'-3"

Open To Below

Bedroom No. 3
13'-9"x12'-3"

Design by
Design Traditions

Design 9996

First Floor: 2,236 square feet
Second Floor: 771 square feet
Total: 3,007 square feet

◆ A neighborly porch embraces three sides of this comfortable home, extending a hearty welcome from its inviting entrance to its warm country kitchen. Inside, rooms open directly onto one another, preserving an old-fashioned farmhouse atmosphere. A soaring, two-story foyer separates the formal living and dining rooms. Openings on both sides of a warming fireplace in the great room lead to a country kitchen where a range top set into a brick chimney arch recalls cooking on an old-time hearth. A sun-drenched breakfast area and an expansive master suite that features a box-bay window and a sumptuous bath bracket the rear porch. Upstairs, dormers accent two family bedrooms and a shared bath, while bonus space can easily become a third bedroom or a convenient home office. This home is designed with a basement foundation.

Design 7294

First Floor: 1,365 square feet
Second Floor: 1,185 square feet
Total: 2,550 square feet

◆ With its brick and siding facade, this farmhouse presents
a strong and solid image while
its covered front porch offers a
cool place to relax. Inside,
flanking the foyer, the formal
living room and the formal
dining room express elegance
in a subtle manner. The family
room at the rear of the home is
graced by a warming fireplace
and has direct access to the
bay-windowed breakfast room
and island kitchen. The sleeping zone is upstairs and is
made up of three secondary
bedrooms that share a full hall
bath with twin vanities and a
master bedroom with a pampering bath and a large walk-
in closet. A bonus room is accessible from the master
bedroom and can be used for
an office, an exercise room or
storage.

Design by
Design
Basics,
Inc.

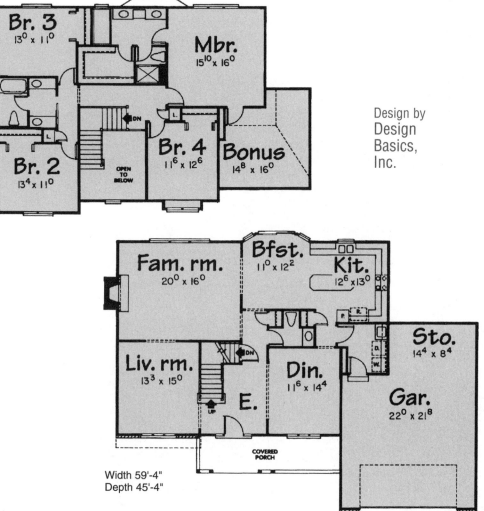

Width 59'-4"
Depth 45'-4"

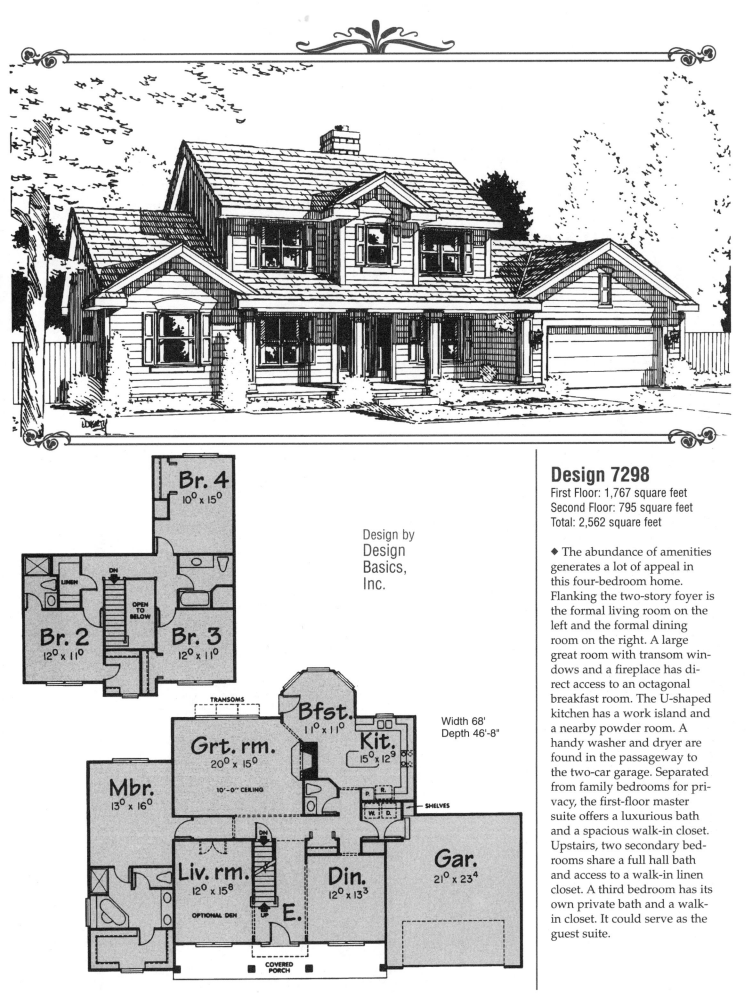

Design 7298

First Floor: 1,767 square feet
Second Floor: 795 square feet
Total: 2,562 square feet

◆ The abundance of amenities generates a lot of appeal in this four-bedroom home. Flanking the two-story foyer is the formal living room on the left and the formal dining room on the right. A large great room with transom windows and a fireplace has direct access to an octagonal breakfast room. The U-shaped kitchen has a work island and a nearby powder room. A handy washer and dryer are found in the passageway to the two-car garage. Separated from family bedrooms for privacy, the first-floor master suite offers a luxurious bath and a spacious walk-in closet. Upstairs, two secondary bedrooms share a full hall bath and access to a walk-in linen closet. A third bedroom has its own private bath and a walk-in closet. It could serve as the guest suite.

Design by
Design Basics, Inc.

Width 68'
Depth 46'-8"

Br. 4 10⁰ x 15⁰

Br. 2 12⁰ x 11⁰

Br. 3 12⁰ x 11⁰

LINEN

DN

OPEN TO BELOW

TRANSOMS

Bfst. 11⁰ x 11⁰

Grt. rm. 20⁰ x 15⁰

10'-0" CEILING

Kit. 15⁰ x 12⁹

Mbr. 13⁰ x 16⁰

P. R.

W. D.

SHELVES

DN

Liv. rm. 12⁰ x 15⁸

OPTIONAL DEN

UP

E.

Din. 12⁰ x 13³

Gar. 21⁰ x 23⁴

COVERED PORCH

183

Design 9997

First Floor: 1,613 square feet
Second Floor: 1,546 square feet
Total: 3,159 square feet

◆ Wood siding, filigree trim above a wide front porch and an inviting board-and batten back porch adorn the front and rear exteriors of this splendid two-story home. The formal living and dining rooms, reminiscent of turn-of-the-century front and rear parlors, open off the right of a wide central stair hall. To the left of the stairs, the casual living areas flow together. Here, a spacious family room joins a window-lined breakfast area connected to a convenient kitchen that opens onto a wraparound rear porch. Sleeping facilities are located on the second floor. Bedrooms 3 and 4 share a full bath, while Bedroom 2 possesses a bath of its own. The relaxing master suite combines with a luxurious master bath to make a spacious hideaway. This home is designed with a basement foundation.

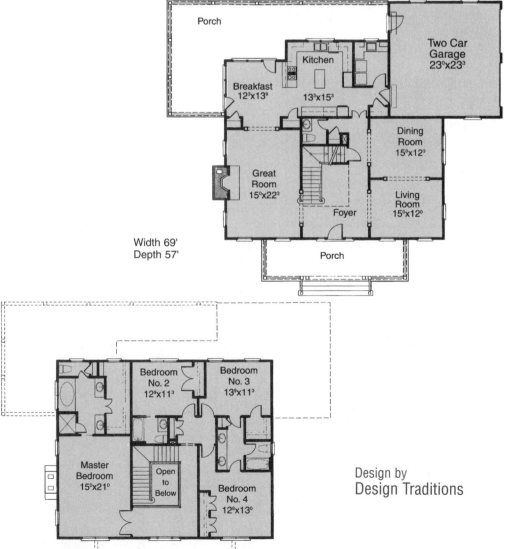

Width 69'
Depth 57'

Design by
Design Traditions

Country Porches

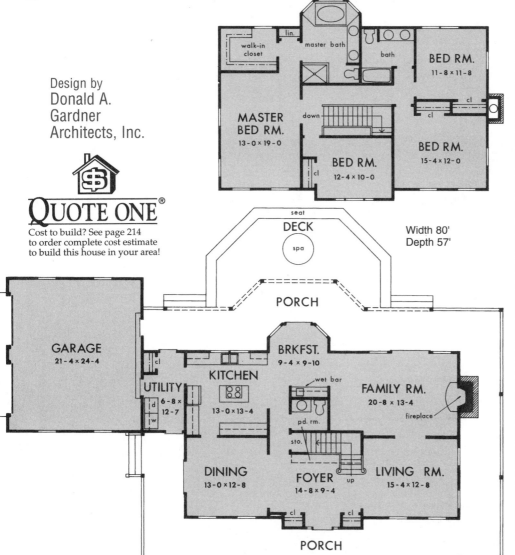

Design by
Donald A.
Gardner
Architects, Inc.

Quote One®

Cost to build? See page 214
to order complete cost estimate
to build this house in your area!

MASTER BED RM.
13-0 × 19-0

BED RM.
12-4 × 10-0

BED RM.
11-8 × 11-8

BED RM.
15-4 × 12-0

walk-in closet

lin.

master bath

bath

down

cl

cl

cl

DECK
spa

seat

PORCH

Width 80'
Depth 57'

GARAGE
21-4 × 24-4

UTILITY
6-8 × 12-7

d
w

cl

KITCHEN
13-0 × 13-4

BRKFST.
9-4 × 9-10

wet bar

FAMILY RM.
20-8 × 13-4

fireplace

pd. rm.

sto.

DINING
13-0 × 12-8

FOYER
14-8 × 9-4

up

LIVING RM.
15-4 × 12-8

cl

cl

PORCH

Design 9667

First Floor: 1,357 square feet
Second Floor: 1,204 square feet
Total: 2,561 square feet

◆ This grand four-bedroom farmhouse with wraparound porch has eye catching features: a double-gabled roof, a Palladian window at the upper level, an arched window on the lower level and an intricately detailed brick chimney. Entry to the home reveals a generous foyer with direct access to all areas. The living room opens to the foyer and provides a formal entertaining area. The exceptionally large family room allows for more casual living. Look for a fireplace, wet bar and direct access to a porch and deck here. The lavish kitchen boasts a cooking island and serves the dining room, breakfast and deck areas. The master suite on the second level has a large walk-in closet and a master bath with a whirlpool tub, a shower and a double-bowl vanity. Three additional bedrooms share a full bath.

Design 9645

First Floor: 1,356 square feet
Second Floor: 542 square feet
Total: 1,898 square feet
Bonus Room: 393 square feet

◆ The welcoming charm of this country farmhouse is expressed by its many windows and its covered, wraparound porch. A two-story entrance foyer is enhanced by a Palladian window in a clerestory dormer above to allow natural lighting. A first-floor master suite allows privacy and accessibility. The master bath includes a whirlpool tub, a shower and double-bowl vanity along with a walk-in closet. The first floor features nine-foot ceilings throughout with the exception of the kitchen area, which features an eight-foot ceiling. The second floor provides two additional bedrooms, a full bath and plenty of storage space. An unfinished basement and bonus room provide room to grow. Please specify basement or crawlspace foundation when ordering.

Width 59'
Depth 64'

QUOTE ONE®

Cost to build? See page 214 to order complete cost estimate to build this house in your area!

Design by
Donald A.
Gardner,
Architects, Inc.

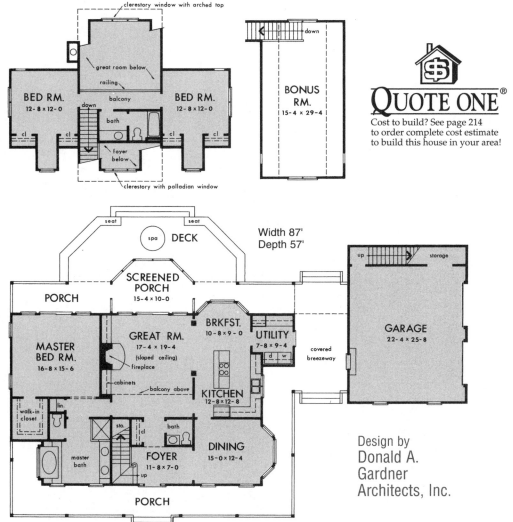

clerestory window with arched top

great room below

railing

BED RM.
12-8 x 12-0

balcony

BED RM.
12-8 x 12-0

down

bath

cl

cl

cl

cl

foyer below

clerestory with palladian window

down

BONUS RM.
15-4 x 29-4

Quote One®

Cost to build? See page 214
to order complete cost estimate
to build this house in your area!

seat   seat

spa   DECK

Width 87'
Depth 57'

SCREENED PORCH
15-4 x 10-0

PORCH

up   storage

GARAGE
22-4 x 25-8

BRKFST.
10-8 x 9-0

UTILITY
7-8 x 9-4

GREAT RM.
17-4 x 19-4
(sloped ceiling)
fireplace

MASTER BED RM.
16-8 x 15-6

cabinets

balcony above

d   w

covered breezeway

KITCHEN
12-8 x 12-8

walk-in closet

lin.

sto.

cl

bath

master bath

FOYER
11-8 x 7-0

up

DINING
15-0 x 12-4

PORCH

Design by
Donald A.
Gardner
Architects, Inc.

Design 9702

First Floor: 1,618 square feet
Second Floor: 570 square feet
Total: 2,188 square feet
Bonus Room: 495 square feet

◆ A wraparound covered porch, an open deck with a spa and seating, arched windows and dormers enhance the already impressive character of this three-bedroom farmhouse. The entrance foyer and great room with sloped ceilings have Palladian window clerestories to allow natural light to enter. All other first-floor spaces have nine-foot ceilings. The spacious great room boasts a fireplace, cabinets and bookshelves. The kitchen, with a cooking island, is conveniently located between a dining room and a breakfast room with an open view of the great room. A generous master bedroom has plenty of closet space as well as an expansive master bath. Bonus room over the garage allows for room to grow. Please specify basement or crawlspace foundation when ordering.

Design 3653

First Floor: 1,216 square feet
Second Floor: 1,191 square feet
Total: 2,407 square feet

L **D**

◆ This home's simple rectangular plan means relatively economical construction costs. Formal areas are located to the front of the plan. Each of the major living areas has direct access to the wraparound porch. The living room is free of annoying cross-room traffic. It even has good blank wall space for effective furniture placement. Upstairs are three bedrooms and a bath with twin lavatories for the kids and a deluxe master suite with a lavish bath. A basement is available for the development of additional recreational and storage space.

Design by
Home Planners

Width 56'
Depth 42'

QUOTE ONE®

Cost to build? See page 214
to order complete cost estimate
to build this house in your area!

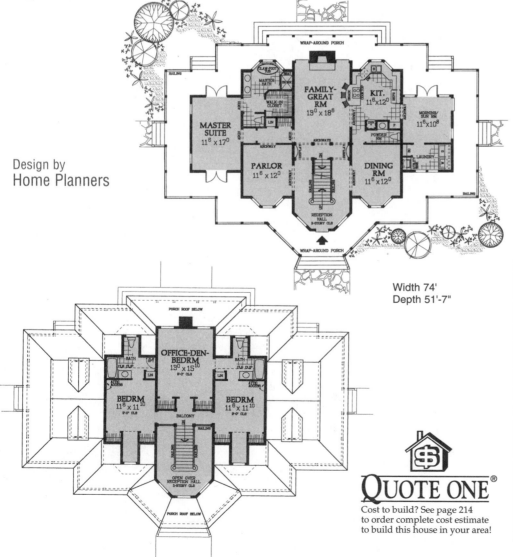

Design by
Home Planners

Width 74'
Depth 51'-7"

Design 3621

First Floor: 1,752 square feet
Second Floor: 906 square feet
Total: 2,658 square feet

L **D**

◆ Delightfully proportioned and perfectly symmetrical, this Victorian farmhouse has lots of curb appeal. The wrap-around porch offers rustic columns and railings and broad steps present easy access to the front, rear and side yards. Archways, display niches and columns catch the eye on the way to the large family great room with a fireplace. Flanking the reception hall are the formal parlor and the dining room. The left wing of the plan is devoted to the master suite. French doors provide direct access to the front and rear porches. The master bath is compartmented and has a bay with a claw-foot tub, twin lavatories, a walk-in closet and a stall shower with a seat. Upstairs, a perfectly symmetrical layout presents a big office/den (or make it a bedroom) flanked by two bedrooms, each with a full bath.

Quote One®

Cost to build? See page 214 to order complete cost estimate to build this house in your area!

Design 9588

First Floor: 1,032 square feet
Second Floor: 870 square feet
Total: 1,902 square feet
Bonus Room: 306 square feet

◆ A wraparound covered porch and symmetrical dormers produce an inviting appearance for this farmhouse. Inside, the two-story foyer leads directly to the large great room graced by a fireplace and an abundance of windows. The U-shaped island kitchen is convenient to the sunny dining room and has a powder room nearby. The utility room offers access to the two-car garage. Upstairs, two family bedrooms share a full hall bath and have convenient access to a large bonus room. The master suite is full of amenities including a walk-in closet and a pampering bath.

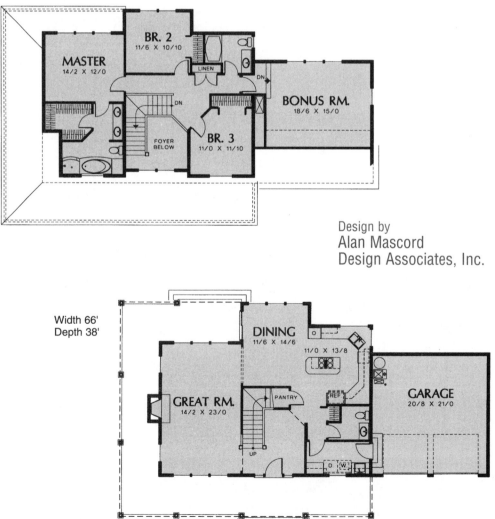

Design by
Alan Mascord
Design Associates, Inc.

Width 66'
Depth 38'

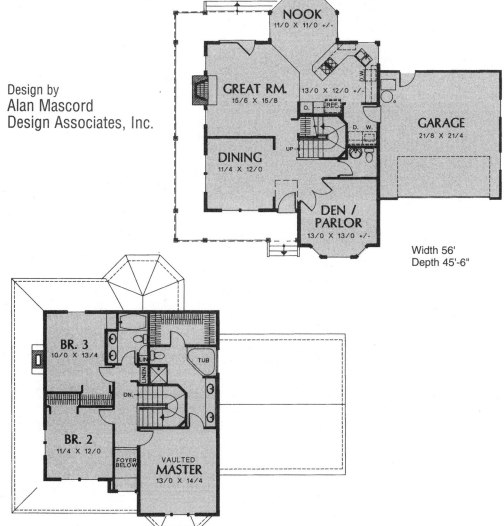

Design by
**Alan Mascord
Design Associates, Inc.**

NOOK
11/0 X 11/0 +/-

GREAT RM.
15/6 X 15/8

DINING
11/4 X 12/0

UP

D.W.

REF.

GARAGE
21/8 X 21/4

DEN /
PARLOR
13/0 X 13/0 +/-

Width 56'
Depth 45'-6"

BR. 3
10/0 X 13/4

TUB

DN.

BR. 2
11/4 X 12/0

FOYER
BELOW

VAULTED
MASTER
13/0 X 14/4

LINEN

Design 9533

First Floor: 1,060 square feet
Second Floor: 898 square feet
Total: 1,958 square feet

◆ A wraparound porch graces the exterior of this plan and provides lots of room for outdoor enjoyment. Inside, a den or parlor opens to the right through double doors. A bright bayed window makes this room even more enjoyable. For dining elegance, take your meals into the formal dining room. The great room with a fireplace also provides rear access to the porch. An angled kitchen serves the attached, light-filled nook. Upstairs, three bedrooms include a vaulted master suite with a luxurious, private bath. The two secondary bedrooms delight in peace and quiet and a nearby hall bath with dual sinks. A two-car garage is set back from the front of the house to further an authentic farmhouse feel.

Design 9910

First Floor: 2,565 square feet
Second Floor: 1,375 square feet
Total: 3,940 square feet

◆ A symmetrical facade with twin chimneys makes a grand statement. A covered porch welcomes visitors and provides a pleasant place to spend cool evenings. The entry foyer is flanked by formal living areas: a dining room and a living room, each with a fireplace. A third fireplace is the highlight of the expansive great room to the rear. An L-shaped kitchen offers a work island and a walk-in pantry for amenities and easily serves the nearby breakfast and sun rooms. The deck is accessible through the great room, the sun room or the master bedroom. The first-floor master bedroom suite is lavish in its luxuries: His and Hers walk-in closets, a sunny bay window and a sumptuous bath. The second floor offers three bedrooms, two full baths and plenty of storage space. This home is designed with a basement foundation.

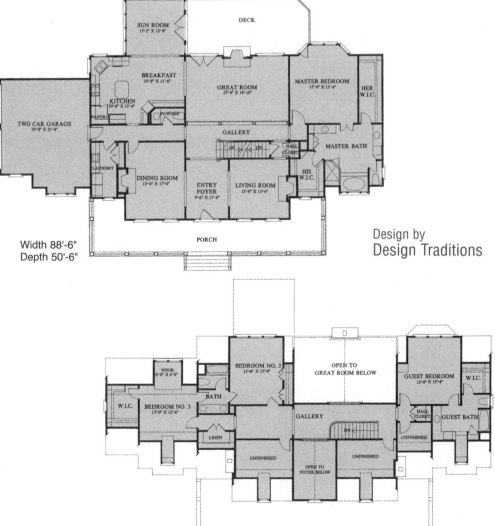

Width 88'-6"
Depth 50'-6"

Design by
Design Traditions

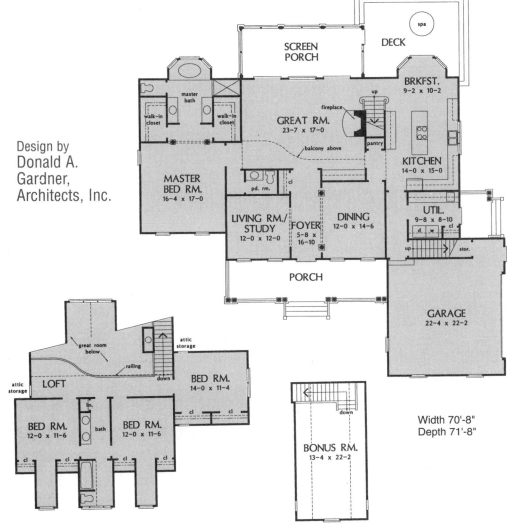

SCREEN PORCH

DECK

spa

master bath

walk-in closet

walk-in closet

GREAT RM.
23-7 x 17-0

fireplace

up

BRKFST.
9-2 x 10-2

balcony above

pantry

KITCHEN
14-0 x 15-0

MASTER BED RM.
16-4 x 17-0

pd. rm.

cl

LIVING RM./ STUDY
12-0 x 12-0

FOYER
5-8 x 16-10

DINING
12-0 x 14-6

UTIL.
9-8 x 8-10

d   w   cl

up   stor.

PORCH

GARAGE
22-4 x 22-2

Design by
Donald A.
Gardner,
Architects, Inc.

great room below

attic storage

railing

down

BED RM.
14-0 x 11-4

attic storage

LOFT

lin.

bath

cl   cl

BED RM.
12-0 x 11-6

BED RM.
12-0 x 11-6

cl   cl   cl   cl

down

BONUS RM.
13-4 x 22-2

Design 7602

First Floor: 2,097 square feet
Second Floor: 907 square feet
Total: 3,004 square feet
Bonus Room: 373 square feet

◆ This wonderful farmhouse offers a casually elegant facade with arched windows, multipane dormers and a welcoming front porch. A formal living room and dining room flank the foyer, with pillars defining the dining room. The large great room is graced by a fireplace and access to the rear screened porch. A luxurious master suite boasts a walk-in closet and a master bath with twin vanities, a separate shower and a sumptuous garden tub nestled in a bay window. A second-floor balcony and loft overlook the spacious great room. Three family bedrooms share a full bath.

Width 70'-8"
Depth 71'-8"

Design 9621

First Floor: 1,325 square feet
Second Floor: 453 square feet
Total: 1,778 square feet

◆ This compact design has all the amenities available in larger plans with little wasted space. In addition, a wrap-around covered porch, a front Palladian window, dormers and rear arched windows provide exciting visual elements to the exterior. The spacious great room has a fireplace, a cathedral ceiling and clerestory windows. A second-level balcony overlooks this gathering area. The kitchen is centrally located for maximum flexibility in layout and features a pass-through to the great room. Besides the generous master suite with a full bath, there are two family bedrooms located on the second level sharing a full bath with a double vanity. Please specify basement or crawlspace foundation when ordering.

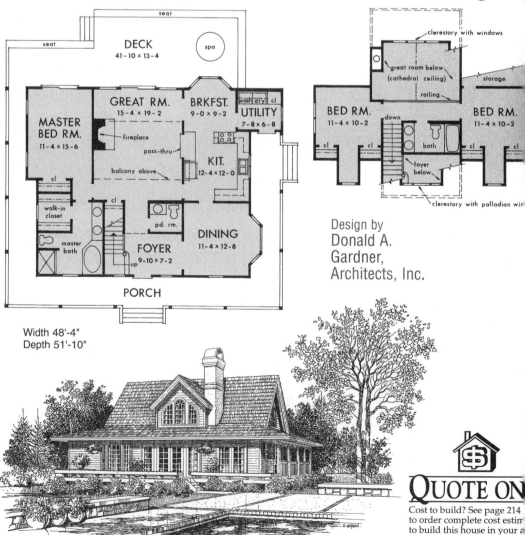

Width 48'-4"
Depth 51'-10"

Design by
Donald A. Gardner,
Architects, Inc.

REAR

QUOTE ON
Cost to build? See page 214
to order complete cost estim
to build this house in your a

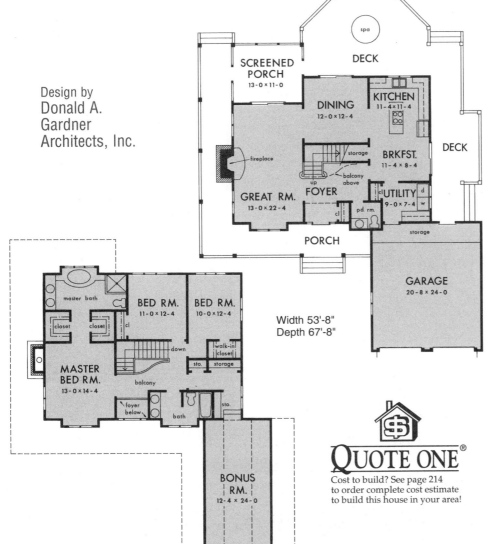

Design by
Donald A.
Gardner
Architects, Inc.

Design 9662
First Floor: 1,025 square feet
Second Floor: 911 square feet
Total: 1,936 square feet

◆ The exterior of this three-bedroom home is enhanced by its many gables, arched windows and wraparound porch. A large great room with impressive fireplace leads to both the dining room and screened porch with access to the deck. An open kitchen offers a country-kitchen atmosphere. The second-level master suite has two walk-in closets and an impressive bath. Two family bedrooms share a full bath and plenty of storage. There is also bonus space over the garage.

Width 53'-8"
Depth 67'-8"

Quote One®
Cost to build? See page 214
to order complete cost estimate
to build this house in your area!

195

Design 9781

Square Footage: 1,246

◆ This one-story home offers tremendous curb appeal and many extras found only in much larger homes. A continuous cathedral ceiling in the great room, dining room and kitchen gives a spacious feel to an efficient plan. The kitchen, brightened by a skylight, features a pantry and a peninsula counter for easy preparation and service to the dining room and screen porch. The deck joins the screen porch for extra entertaining space. The master suite opens up with a cathedral ceiling, a walk-in and linen closets and a private bath including a garden tub and a double-bowl vanity. A cathedral ceiling highlights the front bedroom/study that is separated from the other bedroom by a skylit bath.

Design by
Donald A.
Gardner,
Architects, Inc.

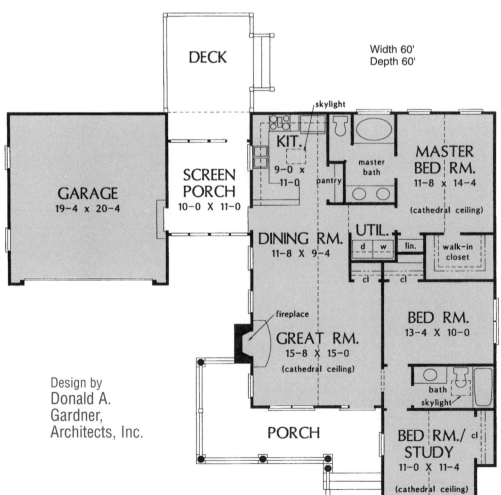

DECK

Width 60'
Depth 60'

skylight

GARAGE
19-4 x 20-4

SCREEN
PORCH
10-0 X 11-0

KIT.
9-0 x
11-0

pantry

master
bath

MASTER
BED RM.
11-8 x 14-4
(cathedral ceiling)

UTIL.
d w   lin.

walk-in
closet

cl   cl

DINING RM.
11-8 X 9-4

fireplace

GREAT RM.
15-8 X 15-0
(cathedral ceiling)

BED RM.
13-4 X 10-0

bath
skylight

PORCH

BED RM./
STUDY
11-0 X 11-4
(cathedral ceiling)

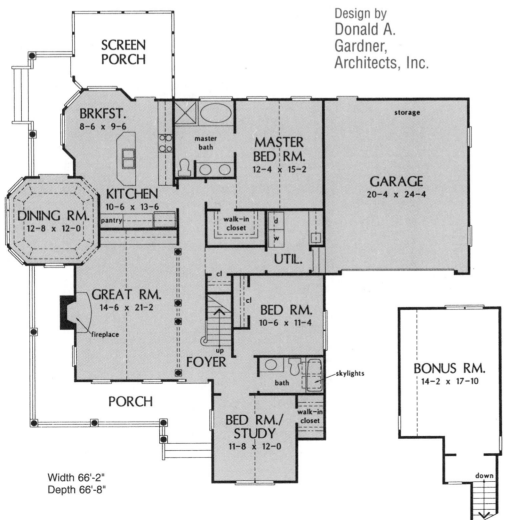

SCREEN PORCH

Design by
Donald A.
Gardner,
Architects, Inc.

BRKFST.
8-6 x 9-6

master bath

MASTER BED RM.
12-4 x 15-2

storage

GARAGE
20-4 x 24-4

KITCHEN
10-6 x 13-6

pantry

DINING RM.
12-8 x 12-0

walk-in closet

d
w

UTIL.

GREAT RM.
14-6 x 21-2

fireplace

cl

cl

BED RM.
10-6 x 11-4

up

FOYER

bath

skylights

BONUS RM.
14-2 x 17-10

PORCH

BED RM./ STUDY
11-8 x 12-0

walk-in closet

down

Width 66'-2"
Depth 66'-8"

Design 7601
Square Footage: 1,787
Bonus Room: 326 square feet

◆ A neighborly porch as friendly as a handshake and a pat on the back wraps around this charming country home, warmly greeting family and friends alike. Inside, cathedral ceilings promote a feeling of spaciousness. To the left of the foyer, the great room is enhanced with a fireplace and built-in bookshelves. A uniquely shaped formal dining room separates the kitchen and breakfast area. Outdoor pursuits—rain or shine—will be enjoyed from the screen porch. The master suite is located at the rear of the plan for privacy and features a walk-in closet and a luxurious bath. Two additional bedrooms, one with a walk-in closet, share a skylit bath. A second-floor bonus room is available to develop later as a study, home office or play area. Please specify basement or crawlspace foundation when ordering.

Design 9242

First Floor: 1,322 square feet
Second Floor: 1,272 square feet
Total: 2,594 square feet

◆ Here's the luxury you've been looking for—from the wraparound covered front porch to the bright sun room at the rear off the breakfast room. A sunken family room with fireplace serves everyday casual gatherings, while the more formal living and dining rooms are reserved for special entertaining situations. The kitchen has a central island with snack bar and is located most conveniently for serving and cleaning up. Upstairs are four bedrooms, one a lovely master suite with French doors into the master bath and a whirlpool tub in a dramatic bay window. A double vanity in the shared bath easily serves the three family bedrooms.

Design by
Design Basics, Inc.

Quote One®

Cost to build? See page 214 to order complete cost estimate to build this house in your area!

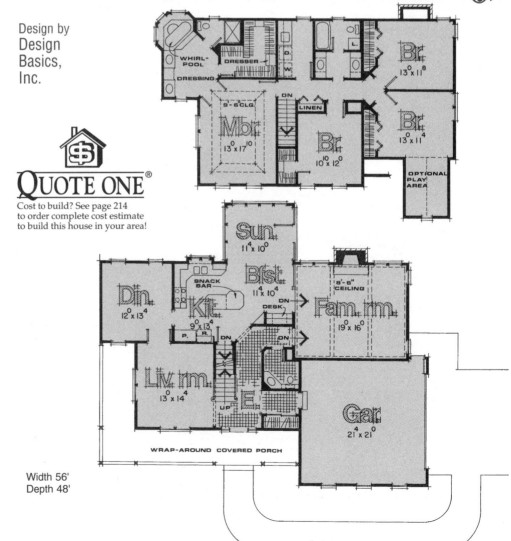

Width 56'
Depth 48'

QUOTE ONE®

Cost to build? See page 214
to order complete cost estimate
to build this house in your area!

Design by
Home Planners

Width 84'
Depth 65'-8"

Design 2694

First Floor: 2,026 square feet
Second Floor: 1,386 square feet
Total: 3,412 square feet

L

◆ This two-story design faithfully recalls the 18th-Century homestead of Secretary of Foreign Affairs John Jay. First-floor livability includes a grand living room with a fireplace and a music alcove, a library with another fireplace and built-in bookshelves, a light-filled dining room, a large country kitchen with still another fireplace and a snack bar and a handy clutter room adjacent to the mud room. Three upstairs bedrooms include a large master suite with a walk-in closet, vanity seating and double sinks. Each of the family bedrooms contains a double closet.

Design 3619

First Floor: 1,171 square feet
Second Floor: 600 square feet
Total: 1,771 square feet

L **D**

◆ There's nothing that tops gracious Southern hospitality—unless it's offered Southern farmhouse style! The entry hall opens through an archway on the right to a formal dining room. Nearby, the efficient country kitchen shares space with a bay-windowed eating area. The two story family/great room is warmed by a fireplace in the winter and open to outdoor country comfort in the summer via double French doors. The first-floor master suite offers room to kick off your shoes and curl up with a good book by the bay window or access the porch through French doors. An abundance of closet space precedes the amenity-filled master bath. The second floor holds two family bedrooms that share a full bath. Plans for an optional indoor swimming pool/spa and detached garage are included.

Quote One®

Cost to build? See page 214
to order complete cost estimate
to build this house in your area!

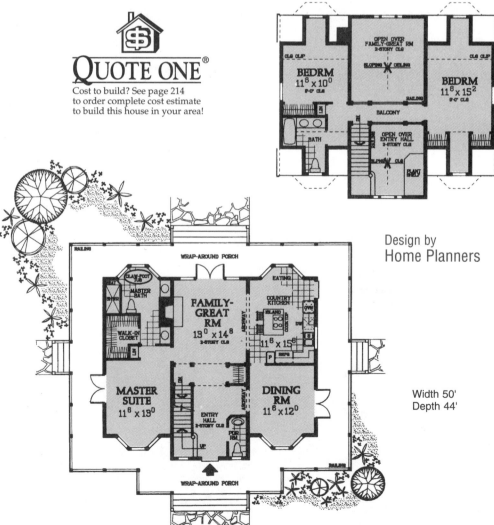

Design by
Home Planners

Width 50'
Depth 44'

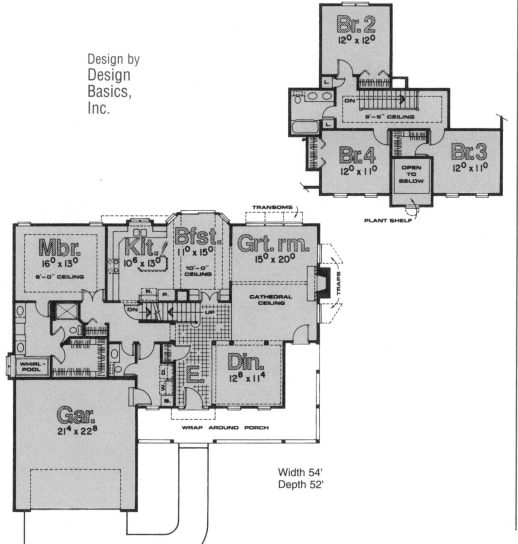

Design by
**Design
Basics,
Inc.**

Br. 2
12⁰ x 12⁰

DN

8'-8" CEILING

Br. 4
12⁰ x 11⁰

OPEN
TO
BELOW

Br. 3
12⁰ x 11⁰

PLANT SHELF

TRANSOMS

Mbr.
16⁰ x 13⁰

9'-0" CEILING

Kit.
10⁶ x 13⁰

Bfst.
11⁰ x 15⁰

10'-0" CEILING

Grt. rm.
15⁰ x 20⁰

CATHEDRAL
CEILING

TRAPS

DN

UP

WHIRL-
POOL

W D

Din.
12⁸ x 11⁴

Gar.
21⁴ x 22⁸

WRAP AROUND PORCH

Width 54'
Depth 52'

Design 9387

First Floor: 1,570 square feet
Second Floor: 707 square feet
Total: 2,277 square feet

◆ A wraparound, covered porch and bright windows create a striking front elevation to this house. The entry offers a tremendous, open view of the dining and great rooms. A fireplace centers on the cathedral ceiling which soars to over sixteen feet high in the great room. French doors to the dinette add a formal touch. The kitchen includes a Lazy Susan, a large food-preparation island and an ample pantry. Double doors access the first-floor master bedroom with a boxed ceiling. The master bath features a large whirlpool tub, dual lavatories, a make-up vanity and a walk-in closet. Three family bedrooms and a full bath are located on the second floor.

Design 2661

First Floor: 1,020 square feet
Second Floor: 777 square feet
Total: 1,797 square feet

L D

◆ It would be difficult to find a starter or retirement home with more charm than this. Inside, it contains a very livable floor plan. An outstanding first floor centers around the huge country kitchen which includes a beam ceiling, a raised-hearth fireplace, a window seat and rear-yard access. The living room with its warming corner fireplace and private study are to the front of the plan. Upstairs are three bedrooms and two full baths. Built-in shelves and a linen closet in the upstairs hallway provide excellent storage.

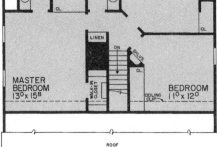

Quote One®

Cost to build? See page 214
to order complete cost estimate
to build this house in your area!

Width 34'
Depth 30'

Design by
Home Planners

202

This home, as shown in the photograph, may differ from the actual blueprints. For more detailed information, please check the floor plans carefully.

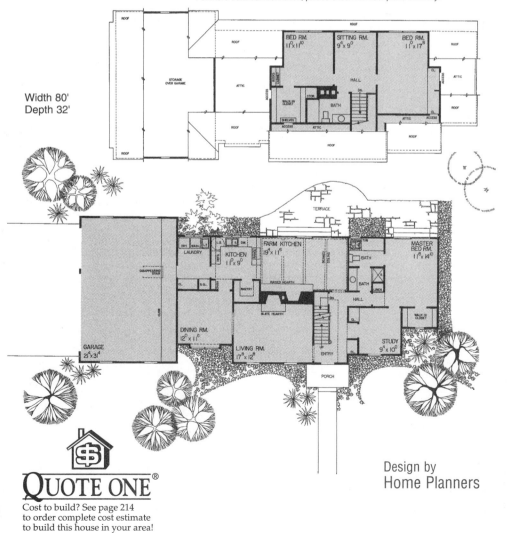

Width 80'
Depth 32'

Design by
Home Planners

Design 2563

First Floor: 1,500 square feet
Second Floor: 690 square feet
Total: 2,190 square feet

L **D**

◆ This charming Cape Cod will capture your heart with its warm appeal. From the large living room with a fireplace and adjacent dining room to the farm kitchen with an additional fireplace, the plan works toward livability. The first-floor laundry and walk-in pantry further aid in the efficiency of this plan. The master bedroom is located on this level for privacy and is highlighted by a luxurious bath and sliding glass doors to the rear terrace. A front study might be used as a guest bedroom or a library. Upstairs there are two bedrooms and a sitting room plus a full bath to accommodate the needs of family members. Both bedrooms have access to the attic. A three-car garage allows plenty of room for vehicles and storage space.

QUOTE ONE®
Cost to build? See page 214 to order complete cost estimate to build this house in your area!

Design 2995

First Floor: 2,465 square feet
Second Floor: 617 square feet
Total: 3,082 square feet

L **D**

◆ This New England Colonial delivers beautiful proportions and great livability on 1½ levels. The main area of the house, the first floor, holds a living room, a library, a family room, a dining room and a gourmet kitchen. The master bedroom, also on this floor, features a sumptuous master bath with a whirlpool tub and a sloped ceiling. A long rear terrace stretches the full width of the house. Two bedrooms on the second floor share a full bath; each has a built-in deck.

Design by
Home Planners

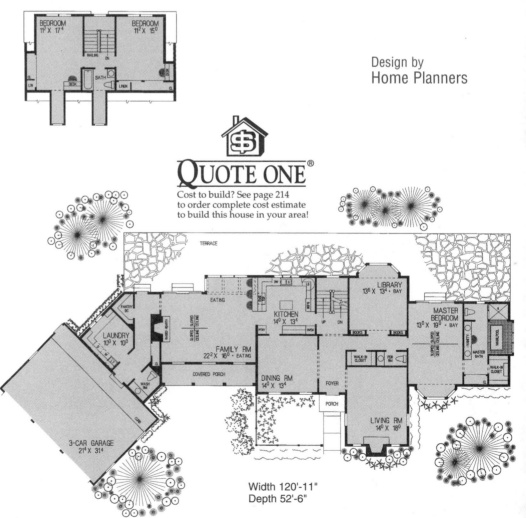

QUOTE ONE®

Cost to build? See page 214 to order complete cost estimate to build this house in your area!

Width 120'-11"
Depth 52'-6"

Photo by Laszlo Regos

This home, as shown in the photograph, may differ from the actual blueprints. For more detailed information, please check the floor plans carefully.

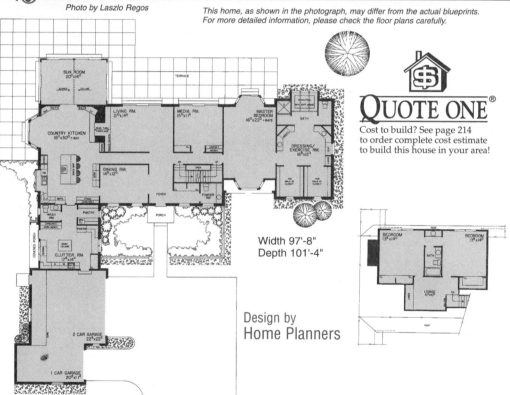

QUOTE ONE®

Cost to build? See page 214 to order complete cost estimate to build this house in your area!

Width 97'-8"
Depth 101'-4"

Design by
Home Planners

Design 2921

First Floor: 3,215 square feet
Second Floor: 711 square feet
Total: 3,926 square feet
Sun Room: 296 square feet

L **D**

◆ Organized zoning makes this traditional design a comfortable home for living. A central foyer facilitates flexible traffic patterns. Quiet areas of the house include a media room and luxurious master bedroom suite with fitness area, spacious closet space and bath, as well as a lounge or writing area. Informal living areas of the house include a sun room, large country kitchen and an efficient food preparation area with an island. Formal living areas include a living area and formal dining room. The second floor holds two bedrooms and a lounge. Service areas include a room just off the garage for laundry, sewing or hobbies.

Design 2880
Square Footage: 2,758
Greenhouse: 149 square feet

L D

◆ This comfortable traditional home offers plenty of modern livability. A clutter room off the two-car garage is an ideal space for a workbench, sewing or hobbies. Across the hall one finds a media room, the perfect place for stereo or video equipment and more. A spacious country kitchen to the right of the greenhouse (great for fresh herbs) is an cozy gathering place for family and friends, as well as a convenient work area. Both the formal living room, with its friendly fireplace, and the dining room provide access to the rear grounds. A spacious, amenity-filled master suite features His and Hers walk-in closets, a relaxing whirlpool tub and access to the rear terrace. Two large secondary bedrooms share a full bath.

Design by
Home Planners

Width 81'-4"
Depth 76'

QUOTE ONE®
Cost to build? See page 214 to order complete cost estimate to build this house in your area!

Design by
Home Planners

Design 3332
Square Footage: 2,168

L

◆ Nothing warms a traditional-style home quite as well as a country kitchen with a fireplace. Additional features include a second fireplace (with raised hearth) and a sloped ceiling in the living room, a nearby dining room with an attached porch, and a snack bar pass-through in the kitchen. Besides two family bedrooms with a shared full bath, there is also a grand master suite with rear terrace access, a walk-in closet, a whirlpool tub and a double-bowl vanity. A handy washroom is near the laundry, just off the two-car garage. A separate terrace is located to the rear of this area.

Width 76'-4"
Depth 46'

TERRACE

WALK-IN CLOSET

MASTER BEDROOM
12⁴ x 17⁶

WHIRLPOOL

BATH

SEAT

BATH

LINEN

LIVING RM
20⁸ x 17⁴

SLOPED CEILING   SLOPED CEILING

RAISED HEARTH

WOOD BOX

STOR.

DN

FOYER

COUNTRY KITCHEN
22⁴ x 13⁰

SNACK BAR

PORCH

DN

DINING RM
11⁸ x 11⁴

BC   PANTRY

WASH RM

RANGE

REF.

CURB

DN

TERRACE

W D

LAUNDRY
9²⁴ x 8⁴

BEDROOM
11⁴ x 11⁰

DESK

BEDROOM
11⁴ x 11⁴

COVERED PORCH

UP

GARAGE
21⁴ x 21⁴

207

Design 9750

Square Footage: 1,575
Bonus Room: 276 square feet

◆ A covered porch and dormers combine to create the inviting exterior on this three-bedroom country home. The foyer leads through columns to an expansive great room with a cozy fireplace, built-in bookshelves and access to the rear covered porch. To the right, an open kitchen is conveniently situated to easily serve the bay-windowed breakfast area and the formal dining room. Sleeping quarters are located on the left, where the master suite enjoys access to the covered porch, a walk-in closet and a relaxing master bath complete with double-bowl vanities, a whirlpool tub and a separate shower. A utility room, two secondary bedrooms and a full bath complete the plan. A bonus room over the garage provides room for future growth.

Design by
Donald A.
Gardner,
Architects, Inc.

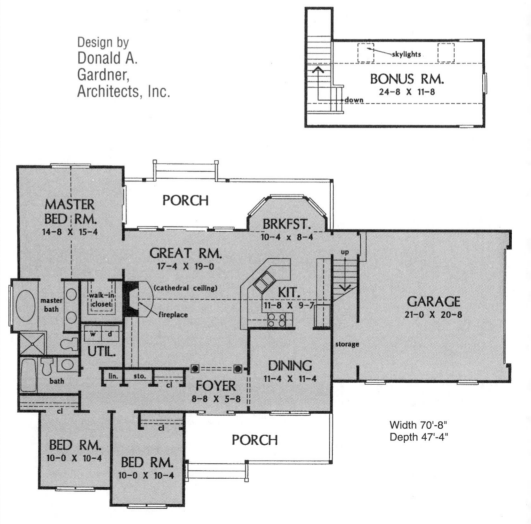

Width 70'-8"
Depth 47'-4"

Design by
Donald A.
Gardner,
Architects, Inc.

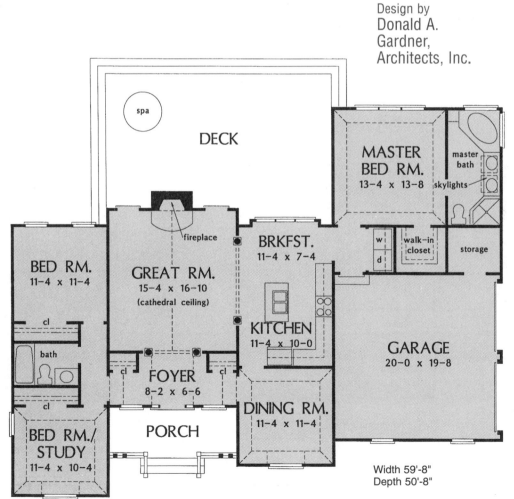

spa

DECK

MASTER
BED RM.
13-4 x 13-8

master
bath

skylights

fireplace

BRKFST.
11-4 x 7-4

GREAT RM.
15-4 x 16-10
(cathedral ceiling)

w
d

walk-in
closet

storage

BED RM.
11-4 x 11-4

cl

bath

cl

KITCHEN
11-4 x 10-0

GARAGE
20-0 x 19-8

cl

FOYER
8-2 x 6-6

cl

DINING RM.
11-4 x 11-4

BED RM./
STUDY
11-4 x 10-4

PORCH

Width 59'-8"
Depth 50'-8"

Design 9726
Square Footage: 1,498

◆ This charming country home utilizes multi-pane windows, columns, dormers, and a covered porch to offer a welcoming front exterior. Inside, the great room with a dramatic cathedral ceiling commands attention; the kitchen and breakfast room are just beyond a set of columns. The tiered-ceilinged dining room presents a delightfully formal setting for dinner parties or family gatherings. A tray ceiling in the master bedroom contributes to its pleasant atmosphere, as do the large walk-in closet and the gracious master bath with a garden tub and a separate shower. The secondary bedrooms are located at the opposite end of the house for privacy. Please specify basement or crawlspace foundation when ordering.

Design 8177
Square Footage: 1,834

◆ Reminiscent of America's farmhouses, this home comes complete with a covered front porch perfect for those hot summer evenings. Inside, the foyer opens to the great room, with a matching pair of double French doors flanking the fireplace and leading out to the rear porch. The dining room adds a formal flair with square columns connected by arched openings. An angled bar design in the kitchen opens the area to the great room and provides a convenient pass-through. The master bedroom features a coffered ceiling and an enormous walk-in closet. Amenities that include a double vanity, a corner whirlpool tub and a shower highlight the master bath. Bedrooms 2 and 3 are located nearby to complete the plan. Please specify crawlspace or slab foundation when ordering.

Design by
Larry E. Belk
Designs

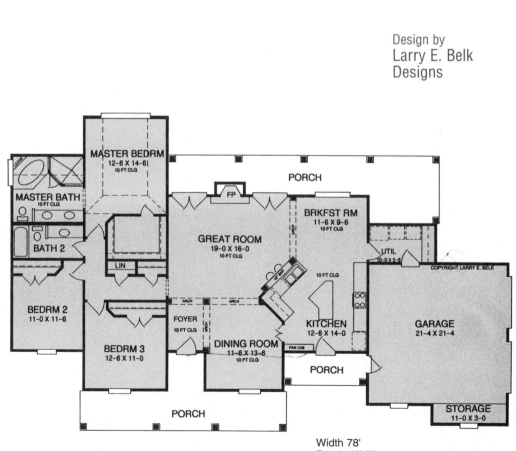

Width 78'
Depth 48'-7"

This home, as shown in the photograph, may differ from the actual blueprints.
For more detailed information, please check the floor plans carefully.

QUOTE ONE®

Cost to build? See page 214
to order complete cost estimate
to build this house in your area!

Design by
Home Planners

Width 154'
Depth 94'-8"

Design 3471

First Floor: 3,166 square feet
Second Floor: 950 square feet
Guest Living Area: 680 square feet
Total: 4,796 square feet

L

◆ Western farmhouse-style
living is captured in this handsome design. The central entrance leads into a cozy parlor—half walls provide a view
of the grand dining room. Entertaining's a cinch with the
dining room's built-in china
alcove, service counter and
fireplace. The country kitchen,
with a large island cooktop,
overlooks the gathering room.
The master bedroom will satisfy even the most discerning
tastes. It boasts a raised
hearth, porch access and a
bath with a walk-in closet,
separate vanities and a
whirlpool. You may want to
use one of the additional first-
floor bedrooms as a study, the
other as a guest room. Two
family bedrooms and attic
storage make up the second
floor. Note, too, the separate
garage and guest house.

When You're Ready To Order . . .

Let Us Show You Our Home Blueprint Package.

Building a home? Planning a home? Our Blueprint Package has nearly everything you need to get the job done right, whether you're working on your own or with help from an architect, designer, builder or subcontractors. Each Blueprint Package is the result of many hours of work by licensed architects or professional designers.

QUALITY

Hundreds of hours of painstaking effort have gone into the development of your blueprint set. Each home has been quality-checked by professionals to insure accuracy and buildability.

VALUE

Because we sell in volume, you can buy professional-quality blueprints at a fraction of their development cost. With our plans, your dream home design costs only a few hundred dollars, not the thousands of dollars that custom architects charge.

SERVICE

Once you've chosen your favorite home plan, you'll receive fast, efficient service whether you choose to mail or fax your order to us or call us toll free at 1-800-521-6797. For customer service, call toll free 1-888-690-1116.

SATISFACTION

Over 50 years of service to satisfied home plan buyers provide us unparalleled experience and knowledge in producing quality blueprints. What this means to you is satisfaction with our product and performance.

ORDER TOLL FREE 1-800-521-6797

After you've looked over our Blueprint Package and Important Extras on the following pages, simply mail the order form on page 221 or call toll free on our Blueprint Hotline: 1-800-521-6797. We're ready and eager to serve you. For customer service, call toll free 1-888-690-1116.

Each set of blueprints is an interrelated collection of detail sheets which includes components such as floor plans, interior and exterior elevations, dimensions, cross-sections, diagrams and notations. These sheets show exactly how your house is to be built.

Among the sheets included may be:

Frontal Sheet
This artist's sketch of the exterior of the house gives you an idea of how the house will look when built and landscaped. Large ink-line floor plans show all levels of the house and provide an overview of your new home's livability, as well as a handy reference for deciding on furniture placement.

Foundation Plan
This sheet shows the foundation layout includ-

SAMPLE PACKAGE

ing support walls, excavated and unexcavated areas, if any, and foundation notes. If slab construction rather than basement, the plan shows footings and details for a monolithic slab. This page, or another in the set, may include a sample plot plan for locating your house on a building site.

Detailed Floor Plans
These plans show the layout of each floor of the house. Rooms and interior spaces are carefully dimensioned and keys are given for cross-section details provided later in the plans. The positions of electrical outlets and switches are shown.

House Cross-Sections
Large-scale views show sections or cut-aways of the foundation, interior walls, exterior walls, floors, stairways and roof details. Additional cross-sections may show important changes in

floor, ceiling or roof heights or the relationship of one level to another. Extremely valuable for construction, these sections show exactly how the various parts of the house fit together.

Interior Elevations
Many of our drawings show the design and placement of kitchen and bathroom cabinets, laundry areas, fireplaces, bookcases and other built-ins. Little "extras," such as mantelpiece and wainscoting drawings, plus moulding sections, provide details that give your home that custom touch.

Exterior Elevations
These drawings show the front, rear and sides of your house and give necessary notes on exterior materials and finishes. Particular attention is given to cornice detail, brick and stone accents or other finish items that make your home unique.

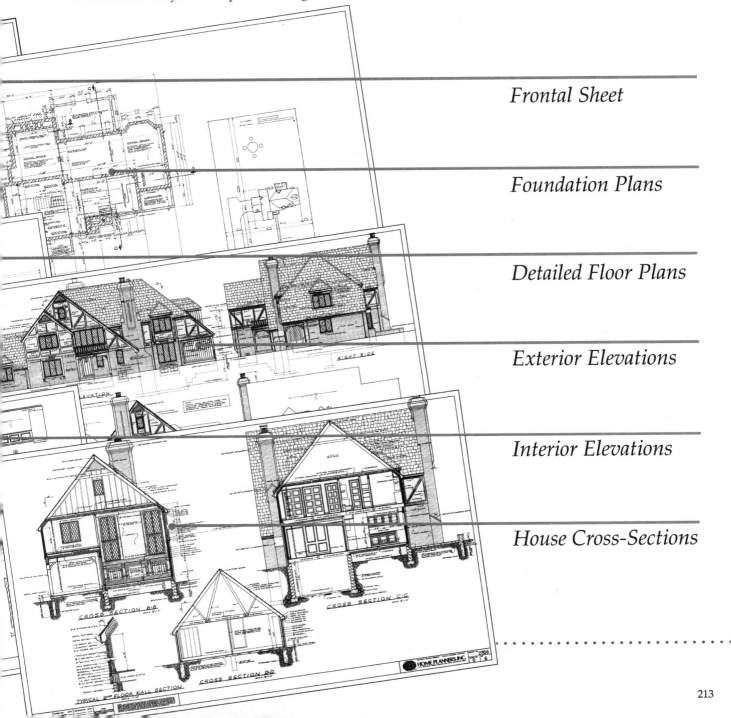

Frontal Sheet

Foundation Plans

Detailed Floor Plans

Exterior Elevations

Interior Elevations

House Cross-Sections

Important Extras To Do The Job Right!

Introducing eight important planning and construction aids developed by our professionals to help you succeed in your home-building project.

MATERIALS LIST

(Note: Because of the diversity of local building codes, our Materials List does not include mechanical materials.)

For many of the designs in our portfolio, we offer a customized materials take-off that is invaluable in planning and estimating the cost of your new home. This Materials List outlines the quantity, type and size of materials needed to build your house (with the exception of mechanical system items). Included are framing lumber, windows and doors, kitchen and bath cabinetry, rough and finish hardware, and much more. This handy list helps you or your builder cost out materials and serves as a reference sheet when you're compiling bids. A Materials List cannot be ordered before blueprints are ordered.

SPECIFICATION OUTLINE

This valuable 16-page document is critical to building your house correctly. Designed to be filled in by you or your builder, this book lists 166 stages or items crucial to the building process. It provides a comprehensive review of the construction process and helps in making choices of materials. When combined with the blueprints, a signed contract, and a schedule, it becomes a legal document and record for the building of your home.

QUOTE ONE®

Summary Cost Report / Materials Cost Report

A new service for estimating the cost of building select designs, the Quote One® system is available in two separate stages: The Summary Cost Report and the Materials Cost Report.

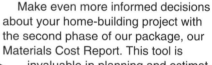

Make even more informed decisions about your home-building project with the second phase of our package, our Materials Cost Report. This tool is invaluable in planning and estimating the cost of your new home. The material and installation (labor and equipment) cost is shown for each of over 1,000 line items provided in the Materials List (Standard grade) which is included when you purchase this estimating tool. It allows you to determine building costs for your specific zip-code area and for your chosen home design. Space is allowed for additional estimates from contractors and subcontractors, such as for mechanical materials, which are not included in our packages. This invaluable tool is available for a price of $110 ($120 for a Schedule E plan) which includes a Materials List. A Materials Cost Report cannot be ordered before blueprints are ordered.

The Summary Cost Report is the first stage in the package and shows the total cost per square foot for your chosen home in your zip-code area and then breaks that cost down into various categories showing the costs for building materials, labor and installation. The total cost for the report (which includes three grades: Budget, Standard and Custom) is just $19.95 for one home, and additionals are only $14.95. These reports allow you to evaluate your building budget and compare the costs of building a variety of homes in your area.

The Quote One® program is continually updated with new plans. If you are interested in a plan that is not indicated as Quote One®, please call and ask our sales reps, they will be happy to verify the status for you. To order these invaluable reports, use the order form on page 221 or call 1-800-521-6797.

CONSTRUCTION INFORMATION

If you want to know more about techniques—and deal more confidently with subcontractors we offer these useful sheets. Each set is an excellent tool that will add to your understanding of these technical subjects.

Plan-A-Home®

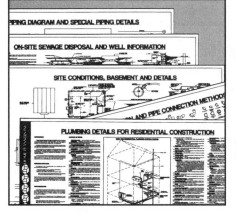

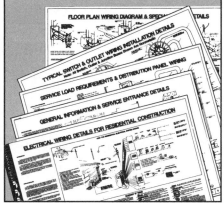

PLUMBING

The Blueprint Package includes locations for all the plumbing fixtures in your new house, including sinks, lavatories, tubs, showers, toilets, laundry trays and water heaters. However, if you want to know more about the complete plumbing system, these 24x36-inch detail sheets will prove very useful. Prepared to meet requirements of the National Plumbing Code, these six fact-filled sheets give general information on pipe schedules, fittings, sump-pump details, water-softener hookups, septic system details and much more. Color-coded sheets include a glossary of terms.

ELECTRICAL

The locations for every electrical switch, plug and outlet are shown in your Blueprint Package. However, these Electrical Details go further to take the mystery out of household electrical systems. Prepared to meet requirements of the National Electrical Code, these comprehensive 24x36-inch drawings come packed with helpful information, including wire sizing, switch-installation schematics, cable-routing details, appliance wattage, door-bell hookups, typical service panel circuitry and much more. Six sheets are bound together and color-coded for easy reference. A glossary of terms is also included.

Plan-A-Home® is an easy-to-use tool that helps you design a new home, arrange furniture in a new or existing home, or plan a remodeling project. Each package contains:

- **More than 700 reusable peel-off planning symbols** on a self-stick vinyl sheet, including walls, windows, doors, all types of furniture, kitchen components, bath fixtures and many more.

- **A reusable, transparent, 1/4-inch scale planning grid** that matches the scale of actual working drawings (1/4-inch equals 1 foot). This grid provides the basis for house layouts of up to 140x92 feet.

- **Tracing paper** and a protective sheet for copying or transferring your completed plan.

- **A felt-tip pen,** with water-soluble ink that wipes away quickly.

Plan-A-Home® lets you lay out areas as large as a 7,500 square foot, six-bedroom, seven-bath house.

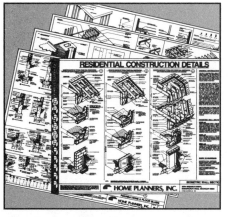

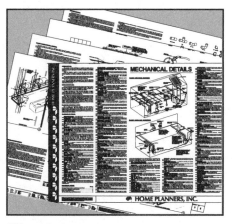

CONSTRUCTION

The Blueprint Package contains everything an experienced builder needs to construct a particular house. However, it doesn't show all the ways that houses can be built, nor does it explain alternate construction methods. To help you understand how your house will be built—and offer additional techniques—this set of drawings depicts the materials and methods used to build foundations, fireplaces, walls, floors and roofs. Where appropriate, the drawings show acceptable alternatives. These six sheets will answer questions for the advanced do-it-yourselfer or home planner.

MECHANICAL

This package contains fundamental principles and useful data that will help you make informed decisions and communicate with subcontractors about heating and cooling systems. The 24x36-inch drawings contain instructions and samples that allow you to make simple load calculations and preliminary sizing and costing analysis. Covered are today's most commonly used systems from heat pumps to solar fuel systems. The package is packed full of illustrations and diagrams to help you visualize components and how they relate to one another.

To Order, Call Toll Free 1-800-521-6797

To add these important extras to your Blueprint Package, simply indicate your choices on the order form on page 221 or call us Toll Free 1-800-521-6797 and we'll tell you more about these exciting products.
For customer service, call toll free 1-888-690-1116.

215

◨ *The Deck Blueprint Package*

Many of the homes in this book can be enhanced with a professionally designed Home Planners' Deck Plan. Those home plans highlighted with a ◨ have a matching or corresponding deck plan available which includes a Deck Plan Frontal Sheet, Deck Framing and Floor Plans, Deck Elevations and a Deck Materials List. A Standard Deck Details Package, also available, provides all the how-to information necessary for building *any* deck. Our Complete Deck Building Package contains 1 set of Custom Deck Plans of your choice, plus 1 set of Standard Deck Building Details all for one low price. Our plans and details are carefully prepared in an easy-to-understand format that will guide you through every stage of your deck-building project. This page contains a sampling of 12 of the 25 different Deck layouts to match your favorite house. See page 218 for prices and ordering information.

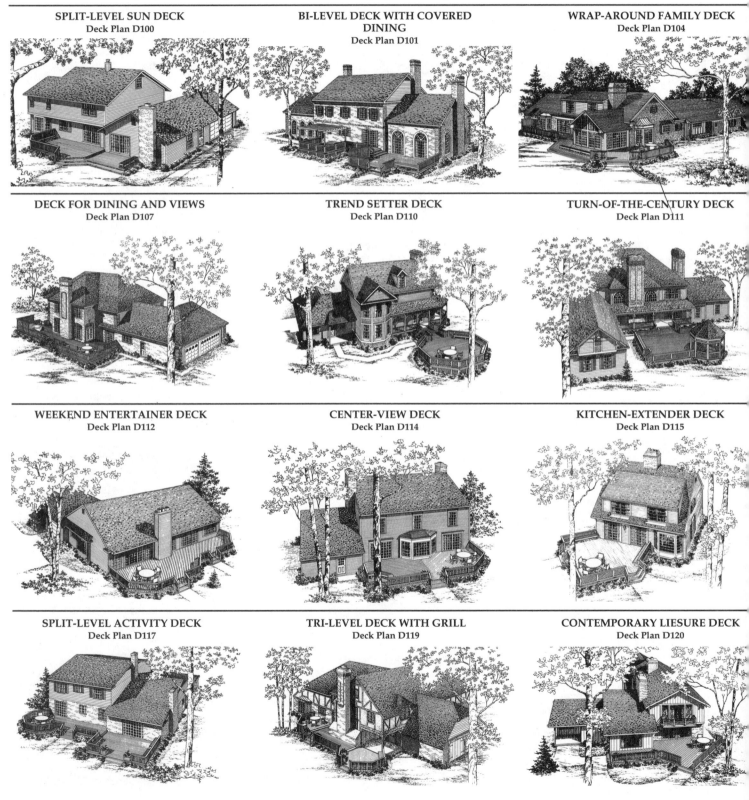

SPLIT-LEVEL SUN DECK
Deck Plan D100

BI-LEVEL DECK WITH COVERED DINING
Deck Plan D101

WRAP-AROUND FAMILY DECK
Deck Plan D104

DECK FOR DINING AND VIEWS
Deck Plan D107

TREND SETTER DECK
Deck Plan D110

TURN-OF-THE-CENTURY DECK
Deck Plan D111

WEEKEND ENTERTAINER DECK
Deck Plan D112

CENTER-VIEW DECK
Deck Plan D114

KITCHEN-EXTENDER DECK
Deck Plan D115

SPLIT-LEVEL ACTIVITY DECK
Deck Plan D117

TRI-LEVEL DECK WITH GRILL
Deck Plan D119

CONTEMPORARY LIESURE DECK
Deck Plan D120

L The Landscape Blueprint Package

For the homes marked with an L in this book, Home Planners has created a front-yard landscape plan that matches or is complementary in design to the house plan. These comprehensive blueprint packages include a Frontal Sheet, Plan View, Regionalized Plant & Materials List, a sheet on Planting and Maintaining Your Landscape, Zone Maps and Plant Size and Description Guide. These plans will help you achieve professional results, adding value and enjoyment to your property for years to come. Each set of blueprints is a full 18" x 24" in size with clear, complete instructions and easy-to-read type. Six of the forty front yard Landscape Plans to match your favorite house are shown below.

Regional Order Map

Most of the Landscape Plans shown on these pages are available with a Plant & Materials List adapted by horticultural experts to 8 different regions of the country. Please specify Geographic Region when ordering your plan. See page 218 for prices, ordering information and regional availability.

Region	1	Northeast
Region	2	Mid-Atlantic
Region	3	Deep South
Region	4	Florida & Gulf Coast
Region	5	Midwest
Region	6	Rocky Mountains
Region	7	Southern California & Desert Southwest
Region	8	Northern California & Pacific Northwest

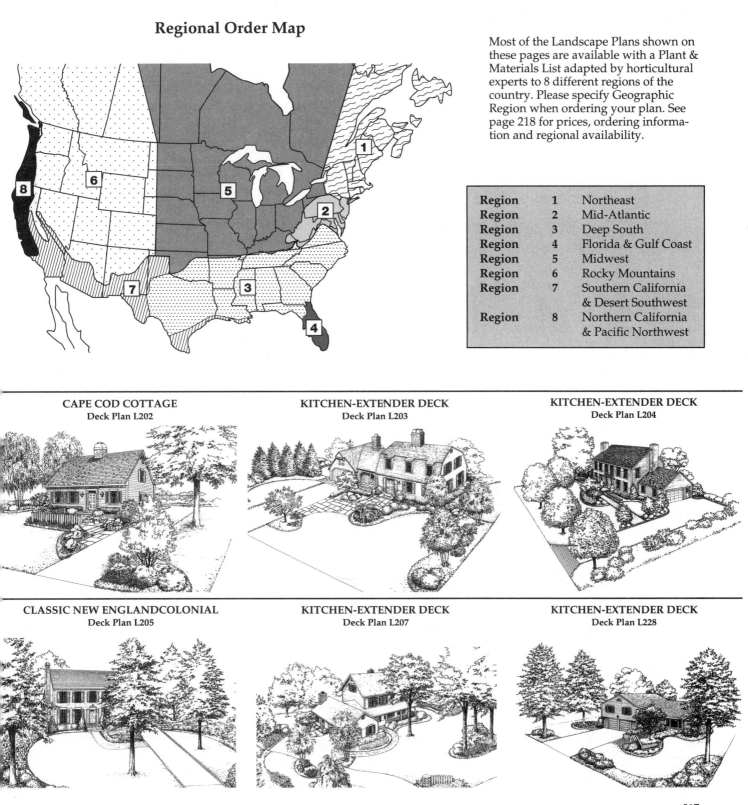

CAPE COD COTTAGE
Deck Plan L202

KITCHEN-EXTENDER DECK
Deck Plan L203

KITCHEN-EXTENDER DECK
Deck Plan L204

CLASSIC NEW ENGLANDCOLONIAL
Deck Plan L205

KITCHEN-EXTENDER DECK
Deck Plan L207

KITCHEN-EXTENDER DECK
Deck Plan L228

Price Schedule & Plans Index

House Blueprint Price Schedule
(Prices guaranteed through December 31, 1999)

Tier	1-set Study Package	4-set Building Package	8-set Building Package	1-set Reproducible Sepias	Home Customizer® Package
A	$390	$435	$495	$595	$645
B	$430	$475	$535	$655	$705
C	$470	$515	$575	$715	$765
D	$510	$555	$615	$775	$825
E	$630	$675	$735	$835	$885

Prices for 4- or 8-set Building Packages honored only at time of original order.

Additional Identical Blueprints in (standard or reverse) same order..$50 per set
Reverse Blueprints (mirror image) with 4- or 8-set order ....$50 fee per order
Specification Outlines ....$10 each
Materials Lists (available only for those designers listed below):
- ▲ Home Planners Designs.....................................$50
- † Design Basics Designs...$75
- ◆ Donald Gardner Designs....................................$50
- ■ Design Traditions Designs..................................$50
- ≠ Larry Belk Designs..$50
- ● The Sater Design Collection...............................$50
- ✳ Larry Garnett Designs...$50

Materials Lists for "E" price plans are an additional $10.

Deck Plans Price Schedule

CUSTOM DECK PLANS

Price Group	Q	R	S
1 Set Custom Plans	$25	$30	$35

Additional identical sets $10 each
Reverse sets (mirror image) $10 each

STANDARD DECK DETAILS
1 Set Generic Construction Details ....$14.95 each

COMPLETE DECK BUILDING PACKAGE

Price Group	Q	R	S
1 Set Custom Plans, plus 1 Set Standard Deck Details	$35	$40	$45

Landscape Plans Price Schedule

Price Group	X	Y	Z
1 set	$35	$45	$55
3 sets	$50	$60	$70
6 sets	$65	$75	$85

Additional Identical Sets....................................$10 each
Reverse Sets (mirror image)..............................$10 each

Index

To use the Index below, refer to the design number listed in numerical order (a helpful page reference is also given). Note the price index letter and refer to the House Blueprint Price Schedule above for the cost of one, four or eight sets of blueprints or the cost of a reproducible sepia. Additional prices are shown for identical and reverse blueprint sets, as well as a very useful Materials List for some of the plans. Also note in the Index below those plans that have matching or complementary Deck Plans or Landscape Plans. Refer to the schedules above for prices of these plans. All Home Planners' plans can be customized with Home Planners' Home Customizer®Package. These plans are indicated below with this symbol: 🏠. See page 221 for information. Some plans are also part of our Quote One® estimating service and are indicated by this symbol: 🏠 . See page 214 for more information.

To Order: Fill in and send the order form on page 221—or call toll free 1-800-521-6797 or 520-297-8200.

DESIGN	PRICE	PAGE	CUSTOMIZABLE	QUOTE ONE®	DECK	DECK PRICE	LANDSCAPE	LANDSCAPE PRICE	REGIONS
▲2174	B	37	🏠		D117	S	L220	Y	1-3,5,6,8
▲2488	A	115	🏠		D102	Q			
▲2563	B	203	🏠	🏠	D114	R	L201	Y	1-3,5,6,8
▲2622	A	63	🏠		D103	R	L200	X	1-3,5,6,8
▲2659	B	60	🏠	🏠	D113	R	L205	Y	1-3,5,6,8
▲2661	A	202	🏠	🏠	D113	R	L202	X	1-3,5,6,8
▲2694	C	199	🏠	🏠			L209	Y	1-6,8
▲2774	B	15	🏠	🏠	D100	Q	L207	Z	1-6,8
▲2776	B	116	🏠		D113	R	L207	Z	1-6,8
▲2826	A	43	🏠	🏠	D116	R			
▲2854	B	25	🏠	🏠	D112	R	L220	Y	1-3,5,6,8
▲2855	B	26	🏠	🏠	D103	R	L219	Z	1-3,5,6,8
▲2880	C	206	🏠		D114	R	L212	Z	1-8
▲2908	B	61	🏠	🏠	D117	S	L205	Y	1-3,5,6,8
▲2921	D	205	🏠	🏠	D104	S	L212	Z	1-8
▲2927	B	45	🏠	🏠	D100	Q			
▲2946	C	14	🏠	🏠	D114	R	L207	Z	1-6,8
▲2947	B	55	🏠	🏠	D112	R	L200	X	1-3,5,6,8
▲2970	D	80	🏠	🏠			L223	Z	1-3,5,6,8
▲2973	B	79	🏠	🏠			L223	Z	1-3,5,6,8
▲2974	A	76	🏠	🏠			L223	Z	1-3,5,6,8
▲2995	D	204	🏠		D106	S	L217	Y	1-8
▲3309	B	75	🏠				L209	Y	1-6,8
▲3313	B	91	🏠	🏠			L200	X	1-3,5,6,8
▲3314	B	100	🏠	🏠			L200	X	1-3,5,6,8
▲3315	D	90	🏠	🏠			L200	X	1-3,5,6,8
▲3316	A	92	🏠	🏠			L200	X	1-3,5,6,8
▲3318	B	89	🏠	🏠	D111	S	L202	Y	1-3,5,6,8
▲3324	E	153	🏠	🏠	D114	R	L207	Z	1-6,8
▲3325	C	152	🏠	🏠	D100	Q	L238	Y	3,4,7,8
▲3330	A	44	🏠	🏠					
▲3332	B	207	🏠	🏠			L200	X	1-3,5,6,8
▲3340	B	73	🏠	🏠			L224	Y	1-3,5,6,8
▲3355	A	128	🏠	🏠	D117	S	L220	Y	1-3,5,6,8
▲3385	C	77	🏠	🏠	D100	Q	L207	Z	1-6,8
▲3461	B	177	🏠	🏠			L204	Y	1-3,5,6,8
▲3462	B	162	🏠	🏠			L207	Z	1-6,8
▲3471	E	211	🏠	🏠			L236	Z	3,4,7
▲3474	B	121	🏠	🏠			L202	X	1-3,5,6,8
▲3487	B	56	🏠	🏠			L209	Y	1-6,8
▲3491	B	52	🏠	🏠	D111	S	L215	Z	1-6,8
▲3498	B	99	🏠	🏠					
▲3510	C	62	🏠	🏠					
▲3605	C	135	🏠	🏠	D111	S	L209	Y	1-6,8
▲3608	D	159	🏠	🏠			L223	Z	1-3,5,6,8
▲3609	C	84	🏠	🏠	D100	Q	L224	Y	1-3,5,6,8

Before You Order . . .

Before filling out the coupon at right or calling us on our Toll-Free Blueprint Hotline, you may want to learn more about our services and products. Here's some information you will find helpful.

Quick Turnaround

We process and ship every blueprint order from our office within two business days. Because of this quick turnaround, we won't send a formal notice acknowledging receipt of your order.

Our Exchange Policy

Since blueprints are printed in response to your order, we cannot honor requests for refunds. However, we will exchange your entire first order for an equal number of blueprints at a price of $50 for the first set and $10 for each additional set; $70 total exchange fee for 4 sets; $100 total exchange fee for 8 sets . . . *plus* the difference in cost if exchanging for a design in a higher price bracket or *less* the difference in cost if exchanging for a design in lower price bracket. One exchange is allowed within a year of purchase date. **(Sepias are not exchangeable.)** All sets from the first order must be returned before the exchange can take place. Please add $18 for postage and handling via regular service; $30 via Priority Service; $40 via Express Service. Returns and exchanges are subject to a 20% restocking fee. Shipping and handling charges are not refundable.

About Reverse Blueprints

If you want to build in reverse of the plan as shown, we will reverse any number of blueprints (mirror image) from a 4- or 8-set packagefor an additional fee of $50. Although lettering and dimensions will appear backward, reverses will be a useful aid if you decide to flop the plan.

Revising, Modifying and Customizing Plans

The wide variety of designs available in this publication allows you to select ideas and concepts for a home to fit your building site and match your family's needs, wants and budget. Like many homeowners who buy these plans, you and your builder, architect or engineer may want to make changes to them. Some minor changes may be made by your builder, but we recommend that most changes be made by a licensed architect or engineer. If you need to make alterations to a design that is customizable, you need only order our Home Customizer® Package to get you started. As set forth below, we cannot assume any responsibility for blueprints which have been changed, whether by you, your builder or by professionals selected by you or referred to you by us, because such individuals are outside our supervision and control.

Architectural and Engineering Seals

Some cities and states are now requiring that a licensed architect or engineer review and "seal" a blueprint, or officially approve it, prior to construction due to concerns over energy costs, safety and other factors. Prior to application for a building permit or the start of actual construction, we strongly advise that you consult your local building official who can tell you if such a review is required.

About the Designers

The architects and designers whose work appears in this publication are among America's leading residential designers. Each plan was designed to meet the requirements of a nationally recognized model building code in effect at the time and place the plan was drawn. Because national building codes change from time to time, plans may not comply with any such code at the time they are sold to a customer. In addition, building officials may not accept these plans as final construction documents of record as the plans may need to be modified and additional drawings and details added to suit local conditions and requirements. We strongly advise that purchasers consult a licensed architect or engineer, and their local building official, before starting any construction related to these plans.

Local Building Codes and Zoning Requirements

At the time of creation, our plans are drawn to specifications published by the Building Officials and Code Administrators (BOCA) International, Inc.; the Southern Building Code Congress (SBCCI) International, Inc.; the International Conference of Building Officials; or the Council of American Building Officials (CABO). Our plans are designed to meet or exceed national building standards. Because of the great differences in geography and climate throughout the United States and Canada, each state, county and municipality has its own building codes, zone requirements, ordinances and building regulations. Your plan may need to be modified to comply with local requirements regarding snow loads, energy codes, soil and seismic conditions and a wide range of other matters. In addition, you may need to obtain permits or inspections from local governments before and in the course of construction. Prior to using blueprints ordered from us, we strongly advise that you consult a licensed architect or engineer—and speak with your local building official—before applying for any permit or beginning construction. We authorize the use of our blueprints on the express condition that you strictly comply with all local building codes, zoning requirements and other applicable laws, regulations, ordinances and requirements. **Notice:** Plans for homes to be built in Nevada must be re-drawn by a Nevada-registered professional. Consult your building official for more information on this subject.

Foundation and Exterior Wall Changes

Most of our plans are drawn with either a full or partial basement foundation. Depending on your specific climate or regional building practices, you may wish to change this basement to a slab or crawlspace. Most professional contractors and builders can easily adapt your plans to alternate foundation types. Likewise, most can easily change 2x4 wall construction to 2x6, or vice versa.

Disclaimer

We and the designers we work with have put substantial care and effort into the creation of our blueprints. However, because we cannot provide on-site consultation, supervision and control over actual construction, and because of the great variance in local building requirements, building practices and soil, seismic, weather and other conditions, WE CANNOT MAKE ANY WARRANTY, EXPRESS OR IMPLIED, WITH RESPECT TO THE CONTENT OR USE OF OUR BLUEPRINTS, INCLUDING BUT NOT LIMITED TO ANY WARRANTY OF MERCHANTABILITY OR OF FITNESS FOR A PARTICULAR PURPOSE.

Terms and Conditions

These designs are protected under the terms of United States Copyright Law and may not be copied or reproduced in any way, by any means, unless you have purchased Sepias or Reproducibles which clearly indicate your right to copy or reproduce. We authorize the use of your chosen design as an aid in the construction of one single family home only. You may not use this design to build a second or multiple dwellings without purchasing another blueprint or blueprints or paying additional design fees.

How Many Blueprints Do You Need?

A single set of blueprints is sufficient to study a home in greater detail. However, if you are planning to obtain cost estimates from a contractor or subcontractors—or if you are planning to build immediately—you will need more sets. Because additional sets are cheaper when ordered in quantity with the original order, make sure you order enough blueprints to satisfy all requirements. The following checklist will help you determine how many you need:

____ Owner

____ Builder (generally requires at least three sets; one as a legal document, one to use during inspections, and at least one to give to subcontractors)

____ Local Building Department (often requires two sets)

____ Mortgage Lender (usually one set for a conventional loan; three sets for FHA or VA loans)

____ TOTAL NUMBER OF SETS

The Home Customizer®

"This house is perfect...if only the family room were two feet wider." Sound familiar? In response to the numerous requests for this type of modification, Home Planners has developed **The Home Customizer® Package**. This exclusive package offers our top-of-the-line materials to make it easy for anyone, anywhere to customize any Home Planners design to fit their needs. Check the index on page 218-219 for those plans which are customizable.

Some of the changes you can make to any of our plans include:

- exterior elevation changes
- kitchen and bath modifications
- roof, wall and foundation changes
- room additions and more!

The Home Customizer® Package includes everything you'll need to make the necessary changes to your favorite Home Planners design. The package includes:

- instruction book with examples
- architectural scale and clear work film
- erasable red marker and removable correction tape
- ¼"-scale furniture cutouts
- 1 set reproducible, erasable Sepias
- 1 set study blueprints for communicating changes to your design professional
- a copyright release letter so you can make copies as you need them
- referral letter with the name, address and telephone number of the professional in your region who is trained in modifying Home Planners designs efficiently and inexpensively.

The price of the **Home Customizer® Package** ranges from $645 to $1085, depending on the price schedule of the design you have chosen. **The Home Customizer® Package** will not only save you 25% to 75% of the cost of drawing the plans from scratch with a custom architect or engineer, it will also give you the flexibility to have your changes and modifications made by our referral network or by the professional of your choice. Now it's even easier and more affordable to have the custom home you've always wanted.

ORDER TOLL FREE!

For information about any of our services or to order call 1-800-521-6797 or 520-297-8200. Plus browse our website: www.homeplanners.com

BLUEPRINTS ARE NOT REFUNDABLE EXCHANGES ONLY

For Customer Service, call toll free 1-888-690-1116.

ORDER FORM

HOME PLANNERS, LLC
Wholly owned by Hanley-Wood, Inc.
3275 WEST INA ROAD, SUITE 110
TUCSON, ARIZONA 85741

THE BASIC BLUEPRINT PACKAGE
Rush me the following (please refer to the Plans Index and Price Schedule in this section):

_____ Set(s) of blueprints for plan number(s) _____. $_____
_____ Set(s) of sepias for plan number(s) _____. $_____
_____ Home Customizer® Package for plan(s)_____ $_____
_____ Additional identical blueprints in (standard or reverse) same order @ $50 per set. $_____
_____ Reverse blueprint fee @ $50 per order. $_____

IMPORTANT EXTRAS
Rush me the following:

_____ Materials List: $50 (Must be purchased with Blueprint set.) $75 Design Basics. Add $10 for a Schedule E-G plan Materials List.$_____
_____ **Quote One**® Summary Cost Report @ $19.95 for 1, $14.95 for each additional, for plans _____ $_____
Building location: City _____ Zip Code _____
_____ **Quote One**® Materials Cost Report @ $110 Schedule A-D; $120 Schedule E for plan_____ $_____
(Must be purchased with Blueprints set.)
Building location: City _____ Zip Code_____
_____ Specification Outlines @ $10 each. $_____
_____ Detail Sets @ $14.95 each; any two for $22.95; any three for $29.95; all four for $39.95 (save $19.85). $_____
❏ Plumbing ❏ Electrical ❏ Construction ❏ Mechanical (These helpful details provide general construction advice and are not specific to any single plan.)
_____ Plan-A-Home® @ $29.95 each. $_____

DECK BLUEPRINTS
_____ Set(s) of Deck Plan _____. $_____
_____ Additional identical blueprints in same order @ $10 per set. $_____
_____ Reverse blueprints @ $10 per set. $_____
_____ Set of Standard Deck Details @ $14.95 per set. $_____
_____ Set of Complete Building Package (Best Buy!) Includes Custom Deck Plan _____.
(See Index and Price Schedule)
Plus Standard Deck Details $_____

LANDSCAPE BLUEPRINTS
_____ Set(s) of Landscape Plan _____. $_____
_____ Additional identical blueprints in same order @ $10 per set. $_____
_____ Reverse blueprints @ $10 per set. $_____

Please indicate the appropriate region of the country for Plant & Material List. (See Map on page 217): Region _____

POSTAGE AND HANDLING	1-3 sets	4+ sets
Signature is required for all deliveries. **DELIVERY** No CODs (Requires street address - No P.O. Boxes)		
•Regular Service (Allow 7-10 business days delivery)	❏ $15.00	❏ $18.00
•Priority (Allow 4-5 business days delivery)	❏ $20.00	❏ $30.00
•Express (Allow 3 business days delivery)	❏ $30.00	❏ $40.00
CERTIFIED MAIL If no street address available. (Allow 7-10 days delivery)	❏ $20.00	❏ $30.00
OVERSEAS DELIVERY Note: All delivery times are from date Blueprint Package is shipped.	fax, phone or mail for quote	

POSTAGE (From box above) $_____
SUB-TOTAL $_____
SALES TAX (AZ, MI & WA residents, please add appropriate state and local sales tax.) $_____
TOTAL (Sub-total and tax) $_____

YOUR ADDRESS (please print)

Name _____

Street _____

City _____ State _____ Zip _____

Daytime telephone number (_____) _____

FOR CREDIT CARD ORDERS ONLY
Please fill in the information below:

Credit card number _____

Exp. Date: Month/Year _____

Check one ❏ Visa ❏ MasterCard ❏ Discover Card ❏ American Express

Signature _____

Please check appropriate box: ❏ Licensed Builder-Contractor
❏ Homeowner

ORDER TOLL FREE!
1-800-521-6797 or 520-297-8200

Order Form Key

TB42

221

Helpful Books & Software

Home Planners wants your building experience to be as pleasant and trouble-free as possible. That's why we've expanded our library of Do-It-Yourself titles to help you along. In addition to our beautiful plans books, we've added books to guide you through specific projects as well as the construction process. In fact, these are titles that will be as useful after your dream home is built as they are right now.

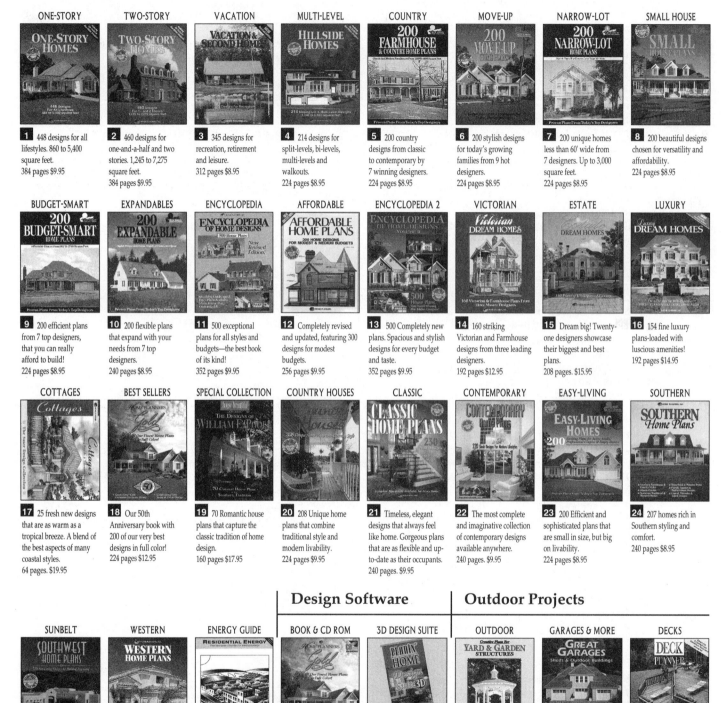

ONE-STORY

1 448 designs for all lifestyles. 860 to 5,400 square feet. 384 pages $9.95

TWO-STORY

2 460 designs for one-and-a-half and two stories. 1,245 to 7,275 square feet. 384 pages $9.95

VACATION

3 345 designs for recreation, retirement and leisure. 312 pages $8.95

MULTI-LEVEL

4 214 designs for split-levels, bi-levels, multi-levels and walkouts. 224 pages $8.95

COUNTRY

5 200 country designs from classic to contemporary by 7 winning designers. 224 pages $8.95

MOVE-UP

6 200 stylish designs for today's growing families from 9 hot designers. 224 pages $8.95

NARROW-LOT

7 200 unique homes less than 60' wide from 7 designers. Up to 3,000 square feet. 224 pages $8.95

SMALL HOUSE

8 200 beautiful designs chosen for versatility and affordability. 224 pages $8.95

BUDGET-SMART

9 200 efficient plans from 7 top designers, that you can really afford to build! 224 pages $8.95

EXPANDABLES

10 200 flexible plans that expand with your needs from 7 top designers. 240 pages $8.95

ENCYCLOPEDIA

11 500 exceptional plans for all styles and budgets—the best book of its kind! 352 pages $9.95

AFFORDABLE

12 Completely revised and updated, featuring 300 designs for modest budgets. 256 pages $9.95

ENCYCLOPEDIA 2

13 500 Completely new plans. Spacious and stylish designs for every budget and taste. 352 pages $9.95

VICTORIAN

14 160 striking Victorian and Farmhouse designs from three leading designers. 192 pages $12.95

ESTATE

15 Dream big! Twenty-one designers showcase their biggest and best plans. 208 pages. $15.95

LUXURY

16 154 fine luxury plans-loaded with luscious amenities! 192 pages $14.95

COTTAGES

17 25 fresh new designs that are as warm as a tropical breeze. A blend of the best aspects of many coastal styles. 64 pages. $19.95

BEST SELLERS

18 Our 50th Anniversary book with 200 of our very best designs in full color! 224 pages $12.95

SPECIAL COLLECTION

19 70 Romantic house plans that capture the classic tradition of home design. 160 pages $17.95

COUNTRY HOUSES

20 208 Unique home plans that combine traditional style and modern livability. 224 pages $9.95

CLASSIC

21 Timeless, elegant designs that always feel like home. Gorgeous plans that are as flexible and up-to-date as their occupants. 240 pages $9.95

CONTEMPORARY

22 The most complete and imaginative collection of contemporary designs available anywhere. 240 pages. $9.95

EASY-LIVING

23 200 Efficient and sophisticated plans that are small in size, but big on livability. 224 pages $8.95

SOUTHERN

24 207 homes rich in Southern styling and comfort. 240 pages $8.95

Design Software

Outdoor Projects

SUNBELT

25 215 Designs that capture the spirit of the Southwest. 208 pages $10.95

WESTERN

26 215 designs that capture the spirit and diversity of the Western lifestyle. 208 pages $9.95

ENERGY GUIDE

27 The most comprehensive energy efficiency and conservation guide available. 280 pages $35.00

BOOK & CD ROM

28 Both the Home Planners Gold book and matching Windows™ CD ROM with 3D floorplans. $24.95

3D DESIGN SUITE

29 Home design made easy! View designs in 3D, take a virtual reality tour, add decorating details and more. $59.95

OUTDOOR

30 42 unique outdoor projects. Gazebos, strombellas, bridges, sheds, playsets and more! 96 pages $7.95

GARAGES & MORE

31 101 Multi-use garages and outdoor structures to enhance any home. 96 pages $7.95

DECKS

32 25 outstanding single-, double- and multi-level decks you can build. 112 pages $7.95

Landscape Designs

EASY CARE	FRONT & BACK	BACKYARDS	BEDS & BORDERS	BATHROOMS	KITCHENS	HOUSE CONTRACTING	WINDOWS & DOORS

33 41 special landscapes designed for beauty and low maintenance. 160 pages $14.95

34 The first book of do-it-yourself landscapes. 40 front, 15 backyards. 208 pages $14.95

35 40 designs focused solely on creating your own specially themed backyard oasis. 160 pages $14.95

36 Practical advice and maintenance techniques for a wide variety of yard projects. 160 pages. $14.95

37 An innovative guide to organizing, remodeling and decorating your bathroom. 96 pages $9.95

38 An imaginative guide to designing the perfect kitchen. Chock full of bright ideas to make your job easier. 176 pages $14 .95

39 Everything you need to know to act as your own general contractor...and save up to 25% off building costs. 134 pages $14.95

40 Installation techniques and tips that make your project easier and more professional looking. 80 pages $7.95

ROOFING	FRAMING	VISUAL HANDBOOK	BASIC WIRING	PATIOS & WALKS	TILE	TRIM & MOLDING

41 Information on the latest tools, materials and techniques for roof installation or repair. 80 pages $7.95

42 For those who want to take a more-hands on approach to their dream. 319 pages $19.95

43 A plain-talk guide to the construction process; financing to final walk-through, this book covers it all. 498 pages $19.95

44 A straight forward guide to one of the most misunderstood systems in the home. 160 pages $12.95

45 Clear step-by-step instructions take you from the basic design stages to the finished project. 80 pages $7.95

46 Every kind of tile for every kind of application. Includes tips on use installation and repair. 176 pages $12.95

47 Step-by-step instructions for installing baseboards, window and door casings and more. 80 pages $7.95

Additional Books Order Form

To order your books, just check the box of the book numbered below and complete the coupon. We will process your order and ship it from our office within 48 hours. Send coupon and check (in U.S. funds).

YES! Please send me the books I've indicated:

☐ 1:VO	$9.95	☐ 25:SW	$10.95
☐ 2:VT	$9.95	☐ 26:WH	$9.95
☐ 3:VH	$8.95	☐ 27:RES	$35.00
☐ 4:VS	$8.95	☐ 28:HPGC	$24.95
☐ 5:FH	$8.95	☐ 29:PLANSUITE	$59.95
☐ 6:MU	$8.95	☐ 30:YG	$7.95
☐ 7:NL	$8.95	☐ 31:GG	$7.95
☐ 8:SM	$8.95	☐ 32:DP	$7.95
☐ 9:BS	$8.95	☐ 33:ECL	$14.95
☐ 10:EX	$8.95	☐ 34:HL	$14.95
☐ 11:EN	$9.95	☐ 35:BYL	$14.95
☐ 12:AF	$9.95	☐ 36:BB	$14.95
☐ 13:E2	$9.95	☐ 37:CDB	$9.95
☐ 14:VDH	$12.95	☐ 38:CKI	$14.95
☐ 15:EDH	$15.95	☐ 39:SBC	$14.95
☐ 16:LD2	$14.95	☐ 40:CGD	$7.95
☐ 17:CTG	$19.95	☐ 41:CGR	$7.95
☐ 18:HPG	$12.95	☐ 42:SRF	$19.95
☐ 19:WEP	$17.95	☐ 43:RVH	$19.95
☐ 20:CN	$9.95	☐ 44:CBW	$12.95
☐ 21:CS	$9.95	☐ 45:CGW	$7.95
☐ 22:CM	$9.95	☐ 46:CWT	$12.95
☐ 23:EL	$8.95	☐ 47:CGT	$7.95
☐ 24:SH	$8.95		

Canadian Customers
Order Toll-Free 1-800-561-4169

Additional Books Sub-Total $_____
ADD Postage and Handling $ 3.00
Sales Tax: (AZ, CA, DC, IL, MI, MN, NY & WA residents, please add appropriate state and local sales tax.) $_____
YOUR TOTAL (Sub-Total, Postage/Handling, Tax) $_____

YOUR ADDRESS (Please print)

Name _____

Street _____

City _____State_____Zip _____

Phone (_____) _____ — _____

YOUR PAYMENT
Check one: ☐ Check ☐ Visa ☐ MasterCard ☐ Discover Card ☐ American Express
Required credit card information:
Credit Card Number_____

Expiration Date (Month/Year) _____/ _____

Signature Required _____

Home Planners, LLC
Wholly owned by Hanley-Wood, Inc.
3275 W. Ina Road, Suite 110, Dept. BK, Tucson, AZ 85741

TB42

Design 9621

OVER 3 MILLION BLUEPRINTS SOLD

"We instructed our builder to follow the plans including all of the many details which make this house so elegant... Our home is a fine example of the results one can achieve by purchasing and following the plans which you offer... Everyone who has seen it has assured us that it belongs in 'a picture book.' I truly mean it when I say that my home 'is a DREAM HOUSE.'"

S.P.
Anderson, SC

"We have had a steady stream of visitors, many of whom tell us this is the most beautiful home they've seen. Everyone is amazed at the layout and remarks on how unique it is. Our real estate attorney, who is a Chicago dweller and who deals with highly valued properties, told me this is the only suburban home he has seen that he would want to live in."

W. & P.S.
Flossmoor, IL

"Your blueprints saved us a great deal of money. I acted as the general contractor and we did a lot of the work ourselves. We probably built it for half the cost! We are thinking about more plans for another home. I purchased a competitor's book but my husband wants only your plans!"

K.M.
Grovetown, GA

"We are very happy with the product of our efforts. The neighbors and passersby appreciate what we have created. We have had many people stop by to discuss our house and kindly praise it as being the nicest house in our area of new construction. We have even had one person stop and make us an unsolicited offer to buy the house for much more than we have invested in it."

K. & L.S.
Bolingbrook, IL

"The traffic going past our house is unbelievable. On several occasions, we have heard that it is the 'prettiest house in Batvia.' Also, when meeting someone new and mentioning what street we live on, quite often we're told, 'Oh, you're the one in the yellow house with the wrap-around porch! I love it!'"

A.W.
Batvia, NY

"I have been involved in the building trades my entire life... Since building our home we have built two other homes for other families. Their plans from local professional architects were not nearly as good as yours. For that reason we are ordering additional plan books from you."

T.F.
Kingston, WA

"The blueprints we received from you were of excellent quality and provided us with exactly what we needed to get our successful home-building project underway. We appreciate your invaluable role in our home-building effort."

T.A.
Concord, TN